The Idea of Global Civil Society

This book evaluates the claim that we need to take global civil society into account if we are to understand the changing social foundations of global power relations today, particularly if we wish to raise ethical questions about the changing political and institutional practices of trans-national governance.

The authors engage directly with the notion of global civil society in order to examine the ethical, social and political conditions that make certain kinds of globalizing practices a reality today. They explore and utilize the normative dimensions of the civil society discourse to further debate about the meaning of citizenship in a world of multi-level governance, as well as the changing characteristics of political community and democracy.

Bridging the normative concerns of political theorists with the historical and institutional focus of scholars of international relations and international political economy, this book will be of broad interest to students and researchers concerned with international relations, civil society, global governance and ethics.

Randall D. Germain teaches international political economy at Carleton University, Canada. He is the author of *The International Organization of Credit* and the editor of *Globalization and Its Critics*.

Michael Kenny teaches political theory at the University of Sheffield. He is the author of *The Politics of Identity* and *The First New Left in Britain*.

RIPE Series in Global Political Economy

This series, published in association with the *Review of International Political Economy*, provides a forum for current debates in international political economy. The series aims to cover all the central topics in IPE and to present innovative analyses of emerging topics. The titles in the series seek to transcend a state-centred discourse and focus on three broad themes:

- the nature of the forces driving globalisation forward
- resistance to globalisation
- the transformation of the world order.

The series comprises two strands:

The *RIPE Series in Global Political Economy* aims to address the needs of students and teachers, and the titles will be published in hardback and paperback. Titles include:

Transnational Classes and International Relations
Kees van der Pijl

Gender and Global Restructuring
Sightings, Sites and Resistances
Edited by Marianne H Marchand and Anne Sisson Runyan

Global Political Economy
Contemporary Theories
Edited by Ronen Palan

Ideologies of Globalization
Contending Visions of a New World Order
Mark Rupert

The Clash within Civilisations
Coming to Terms with Cultural Conflicts
Dieter Senghaas

Global Unions?
Theory and Strategies of Organized Labour in the Global Political Economy
Edited by Jeffrey Harrod and Robert O'Brien

Political Economy of a Plural World
Critical Reflections on Power, Morals and Civilizations
Robert Cox with Michael Schechter

A Critical Rewriting of Global Political Economy
Integrating Reproductive, Productive and Virtual Economies
V. Spike Peterson

Contesting Globalization
Space and Place in the World Economy
André C. Drainville

Global Institutions and Development
Framing the World?
Edited by Morten Bøås and Desmond McNeill

Global Institutions, Marginalization, and Development
Craig N. Murphy

Routledge/RIPE Studies in Global Political Economy is a forum for innovative new research intended for a high-level specialist readership, and the titles will be available in hardback only. Titles include:

1. Globalization and Governance *
Edited by Aseem Prakash and Jeffrey A. Hart

2. Nation-States and Money
The Past, Present and Future of National Currencies
Edited by Emily Gilbert and Eric Helleiner

3. The Global Political Economy of Intellectual Property Rights
The New Enclosures?
Christopher May

4. Integrating Central Europe
EU Expansion and Poland, Hungary and the Czech Republic
Otto Holman

5. Capitalist Restructuring, Globalisation and the Third Way
Lessons from the Swedish Model
J. Magnus Ryner

6. Transnational Capitalism and the Struggle over European Integration
Bastiaan van Apeldoorn

7. World Financial Orders
An Historical International Political Economy
Paul Langley

8. The Changing Politics of Finance in Korea and Thailand
From Deregulation to Debacle
Xiaoke Zhang

9. Anti-Immigrantism in Western Democracies
Statecraft, Desire and the Politics of Exclusion
Roxanne Lynn Doty

10. The Political Economy of European Employment
European Integration and the Transnationalization of the (Un)Employment Question
Edited by Henk Overbeek

11. Rethinking Global Political Economy
Emerging Issues, Unfolding Odysseys
Edited by Mary Ann Tétreault, Robert A. Denemark, Kenneth P. Thomas and Kurt Burch

12. Rediscovering International Relations Theory
Matthew Davies and Michael Niemann

13. International Trade and Developing Countries
Bargaining Coalitions in the GATT & WTO
Amrita Narlikar

14. The Southern Cone Model
The Political Economy of Regional Capitalist Development in Latin America
Nicola Phillips

15. The Idea of Global Civil Society
Politics and Ethics in a Globalizing Era
Edited by Randall D. Germain and Michael Kenny

16. Governing Financial Globalization
International Political Economy and Multi-Level Governance
Edited by Andrew Baker, David Hudson and Richard Woodward

* Also available in paperback

The Idea of Global Civil Society

Politics and ethics in a globalizing era

Edited by Randall D. Germain and Michael Kenny

Routledge
Taylor & Francis Group
LONDON AND NEW YORK

First published 2005
by Routledge
2 Park Square, Milton Park, Abingdon, Oxfordshire, OX14 4RN

Simultaneously published in the USA and Canada
by Routledge
270 Madison Ave, New York, NY 10016

Routledge is an imprint of the Taylor & Francis Group

Typeset in Baskerville by Taylor & Francis Books Ltd
Printed and bound in Great Britain by The Cromwell Press, Trowbridge, Wiltshire

British Library Cataloguing in Publication Data
A catalogue record for this book is available from the British Library

Library of Congress Cataloging in Publication Data
The idea of global civil society / edited by Randall D. Germain and Michael Kenny.
p. cm.
Includes bibliographical references and index.
1. Globalization. 2. Civil society. 3. World citizenship. 4. World politics—1989- I. Germain, Randall D., 1961- Kenny, Michael.
JZ1318.I33 2005
2004011718

ISBN 0–415–34942–7

Contents

Contributors

Louise Amoore is Lecturer in International Politics at the University of Newcastle upon Tyne.

Nigel Dower is Senior Lecturer in Philosophy at the University of Aberdeen.

Mervyn Frost is Professor of International Politics at Kings College, London.

Andrew Gamble is Professor of Politics at the University of Sheffield.

Randall D. Germain is Associate Professor of Political Science at Carleton University.

Kimberley Hutchings is Reader in International Relations at the London School of Economics.

Michael Kenny is Professor of Politics at the University of Sheffield.

Paul Langley is Lecturer in Politics at the University of Northumbria at Newcastle.

Nicholas Onuf is Professor of Political Science at Florida International University.

Anne Showstack Sassoon is Emeritus Professor of Politics at Kingston University, UK.

Nick Stevenson is Senior Lecturer in Sociology at the University of Nottingham.

Rorden Wilkinson is Senior Lecturer in International Politics at the University of Manchester.

Series preface

The confrontations that took place between state authorities and demonstrators during the autumn of 1999 and spring of 2000 ignited a wave of academic interest in the possibilities and problems of global civil society that drew upon post-cold war examinations of the role of non-state actors in world politics. Yet few of the studies that emerged thereafter subjected the idea of a global civil society to a sustained intellectual examination. The group of scholars brought together by Randall Germain and Michael Kenny seek to add to knowledge in this area by engaging in a wide-ranging interrogation of the idea of civil society at the global level. Although all are critical of the concept of global civil society, several contributors see in it a new and fruitful avenue of inquiry for understanding how world order is fashioned under changing economic, political, social and ideological conditions. This volume can therefore be read profitably by all scholars concerned with understanding the political economy of world order in the contemporary era.

The Idea of Global Civil Society: politics and ethics in a globalizing era is a valuable collection of essays in another important way. Enquiries into the form and function of global civil society have so far tended to be confined within individual intellectual boundaries. Although scholars from a number of disciplines (political science, international relations, sociology, political theory, international political economy, to identify only a few) have begun to think seriously and systematically about civil society, few examinations have ventured across disciplinary divides, or tried to sew together the broader tapestry with their individual (disciplinary) threads. A key attraction of Germain and Kenny's edited volume is that it has been explicitly conceived as a dialogue between and across three disciplines: international relations, political theory and international political economy. And while the conclusions sometimes sit uneasily one with another, they offer many more suggestive and insightful claims about how we might conceive of the idea of global civil society than analyses confined to a single disciplinary perspective.

The Routledge/RIPE Series in Global Political Economy seeks to publish innovative and cutting edge scholarship that pushes forward our understanding of how the world is organized, why it is developing in particular directions, and how globalizing tendencies across a range of social relations are reinforcing or undermining these changes. This volume fits in with this mandate because it closely examines a new and potentially helpful analytical category for understanding world order, but one which has not yet been thoroughly and systematically assessed to our satisfaction. As a result, Germain and Kenny's volume advances the debate on the analytical utility of the idea of global civil society without at the same time invoking any kind of intellectual closure. For these reasons we are pleased to include it in the Series.

Louise Amoore
University of Newcastle upon Tyne, UK

Randall Germain
Carleton University, Canada

Rorden Wilkinson
University of Manchester, UK

Preface

At 2:30 in the afternoon of 11 September 2001 I had just finished a talk on 'Ethics and Global Civil Society' to two other American International Relations experts and twenty-one of our leading British colleagues gathered at Gregynog, the rural retreat site of the University of Wales, Aberystwyth, the institution where the academic study of International Relations began, the place where what some of us think of as the practice of 'citizens talking to citizens about the politics of princes' had started nearly a century before.

I was happy. I had kept all my distinguished colleagues awake throughout the deadly hour after lunch by claiming to unmask our field's pretence of academic objectivity about voluntary transnational networks that do things like build hospitals, push for workers' rights, and set up credit schemes for impoverished women. Studying global civil society was all the vogue, I argued, because we tender-hearted scholars really just like the groups that constitute it. We think those groups do great good, or that they have the potential for doing great good, even if we have a slightly distorted view of the population of groups that makes up 'civil society' at a the transnational level. Most of the groups that do the range of things we find so admirable are not the Western non-governmental organizations that we often think of, such as Médicins sans Frontières, Amnesty International and the like. Instead, they are, more typically, faith-based development organizations funded by co-religionists from richer nations. This part of global civil society picks up much of the work where the state has failed, or has been forced to fail when leaders follow the advice of Western-trained social scientists like ourselves, the necessary condition for loans to keep their debt-ridden governments afloat.

As I confidently answered questions and accepted criticism, one of the staff of the Welsh conference center broke into the meeting to demand the attention of one of our hosts. Twenty minutes later, our colleague returned to tell us a fantastic story of passenger planes from Boston crashing into New York's World Trade Center. Stunned, unbelieving, we descended to the conference-center game room and joined the rest of the world watching TV images of the planes and the towers, entering, exiting, and falling, again and again.

Within hours, the conference site began to empty. Some left for London, seconded to the media or government. We Americans, suddenly all-too-conscious of a cell-phone dead-spot in the center of Wales, waited for precious minutes on the center's phone to reassure ourselves. Some of our hosts from the University of Wales and the more junior of our British colleagues waited with us. None of us was ready for dinner. A friend tried to pull me out of myself, out of my cataloging of acquaintances and friends of friends who could have been on those early morning flights from my home in Boston, by getting me to pull on my running shorts and slog with him along wet and rutted Welsh roads. As we ran past clumps of sheep, cows, horses, and men still working the picture-book farms, we talked about what had happened, why it occurred, what the consequences would be. We were, after all, experts on International Relations.

We rapidly agreed to work from the hypothesis that Al Qaeda, or a similar group was responsible. The conference topic made us think about how fuzzy the lines could be between the unambiguously well-intentioned groups that gathered expatriate donations and foreign charity to build clinics and schools for forgotten people, and networks of zealots convinced they can make a more just world through mass murder. As we ran, my friend's conversation turned to the particular type of hopelessness that made it possible for Al Qaeda to survive, to how the covert US war against the Soviet-backed regime in Afghanistan had helped empower Osama bin Laden and how American attachment to Israel and oil had fueled hatred in so much of the Arab world.

Yet, as we ran, I couldn't be the International Relations expert. I kept thinking about untenured American colleagues whose analysis of the etiology of this crime would be the same as my running partner's, but who would risk losing their jobs if they were to speak out as directly and passionately. I worried about my family, my neighbors, my country, and only then about the larger world. On the long-delayed flights back to Boston and then over the following months, I kept wondering whether the field of International Relations could ever be the same, whether we would ever return to the easy way we once talked about the violence and destitution that makes up so much of our subject, even at a conference about global civil society.

Remarkably, this book came out of that conference. Its essays are not part of that facile genre that, in fact, returned very quickly. They engage directly with the ideological struggles that divide the 'voluntary' transnational world. They place global civil society within the networks of power that both create and are sustained by the violence and destitution that mark our world. Moreover, they are deeply self-reflective; they are conscious of the role of our scholarly communities within international civil society, and of the way in which, for so many of us, this particular community is so deeply a part of who we are that some of its faces would flash before our eyes in moments of crisis. The book, and its particular context, remind us that International Relations, itself, provides one grain of sand in which the universe of global civil society can be seen.

Craig N. Murphy
May 2004
Boston (USA)

Acknowledgements

Nearly all of the chapters collected in this volume were first delivered at a specially convened meeting in the pastoral, mid-Wales setting of Gregynog, the conference facility of the University of Wales. This gathering began on 10 September 2001, and broke on the 12th. The world we rejoined seemed frighteningly different to the one we had left. In the course of what was proving to be a congenial and highly stimulating scholarly meeting, news filtered through of the events of the morning of 11 September in New York. Like millions of others, we too experienced the mixture of shock, disbelief and anxiety that those events provoked. That this tragic event occurred during a meeting devoted to an idea that appears to herald a peaceful and more co-operative international order was an irony lost on none of the participants at this event. We all struggled to juxtapose our academic discussion of this ideal with the violent and shocking reality replayed ad infinitum on the small television screen that constituted our main link with the outside world.

With hindsight, it is clear that the polarized response of our own gathering to this juxtaposition is highly revealing about the ambivalent status of the notion of a transnational or global civil society. For some, the day's events were the most brutal revelation of the truths that in the end what counts in international politics is the exercise of force, and that the development and character of the global order depend upon the actions and reactions of the sole wielders of legitimate force – states. Yet others at the conference saw in these events a pathological symptom of the limitations of a world order shaped by the hegemony of a large superpower. To holders of this view, only the reaffirmation of a cosmopolitan morality closely associated with a globalizing civic culture and universal moral norms, can foster peaceful terms of co-existence at the trans-national level. A rather uncomfortable, and more ambivalent third view was also aired in our discussions. This highlighted the defensiveness, insecurity and anger that the new kinds of social interdependencies and cultural encounters associated with globalization generate within world politics. A globalizing civil society may well intensify and deepen hostility to Western values and cultural codes. At the same time, we all understood that to appreciate adequately the new terrorist networks involved in the attack on the twin towers, it is necessary to develop a sensitivity to the distinctively modern conditions spawned by the forces of economic globalization.

These include mass migration between South and North, increased marginalization within societies, growing inequality arising out of uneven economic growth patterns, cultural responses to the global aspirations of Western media outlets, and the spread of activities associated with the 'covert world'.

Each of these views possesses analytic and normative value, and all appear at places in this book. But it is the third that approximates most closely to the guiding ethos of this collection. A cautious but nevertheless critical assessment of global civil society underpins the different contributions to this volume. Such a stance is hard to translate into a simple moral or political formula about the dangers or merits of this idea. What can be said about the generic approach of these authors is that all accept that 'global civil society' provides us with an analytical handle upon various important social, cultural and political developments. And all urge greater sensitivity to the merits and dangers of this idea.

Edited volumes always generate multiple debts of gratitude, and this one is no exception. The editors are grateful to all who participated at the meeting where many of these ideas were first aired: both for the stimulating nature of the discussions and the congeniality which characterized this event. The contributors to this volume have been models of patience and co-operation during the occasionally tortuous journey from conference to published volume, a journey which has seen one editor begin a family and the other move with his across the Atlantic. We are especially indebted to Rorden Wilkinson, Louise Amoore and Paul Langley for kindly agreeing to provide additional chapters in areas that the original meeting neglected. Their initial enthusiasm to participate in the conference enabled them to fashion their contributions in the wake of the stimulating discussions we had at Gregynog. We would also like to acknowledge and thank the other participants at this conference whose contributions strengthened the ideas contained in these chapters, including Ken Booth, April Carter, Ian Clark, Michael Cox, Alan Finlayson, Tony Heron, Craig Murphy, Tony Payne, Jan Aart Scholte and Steve Smith. Craig Murphy's enthusiasm for this project extends to writing the preface, for which we are very appreciative.

We wish also to acknowledge and thank the institutions that helped fund this conference: the Department of International Politics at the University of Wales, Aberystwyth; the British Academy; the University of Wales Gregynog Colloquia Fund; the Political Economy Research Centre at the University of Sheffield; and the Pro-Vice Chancellor's Office at the University of Wales, Aberystwyth. We would like to highlight the generosity of the Department of International Politics at Aberystwyth, which showed tremendous enthusiasm for this project at a very early stage. Randall Germain would also like to gratefully acknowledge the assistance of Sophie Hague, who compiled the bibliography and organized the final draft of the manuscript far more efficiently and cheerfully than he could ever have done.

Finally, we would like to thank Cambridge University Press, for permission to publish Chapter 9. This was written especially for this volume, but due to the logistics of publication it appeared originally in the *Review of International Studies* (Vol. 30, no. 1, 2004). We are also grateful to Lynne Rienner Publishers, for permission to publish Figure 1 in Chapter 11, which first appeared in Randall Germain, 'Global Financial Governance and the Problem of Inclusion', *Global Governance* (Vol. 7, no. 4, 2001), and to Taylor & Francis for permission to publish Figure 2 in Chapter 11, which first appeared in 'Globalizing Accountability within the International Organization of Credit: financial governance and the public sphere', *Global Society* (Vol. 18, no. 3, 2004).

Michael Kenny
Sheffield University, Sheffield, UK

Randall Germain
Carleton University, Ottawa, Canada

1 The idea(l) of global civil society

Introduction

Michael Kenny and Randall Germain

Introducing global civil society

The idea of a 'global civil society' has now become a common place term of the popular imagination. Starting with the collapse of the Berlin Wall and the end of the cold war in 1989, the vision of a growing web of voluntary civic associations engaged in dialogue, debate and struggle over the unfolding direction of the economic and political organization of the world has been a powerful one. This vision has provided us with explanations of the collapse of communism (Keane 2001b), of the demise of rich-country initiatives such as the Multilateral Agreement on Investment (Johnston and Laxer 2003), and even of some of the limits to globalization as demonstrated by such events as the 'Battle of Seattle' (Scholte 2000a). It has also invested in non-governmental organizations (NGOs) a new legitimacy based on their political claim to represent citizens more adequately than traditional political institutions (Chandhoke 2002).

Scholars have spent the last years of the twentieth century examining the idea of global civil society for analytical insights concerning new and important political developments. Political theorists have turned to the idea of civil society and its global corollary in an effort to better understand the new configurations of public authority in the contemporary period (Seligman 1992; Walzer 1995). International relations scholars have enlisted the idea of global civil society to help explain the resurgence of interest in human rights, global justice and humanitarian assistance and intervention (Shaw 1994; Dunne and Wheeler 1999; Frost 2002). And international political economy scholars have engaged critically with the idea of a global civil society to help explain the transformation of hegemony in the global capitalist system (Murphy 1994; Cox 1999; Drainville 1994). These efforts suggest that a deep intellectual need exists to consider the changing modalities of global political order within the context of a renewed debate over the role and place of individual and collective agency.

The terminology of global civil society has also been used to highlight the expansion of moral, civic and political possibilities associated with the appearance of an overlapping and patchy set of transnational publics. Among the most crucial elements of these publics are networks of virtual communication, broad-based social movements engaged in criticism of existing political and social relations, media conglomerates that are often attempting to establish media cultures that span territorial boundaries, erode cultural exclusivity and bridge geographical distance, and the growing legitimacy of the moral vocabulary of human rights. While claims about the political efficacy and moral worthiness of this supposedly novel 'space' vary considerably, even the most enthusiastic proponents of global civil society remain cautious about the idea that any kind of new social order associated with it represents the demise of the power and authority of nation-states and/or nationally constituted authorities. Nevertheless, given the popularity of a mode of argument that projects the idea of a global civil society as the societal accompaniment to the supposedly inexorable and unalterable processes of economic and cultural globalization, it is not surprising that this label has come to be associated with some of the grandest claims about the character and reach of politics and community in a globalizing era.

In this book we have assembled a group of authors to examine the historical, normative and political implications of the idea of global civil society, in light of the growing scholarly attention it is receiving. They have done so in arguments and analyses that consider some of its main ideological usages and associated normative claims from different sub-disciplinary backgrounds, including normative political theory, the study of ideological change, the evaluation of theories and trends in international political economy, and the scholarly analysis of particular institutions and developments in international politics. As editors, we were particularly concerned that the contributors explore two aspects of the idea of global civil society. First, we wanted them to consider the oft-neglected dimension of power in relation to this ideal, and to trace the many connections between global civil society and the various aspects of hegemony that continue to inform the practice of international politics. We also wanted our contributors to direct attention to the moral and ethical possibilities represented by this idea, including how it enables certain kinds of normatively grounded critiques of existing social, economic and political arrangements, and provides a basis for programmatic plans to move beyond them.

Second, we directed the contributors to focus critical attention on the different ways in which the idea of an emergent transnational civic culture has been deployed in the various scholarly sub-fields of international politics. The idea of a 'global civil society' has become a staple across a wide range of academic and practitioner circles, including political and social scientists, political activists, policy practitioners, campaigning groups and individual citizens concerned to debate the character of global politics. Just a few years ago, such a notion was at best a minority intellectual concern. Yet now, the vision of an increasingly influential and independent web of interlocking civic associations, campaigning organizations, transnational institutions, and international voluntary groups, committed to debate and struggle over the unfolding direction of the economic and political organization of the world, is pervasive. Some of its advocates claim that the growth of a globalizing civil society offers one explanation for the swift collapse of the official communist regimes of Eastern Europe, while others stress its role as a crucial resource and inspiration for those resisting globalization and campaigning for democratization in Latin America and Africa (Macdonald 1997; MacLean, Quadir and Shaw 2000). An alternative radical perspective regards global civil society as a vital outcome of the diffuse anti-globalization movement that has emerged in recent times (Gills 2000).

The relative attractiveness of this concept-idea can also in part be attributed to its role as a handy weapon for those engaged in some intractable, on-going scholarly disputes. For some Anglo-American political theorists, the idea of global society brings a new dimension to long-established arguments about the character and possibility of political community and ethical solidarity beyond the reach of the territorially bounded nation (Hutchings and Dannreuther 1999; Keane 2003). For various International Relations scholars meanwhile, the term is an integral part of explanatory accounts of the resurgence of interest in Western democracies for the ideas of human rights and global justice (Dunne and Wheeler 1999). It figures too within the vocabulary of those seeking to make a case for interventionist policies towards rogue states on 'humanitarian' grounds (Ignatieff 2004). And for scholars in the field of international political economy, this has become an important term within the lexicon of those seeking to explain the transformation of hegemony in the global capitalist system (Murphy 1994; Cox 1999; Drainville 1994); and especially for those committed to locating a putative source of counter-hegemonic, subaltern struggle to the globalization thus far orchestrated 'from above' (Gills 2000; Gill 2003).

As with all of the political terms that have entered the vocabulary of English-speaking social science with the prefix 'global' attached to them, however, the notion of a global or transnational civil society has its share of critics. For some, this idea represents an overly benign characterization of changes that are in fact dangerous and regressive in character (Pasha and Blaney 1998; Young 1995). One kind of criticism suggests that global civil society is the product of the machinations of elite Western interests, corporate moguls, and institutions like the World Trade Organization (WTO) and World Bank (cf. Scholte and Schnabel 2002). On this view, transnational social order has been brought into being in order to pursue the imperatives favoured by global capitalism, and, in particular, to disseminate and legitimate the norms of neo-liberalism. Others are skeptical on different grounds. They heap scorn upon the notion that there are real-world social developments to which a term such as this corresponds. For them, civil society represents a hopeless piece of intellectual narcissism, a fantasy that revives the cosmopolitan aspirations of Enlightenment theorists at a time when world order is in fact being shaped by a singularly powerful hegemon and an array of corporate interests. What matters in this view are inter-state rivalries and the willingness of the United States and its principal allies in the society of states to bring outlaw states into line with its constitutive norms (Hirst 2002). However, such skeptics are still faced with the challenge of offering a plausible explanation of why this notion has been taken up so widely in both the political and scholarly worlds. It to this question that we now turn.

The emergence of an idea

A global and civil society

We suggest that understanding the conditions shaping the dissemination of this idea is not possible until we acknowledge the unique and recent coalescence of two separate intellectual–political impulses. These imperatives are neatly conveyed by the conjoining of two terms that have traditionally occupied distinct and separate intellectual domains. The first of these is the word 'global', which since 1960 has been indelibly associated with the process of globalization (Waters 1995). Globalization represents most importantly the triumph of a set of globally oriented social, political, economic and cultural forces that recast the behavior of institutions on a worldwide basis (Cox 1999; Germain 2000). These have redrawn the parameters of state–society relations (Schechter 1999), enlarged the scope of market activities, and reconfigured the role of the state (Cerny 2000; Strange 1996). In placing emphasis upon the 'global', commentators point to one of the defining characteristics of the contemporary period, namely, that the impulse to globalize is led by the many transnationally organized social forces operating through institutions, social classes, and cultural and kinship groups.

The second impulse is associated with the revival of the ideal of civil society in Anglo-American political thought and debate since the early 1980s. This notion has a long and distinguished pedigree in Western political thought (Kaviraj and Khilnani 2001), and has assumed a wide variety of meanings and associations over time (Cox 1999). While the story of the revival of the idea of civil society is complex, for our purposes it is important to stress how the concept was taken up by a number of intellectuals in the West keen to advance a more democratically inclined and less statist interpretation of democratic socialism (Keane 1998a). Around the same time, civil society was advocated as both an independent moral value and, instrumentally, as the social condition through which other democratic values might be achieved (Lively and Reeve 1997; Fine 1997). It also became used as an analytic-empirical description of the growth of independent associational activities in various regional contexts, notably Eastern Europe, Latin America and Africa, where different democratizing movements are salient (Keane 1988a; Risse 2000). Within this milieu, it did not take long for the idea of civil society to acquire an analytical power and a normative sheen congenial to liberal explanations of change.

From our perspective, what is most interesting is the way in which these two impulses combined to confirm the attractiveness of an idea whose main contours fit so well with some of the most salient contemporary social, economic and political dynamics. The demise of the political and intellectual polarities enshrined by the cold war created a space for a revival of interest in associational activity that emerged beyond the reach of powerful states, and independently of familiar ideological paradigms. The emergence of a more fluid international context in the 1990s, including the recognition of globalization as perhaps the era's defining social condition, meant that political authority was taking on transhistorical attributes. And the adoption at this time of a generic, democratically inclined vocabulary by different subaltern movements and struggles provided the possibility of a consensual model of social relations with concrete normative attractions. Within this context it is not surprising that the conjunction of 'global' and 'civil society' assumed such a powerful logical and political force.

The demise of the cold war provides a useful demarcation point in this narrative. With its termination, a host of hitherto marginalized and repressed alternative possibilities reappeared in international political life. Indeed some of global civil society's major advocates see in the struggles of peace campaigners operating in both 'East' and 'West' before 1989 the first glimmerings of this later development (Kaldor 2000; 2004). More importantly, a subtle intellectual shift began to take place in Western political thinking around this time. This involved a discernible recalibration by policymakers, political actors, subaltern movements and academics of the limits, purposes and boundaries of political authority.

In the West, political authority within a democratic liberal polity has over the post-1945 period become bound up with the increasing bureaucratization of the state and its attendant political parties, precisely in order to control the extension of social and political benefits among the wider population. Recently, economic globalization has eroded this form of authority by redrawing the parameters of state/society relations, in many cases forcing states to reconfigure and/or withdraw these benefits (Strange 1996; Keohane and Milner 1996). Opposition to these developments through the traditional bureaucratic channels of state and political party has met with limited success. One response favoured by Anglo-American theorists has been to shift attention to civil society as a new terrain of democracy and a possible site of social solidarity at transnational levels (Seligman 1992; Walzer 1995).

For others keen to promote alternatives to the existing system of political authority – both nationally and globally – the idea of a globalizing version of civil society is attractive for a different reason. It offers an effective critical yardstick with which to attack the limits of representative democratic politics, and a means of announcing that the new anti-globalization politics eschews a political vision steeped in statist and national collectivist assumptions (Falk 1995b). Critical, normative aspirations have also informed the appropriation of the term by moral philosophers and international political theorists keen to demonstrate the arbitrary and contingent character of intellectual traditions that conflate ethical life with the territorial boundaries of the nation-state (Linklater 1998; Held 2003). Thus, the ancient dreams of a world citizenship and a planetary-wide political community are strikingly revivified by talk of a globalizing civil society. Just as importantly, this term is bound up with the increasingly significant role in international society of notions of universally applicable human rights (Wheeler 2000). The idea that there are certain inviolable rights-claims that anybody can make on a state, irrespective of their own national membership, has been given an important boost by the assertion that technological, social and cultural developments are all creating a social basis for an actual cosmopolitan political community.

Among the influences at work upon the dissemination of this idea, then, are the possibilities of refashioning or renewing global political order after the breakdown of the cold war. The task of understanding the trajectory of world order in a tumultuous era – where familiar institutional channels and state powers seem to be atrophying or even decaying – suggests a renewed focus on the foundational elements of order that are operative beyond the reach of, as well as above and below, individual states. The idea of global civil society has to some degree met this analytical need, and thus became a fruitful theoretical category to explore, as well as an apparently benign value to promote.

There is much, then, to be gained from considering the history and implications of the emergence of global civil society as an idea independently from the kind of enquiry that takes its existence as an empirical 'given'. While there may be a case for deploying this term as a reference for various kinds of technological changes, social developments, communicative interactions and associational networks, a more rounded appreciation of the meanings of civil society – and its purportedly transnational character – is needed before any stable sense of its empirical reference can be achieved. At the same time, retaining a focus upon the historical emergence of this ideal opens up a promising and uncharted intellectual terrain.

Contending narratives

The notion of a global civil society arises at an interesting point of intersection between some of the leading ideological narratives competing in transnational political life. Within the Anglo-American world, it is possible to discern an influential perspective that uses civil society to promote the merits of individual rights and voluntary association, a contractual and delimited state structure, and a market economy in which the relations of private property are sacrosanct. Civil society in this narrative refers both to the processes of associational formation and interaction, and to the imputed exercise of voluntary preference by individual citizens through these bodies. As has been widely observed by historians of liberalism, it has been important for Anglo-American liberals to posit the domain of civil association as insulated from, and naturally antithetical to, the political and economic orders (Chandhoke 2002).

Also significant within liberal constructions of civil society is the separation effected between public life and the (implicitly excluded) private domain, centred upon the institution of the family. A recurrent theme in the writings of Western liberal intellectuals is the consensual participation in civic life of sovereign individuals who undertake to reinforce and extend their individual agency through collective means. This perspective sees contestation and struggle within civil society as originating in the pursuit of individual desires and interests, yet as tempered in a free society by the ethical lessons learned from associational life. It sustains a picture of civil association as a space where individuals can realize their interests, defend their liberties against an encroaching state and/or market, and learn the 'habits of the heart' – such as the art of compromise, restraint and tolerance –

required for the practice of democratic citizenship (Barber 1998; Walzer 1995; Bellah 1996). The logical implication of the extension of this perspective onto politics at the global level is that individuals are simply deciding to carry their preferences and actions beyond the confines of their own society on the understanding that others will engage in interaction and cooperation with them.

One of the main challenges to this version of global civil society comes from a perspective rooted in the work of the Italian Marxist theorist Antonio Gramsci. As opposed to the (stylized) liberal narrative described above, scholars from within this tradition suggest that it is the inequitable relationships relating to social class that constitute the kernel of civil society. But even if classes themselves are the product of social relations arising out of particular modes of production, their engagement with the state and organized political power is mediated by the varied perceptions that social groups hold of their own socialized forms of agency at any particular moment. Scholars in this tradition typically acknowledge that although classes might be said to exist in an objective and material sense, the form which their agency takes at given points in time can only be the product of their material conditions of existence as filtered by their consciousness and cultures (cf. Gramsci 1971: 181–2). This sensitivity to the importance of morals, values and ideals distinguishes the neo-Gramscian narrative of civil society, by elevating consciousness and the formation of subjectivity to the status of a major analytical concern. Civil society on this reading represents the key terrain upon which collective subjectivity is formed through quasi-voluntary acts of association outside the structures of both market relations and state power. It is, as Craig Murphy (1994: 32) argues, the place where 'I' becomes 'we'. The significance of civil society and its global corollary lies not so much in the way in which it sits as a third force between market relations and the state, but in its position as an enabling or disabling mechanism for achieving hegemony over entire social formations.

Other characterizations of global civil society fit with neither of these perspectives. For some radical critics of a rapidly globalizing economy, and free trade in particular, global civil society describes the advent of uncontainable opposition to the current global order. It figures within this subalternist narrative as a myriad of interconnected movements of resistance to global capitalism, state elites and human rights abuses. In the hands of one of the anti-globalization movement's main 'organic intellectuals', Richard Falk (1999), it has come to possess a totemic as well as analytical force – the expression of the processes of revolt and opposition, and the proclamation of a 'counter-public' sphere, laden with the promise of a new ethical order. There are different versions of this narrative, too, but it has helped sustain a broadly generic set of ambitions and aspirations for various intellectual radicals, globalization critics and social movement activists.

This brief rehearsal by no means exhausts the gamut of ideological constructions of global civil society. The importance of rival liberal perspectives, specifically those inspired by the communitarian and republican lineages in world politics, is central to the contributions of Andrew Gamble and Michael

Kenny, as well as Nicholas Onuf, in this volume. A consideration of the ideological factors that have shaped the production and meanings of this idea remains an under-emphasized component of its analysis. An awareness of the competing histories and claims of these views offers a simple way of illustrating that there are rival ways of thinking about a putatively globalizing form of civil society. Each of these narratives privileges a certain form of political agency, and each tends to understand the character and purpose of global civil society in a different way. Their points of departure inform some of the most important philosophical and ethical debates about transnational society.

The normative implications of global civil society

We also maintain that the idea of a global civil society has become relevant for established philosophical and political arguments about the appropriate domain and character of the status and practice of citizenship in particular. In recent Anglo-American philosophical discourse, this term has served to reanimate an established cosmopolitan ethical tradition. Some contemporary Kantian theorizing sees in the social networks of civil society the putative realization of various universalizable moral norms. Among the many kinds of claims advanced in relation to this idea is the intriguing and contentious suggestion that certain kinds of non-state actors enjoy a legitimacy that is increasingly denied to states (Scholte 2000b).

An important debate has therefore developed concerning the relation of a putative transnational civic domain to the changing character of global social order. This theme has been explored in a variety of commentaries, ranging from the optimistic to the pessimistic in character. For some, a commitment to the existence of an emergent global civil society supports the claim that the principles and mechanisms of global order must be organized and operationalized in relation to putative public spaces that lie beyond the control of powerful states or corporate elites (Keane 2001). Not surprisingly, such a perspective presents transparency as one of the chief hallmarks of civil society. These accounts stress the increased ease with which marginal perspectives and oppressed groups can touch the consciousness of others, and the putative emergence of a 'mode of public reasoning' recognized and understood across a variety of cultures, religious traditions, and political perspectives (Bohman 1998).

This kind of claim has been criticized for its broadly Western (or perhaps more accurately Anglo-American), liberal and cosmopolitan aspirations. It has been argued that these generate political and cultural tensions, given that the normative presuppositions of Enlightenment liberalism and its relationship with different episodes in the history of empire, are increasingly subject to critical appraisal (Young 1995). Yet it is important to note here that the choice between a form of 'liberal imperialism' and a morally attenuated post-liberal pluralism is not the only one available to liberal-inclined thinkers and activists. Some of the most perceptive and challenging arguments in this field defend a brand of liberalism that is acutely aware of its own cultural biases, more respectful of other, non-liberal cultures, and keen to transplant the values of toleration, peaceful co-existence and the civil resolution of conflicts to spaces beyond the national (Walzer 1995; Bohman 2001). Such a position links several contributions in this volume. In contradistinction to the legalism associated with Kantian cosmopolitanism, and some Western understandings of the current human rights agenda, thinkers drawing upon other adjacent traditions to liberalism – for instance, republicanism – advocate the merits of the more substantive value of 'civility' within transnational arenas (cf. Onuf and Frost in this volume; Kenny 2003).

Global civil society can provide an important background to, and perhaps support for, these normative ventures. Rather than read as a process of inexorable Westernization, the advent of transnational civil society may signal the social realization of a universalizable interest in peaceful inter- and intra-communal co-existence. Civility on this view is less about 'civilizing' various (non-Western) others; rather it involves ensuring that all live in circumstances which do not inhibit the formation of viable political communities and, more ambitiously, a fully functioning self (Sen 1999). In relation to the argument regarding international distributive justice, a key question is whether the bonds, ties and connectedness that the idea of a global civil society supposedly describes, can provide an equivalent to the forms of solidarity among national co-citizens that Rawls regards as a prerequisite for the achievement of his conception of justice (Rawls 1971).

Increasingly, thinkers and activists are starting to ask whether the nation-state remains the meaningful site at which political community can be constructed and civic identity sustained. The intellectual fall-out from such a question pivots on arguments about the actuality and potentiality of the practice of a degree of 'civic virtue' at different spatial and territorial scales; and upon long-established tensions between rights-driven and identity-orientated accounts of citizenship itself (Kymlicka and Norman 2000). A crucial sub-set of current debates about world citizenship in this context is the question of the character and scope of the participative opportunities associated with a globalizing civil society. Cosmopolitan democrats maintain that with the establishment of a world society a meaningful right to be consulted about decisions that affect communities and individuals has come into being. Such claims raise a host of empirical and normative complexities that deserve more sustained consideration.

Participation emerges as an important theme too in the plethora of (purportedly neutral) descriptive accounts of emergent patterns of global governance, and its attendant sites of decision-making. If a unified and transnational society can or should be said to be in existence, then this may have a huge bearing upon understandings of the accountability, legitimacy, democratic scrutiny and representativeness of global decision-making networks (Germain 2004). In the key arenas of transnational decision-making, 'rights claims' have been pursued by focusing on arguments about who should participate in such decisions and how this participation should be organized. Decision-making at the international level has traditionally been confined to states and their international surrogates such as the International Monetary Fund (IMF) and WTO. Increasingly, however, the decisions of particular states are being challenged by social movements claiming to represent marginalized voices or excluded constituencies and communities that are affected by these decisions (O'Brien *et al.* 2000; Woods 2001; Scholte and Schnabel 2002).

What these groups claim to represent is a nascent moral authority that established channels of political decision-making must acknowledge and engage if their decisions are to become acceptable to a global audience. A considerable part of the appeal of global civil society is its capacity to provide an attractive and apparently sinuous normative anchor for those who want to hold governments and international institutions to account for the policies they impose on subaltern peoples. Its appeal lies in the moral aspirations invested in the social developments it purports to describe. But, just as importantly, the critical vantage-point it supplies for those worried about the democratic and legitimacy deficits associated with current patterns of global governance and institutional configuration also rank highly (Schechter 1999).

More sceptically inclined scholars, however, see in transnational society the potential for a tightening of the grip of leading states, regional elites and multinational corporations. They remind us that the voluntaristic and emancipatory properties attributed by Western liberals and socialists to civil society rely upon moments, actions and relationships that are essentially coercive, and sometimes violent. The idea of global civil society represents a powerful lever for Western-dominated institutions that want to exclude or delegitimate groups or practices that they consider to be 'uncivil' (Wilkinson in this volume). Thus, some critics observe the integral role played by Western states in encouraging and facilitating international civil society; while radical critics see in talk of a global civil order a tool for the most powerful states to use to get their way in relation to the less potent (Robinson and Harris 2000). The concern here is that the romance and voluntarism bound up with transnational society obfuscates growing disparities of wealth, living condition and power between and within North and South. Among the key questions facing analysts of global politics is whether the 'comprehensive' and confident ideals that Western liberalism invests in the idea of civil society makes this a mystificatory, culturally imperialist idea when applied to contemporary geopolitical affairs (Kaviraj and Khilnani 2001; Young 1995).

The seriousness and complexity of this question is not as yet reflected in the academic literature devoted to global civil society. Thus, the almost ubiquitous assumption that civil society represents a distinct 'third sector' that is intrinsically benign, because of its opposition to the modalities of power enshrined in state and market, is debilitating in analytical and normative terms. Such a separation (which was itself powerfully criticized by some of the central figures of nineteenth-century European thought) has passed, largely unquestioned, into contemporary intellectual usage (Fine 1997; Lively and Reeves 1997). But positing such a sharp analytical separation between economic, political and social phenomena, which are more properly considered in direct relation to each other, injects into Western liberal applications of global civil society an idealizing bias, and a tendency to romanticize NGO activities and civic organizations. Against this position, we would assert that a central part of the suggestiveness associated with this term concerns its relationship to, not separation from, political and economic affairs (Cox 1999). Civil society, the state and the market are mutually constituted, as well as sometimes in tension. To conceptualize them, on an a priori basis, as perpetually arranged in conflict or enmity, is to deplete the interpretative arsenal available to those seeking to understand global politics today.

Too often civil society is reduced to the world populated by NGOs, and most alarmingly to so-called 'progressive' NGOs such as Amnesty International or Médicins Sans Frontières. In empirical terms, such rose-tinted spectacles deflect attention from the increasingly significant task of interpreting the appeal and strength of the many anti-liberal groups that populate and mark out transnational spaces – for instance, fascist organizations or criminal gangs which exist in what Robert Cox (2002) identifies as the 'covert world'. Just as importantly, such a reading of civil society tends to overlook the many forms of coercion that exist within associational life, in terms either of direct intimidation and violence or indirect forms of pressure and influence.

For this reason in particular, one of the central motifs in this collection concerns the question of power, and specifically whether the concept of a globalizing civil society might sustain moral challenges and forms of redress for some of the most obdurate and debilitating inequities in the current world order. One aspect of 'power' that is therefore engaged by some of our contributors concerns its protean nature: its visible and invisible forms, and the variety of sites and modalities through which it is exercised. In relation to these dimensions, the idea(l) of a transnational society seems to possess strengths and limitations. One of the main arguments of those interested in the idea of global civil society concerns the importance of shifting the focus of analysis away from a formally demarcated sphere of politics towards the apparently voluntary and consensual domain of social relationships. Unless the latter are seen as inherently benign and non-coercive (as is true of some liberal usages), there is no reason why the civil society framework cannot be used, *pace* Gramsci, to stimulate thinking about the inequitable social terrain upon which identities and collectivities are generated, and to attend to the importance of ideological struggles in cementing and justifying extant relations of power.

Scholars who deploy the idea of global civil society in this way are led to look beyond the way in which formal instruments of power (that is, the police, courts and military; or what Gramsci identified as the 'apparatus of state coercive power' (Gramsci 1971: 12)) are wielded to produce order. In this respect, the idea of civil society looks promising because it points towards the problematic of establishing and/or challenging social order at different political levels, even as it encourages us to consider the factors and struggles pertinent to the achievement and disruption of order beyond the formal process of political institutionalization and mobilization. In this sense, this term helpfully alerts us to a new and potentially significant domain wherein power relationships are organized. Here the idea of a global civil society is useful precisely because it casts a different conceptual lens upon the configuration of current geopolitical power relations.

Plan of book

The different contributions collected in this volume have not been selected because they advocate a particular policy or programmatic response premised upon the reality of a global civil society, nor (as will become clear) do they necessarily share a common theoretical position towards this idea. But they do exhibit what we believe is an appropriately critical sensibility, particularly towards the main ideologically shaped understandings of global civil society. The first of these arises from the presumption that this domain belongs to the forces of historical progress, gathered in unified opposition to neo-liberal globalization. There also emanates from these essays a generalized scepticism about facile conceptions of a supposedly zero-sum relationship between global society and state power. While talk of a globalizing economy and civic culture makes sense for a host of analytical and empirical reasons, to extend such a claim to the realm of state formation is a step in the wrong direction. A persuasive characterization of global politics must acknowledge the legacy of state sovereignty and the intellectual force behind the idea of 'national interests' (Shaw 2000; Wendt 1994). For too long, scholars in the fields of International Relations and International Political Economy have failed to pay close attention to the complex exercise of power across the entire fabric of global order. Rectifying this omission represents one of the principal analytical advantages of the idea(l) of global civil society.

Part I of the book explores the different intellectual and narrative traditions with which those who are trying to use the idea of global civil society must contend. In the first chapter of this section, Andrew Gamble and Michael Kenny draw attention to some of the main ideological battles that have been displaced from the national to the global political level. These authors argue that global civil society is emerging as a central term within an ideological contest between rival versions of liberalism (as well as conservative and neo-socialist positions). They question the familiar radical contrast between an all-conquering Western liberal individualism and a radical subaltern alternative.

Anne Showstack Sassoon focuses on one especially influential theorist in debates about the political character of global civil society: Antonio Gramsci. She asks whether his influential, and still debated, understanding of civil society can be meaningfully 'globalized' as various radical thinkers assume. We cannot, she maintains, divorce the sphere of civil society from political authority, most importantly because the voluntary and consensual nature of civil society itself depends on the coercive arm of the state, particularly through its legal institution. The very idea of a creative, fluid and autonomous civil society is an unhelpful fantasy and runs counter to Gramsci's own analytical conception of its intertwined relationship with the coercive apparatus of the state. If we want to democratize a polity, Sassoon argues, we cannot merely turn to civil society separately from, or prior to, the legal and political institutions associated with the state.

In the last chapter in this section, Nicholas Onuf also rejects any conception of civil society as an unstratified social space, although from a different intellectual vantage point to Sassoon. He sees civil society as the social and ethical outcome of modernity, highlighting the processes of institutionalization and differentiation discussed by the nineteenth-century German thinker, G.W.F. Hegel. Onuf follows Hegel in suggesting that it is modernization that has brought civil society into being, and that the generation of various kinds of institutional stratification and novel social roles are indispensable conditions for moderns to become agents. Status is an inescapable part of modern social distinctions, and relates to three central social processes – participation, representation and recognition. These constitute central dimensions and consequences of contemporary social processes, and have produced what Onuf calls 'late modern' civil society, where the chief status markers are now wealth and poverty.

The essays in Part II take as their shared focal point the normative character and potential of global civil society for understanding the practice and idea of world citizenship. Nick Stevenson considers how an extension of our feelings of social solidarity from the national to the transnational levels can be both furthered and stymied by the workings of the Western-dominated media system. He cautions against adopting a view of such technologies that simply denigrates or celebrates their cosmopolitan impacts, arguing that they enable and frustrate certain kinds of civic awareness. He is especially keen to disabuse us of the view that access to images of suffering will somehow activate our ethical threshold; it is the moral rather than the spatial or temporal distance between people that counts, and technology by itself cannot easily plug that gap.

The chapters by Kimberley Hutchings and Nigel Dower consider established philosophical accounts of world citizenship, and its possible relation to global civil society, and draw opposed conclusions about the former. Hutchings is sceptical of the possibility of a globalized version of citizenship given the absence of a world polity and its associated powers of coercion; both of which are, to her mind, necessary to underpin such claims. She stresses the politically contingent character of citizenship and its ambiguity with respect to a globalized vision of civil society, especially where such a society is conceived without some form of state structure. Shorn of its anchor in a polity, Hutchings maintains, claims to a global citizenship draw upon a pre-modern republican lineage, in which an exclusive elite feel themselves to be obligated to norms and principles based effectively on *noblesse oblige*. In the modern world where ideas of human rights are increasingly important, this is a problematic reversion because it does not speak to the actual experiences of individuals as either citizens or subjects of particular states.

Nigel Dower picks up this call to secure a modern basis for global citizenship by arguing, from within Anglo-American liberalism, that it must ultimately appeal to individuals as rational, value-bearing human beings. He situates the idea of global citizenship in an emergent transnational social space, and explores how the claims of such a citizenship can be related to other discourses such as global governance and global democracy. For him, the idea of world citizenship builds upon these discourses and supersedes them in the sense that it speaks directly to individuals *qua* individuals. Global citizenship may be sustained by a global civil society, but it also occupies a senior claim insofar as it is more inclusive than the latter, both ethically and aspirationally.

Such an ethical dimension is also of central concern to Mervyn Frost, who explores the tensions that emanate from the dual position of individuals in current geopolitical conditions: as civilians who are constituted by their membership in the 'open practice' of global civil society; and as citizens of particular states. He maintains that the ethicality which underpins our position as civilians can no longer be trumped by claims to the exclusive sovereign jurisdiction of states where those states are not well-formed democratic states. With the emergence of a global civil society, we are now in a position to move the demand for 'first generation' rights from within states to a transnational level.

In Part III, the focus shifts to an examination of the various ways in which the idea(l) of global civil society is tied up with, and subversive of, the processes collected under the heading of 'global governance'. Louise Amoore and Paul Langley set out to interrogate the discursive patterns in which the latter is set. In their analysis, the idea of a neutral global public sphere is rejected in favour of a Foucauldian imaginary in which the social relations within civil society are regarded as infused by relations of power/knowledge. Prevailing attempts to develop an 'objective' or closed conception of what constitutes global civil society is then seen as a movement to normalize a particular mode of governing anchored in a broadly neo-liberal view of governmentality. These authors are sceptical too of radical, subalternist narratives of civic-political agency.

The final two chapters in the volume provide case studies of the political implications and character of the global governance/civil society nexus. Both chapters throw some of the broadly enunciated normative and analytical questions that figure in the earlier chapters into sharper relief. They also develop counter-opposed assessments of the political implications of this inter-relationship. In Rorden Wilkinson's chapter, a focus upon the particular ideological character of the notions of global governance and civil society is offered. He concentrates upon the efforts of the WTO to justify policy objectives and practices on the basis of its particular characterization of 'good' global civil society agents. Analysing the WTO's highly selective engagement with NGOs, he detects some powerful political motivations at work, and links these to the normative discourse of civil society. He criticizes the legitimacy deficit that such manoeuvres generate for this global institution, and considers the dilemmas this poses for NGOs that seek constructive engagement with it. The broader implication of his assessment echoes the arguments of other contributors: a healthy dose of scepticism about claims to representativeness made by and on behalf of the new patterns of global governance seems appropriate.

By contrast, Randall Germain engages the global governance/civil society relationship in the context of the exigencies of global financial governance. He argues that in the current world order, a distinctive financial public sphere has become integral to the regulation and governance of this domain. This public sphere is anchored in several different configurations of power, including civil society at the global level. The increasingly public character of this transnational system of financial governance means that for purposes of legitimation, it needs to bring civic organizations of various kinds into its ambit. This generates an important opportunity for different political issues and priorities to be raised in some of the most powerful centres of global economic decision-making.

In the concluding chapter, Randall Germain and Michael Kenny propose several avenues for further inquiry that arise out of the critical and normative insights generated in these essays. Continuing the analytical emphasis suggested above – upon the production, dissemination and variable implications of the idea of global civil society – they argue for focused research into three areas: 1) its status as the site of and source of ideological contestation at both national and transnational levels of political community; 2) its relationship with the practice and theorizing of citizenship; and 3) its significance as a theatre of power relations, inequalities and vital social struggles. Such research will help to highlight how the idea (and ideal) of global civil society is a constituent element in the construction of global political order.

Summary

Debates over the ideal of global civil society represent an important contribution to our broader understanding of global order in the contemporary period. Globalization, the end of the cold war and the 'retreat of the state', all suggest that traditional accounts of global order need to be recalibrated. Particular emphasis is given in this collection to the material, ideational, cultural and civilizational dimensions of global order, alongside the more conventional themes of state power and economic dominance. This broadened analytical focus, we suggest, is especially important as we enter an era when the world's leading superpower confronts an environment in which its hegemony is apparently impossible to sustain, despite the possession of overwhelming military, political and economic power. The ethical and normative possibilities closely associated with the idea of global civil society provide a potentially powerful lever for those trying to understand, and intervene within, struggles over global social order. It is therefore the responsibility of social scientists to subject this idea to rigorous critical scrutiny from as broad an array of intellectual sources as possible.

Part I

Contesting global civil society

2 Ideological contestation, transnational civil society and global politics

Andrew Gamble and Michael Kenny[1]

In the wake of the events of 11 September 2001, and the subsequent 'war' that began in Afghanistan and is now spreading beyond its borders, a marked convergence of focus between the world of politics and that of social scientific analysis is apparent. Over the last decade, analysts of political ideas, public policy, international politics and political economy have grappled with an increasingly common set of concerns as they try to make sense of transformations within the global economy and the related, but unsynchronized, emergence of a global society, partial and plural global public spheres, and a complex pattern of global governance across a range of policy issues. Coming to an understanding of the nature of these developments has encouraged individual analysts to step beyond the horizons of their sub-disciplines and to develop a shared pool of conceptual tools – including such notions as global governance, globalization and global civil society. All of these concepts are normative as well as analytical, and much debate within the social sciences is currently driven by attempts to unpack and contest the implications of these terms.

But this emergent vocabulary, and the concerns it reflects, is not confined to the academy. Even prior to the events of 11 September 2001, globalism and a new ethical internationalism had permeated the discourse of leading political actors. Debate continues about the motives and implications of the multi-lateralism advocated by, for instance, Tony Blair (a discourse clearly prefigured in the tentative articulation of a 'Third Way' International when Clinton was in the White House). But this trend is not confined to Blair. Various centrist politicians in Europe have begun to articulate a species of liberal internationalism (or 'liberal patriotism' as David Marquand (2002) suggests) – in which human rights are regarded as underpinned by strong universal norms of conduct and it is the duty of individual states, as well as such bodies as the UN, to enforce these rights (Dunne and Wheeler 1999).

The implications of this new internationalism, whatever domestic purposes may have helped shape it, are quite profound. It represents a considerable development upon states' understanding of the scope of the application of international law, exercised since 1945 primarily in relation to war crimes. What is particularly striking is that influential state actors are promoting the extension of international law, the logic of which is to limit the sovereign authority of states over their own subjects and their conduct towards others. Related to these arguments are the debates on the constitutional architecture of new kinds of regional authority, notably the European Union which has established a Constitutional Convention under the chairmanship of Giscard d'Éstaing to bring forward proposals about the future constitutional shape of Europe, as well as debates about what kind of public spaces can be guaranteed by appropriate laws and executive authorities.

Meanwhile, within some of the institutional forums within which decisions affecting the global economy are made, much the same language as that favoured by academic theorists is current: 'good' governance, civil society, social capital and the idea of a global civic culture all figure prominently within the vocabularies of those shaping the policy priorities of agencies such as the World Bank and the WTO, and it is not just at the elite level that such notions are in circulation (Wilkinson 2000). One of the most eye-catching social movements of recent times, the broadly based 'anti-globalization' coalition, has contributed to the new internationalism by focusing on the 'democratic deficit', the lack of transparency and accountability in the decision-making of such institutions as the WTO, and has brought these to the consciousness of a wide international public (Kaldor 1999a; 2000).

While the number and range of voices calling for the constitution of new kinds of public space, governance structures and mechanisms of accountability at levels beyond the nation-state is impressive, what will emerge from these debates is still open-ended and unclear. Sceptics have lined up to question both the motivations and the consequences of the construction of some kind of global political order. Many critics perceive the strategic interests of the United States, the undisputed superpower in the wake of the cold war, behind calls for 'good' global governance and the idea of international justice. They point to the inconsistency with which international norms are applied in the world order, observing that these tend to be enforced only when state failure or ethnic cleansing threatens American economic or security interests (Pilger 2002). When these norms appear to constrain powerful corporate interests, in the form of multilateral agreements on harmful emissions into the atmosphere, for example, the US government quickly brushes them aside. As Perry Anderson has recently put it: 'The tattered, if victorious flag of the Free World has been lowered. In its place the banner of "human rights" has been erected – that is, first and foremost the right of the "international community" to blockade, to bomb, to invade peoples or states that displease it . . . and to nourish, finance, and arm states that appeal to it' (2002a: 3). On this reading, the 'international community' is simply a euphemism for the national interests of the United States and its allies.

There are major criticisms also of the implications and influence of the emerging transnational civil society (Dunn 2002). Some dismiss the activities and networks of international non-governmental organizations, pressure groups and social movements as Lilliputians standing at the feet of the global Gulliver (Halliday 2000). For others, global civil society is elitist, Western-orientated and unaccountable to the global 'public' it claims to represent (Marden 1997) or to national democracies. More recently, a new kind of criticism of the project of creating a global civil society has emerged: critics detect in its 'civilising' message an attempt by Western elites to disseminate the norms of Western capitalism (Colás 2001). They point to the way in which such institutions as the World Bank deploy a highly normative idea of 'civil society' to legitimate particular kinds of intervention in recipient states and to delegitimate indigenous forms of cultural expression or anti-capitalist social forces (Wilkinson 2000). While the project of building a global civil society sounds benign and entirely progressive, in reality, according to these critics, it offers a human face to the ugly practices of global corporate capital.

These are large and intellectually challenging issues, on which there can be no final or easy answers. In this chapter we consider the role of ideology in shaping some of the leading accounts of the character of the emerging system of global governance and transnational civil society. In particular, we question the way in which critics of these processes, from both left and right, are prone to designate an all-powerful Western liberalism as the guiding force behind contemporary developments. Such a perception is too simplistic because it neglects the continuing significance of conservative thinking about national and international affairs, and mistakenly collapses a number of significantly different liberal and conservative arguments into one all-conquering reified orthodoxy of neo-liberalism. The wide range of liberal political ideas that developed from the nineteenth century onwards continues to provide a rich source for contemporary thinking about the moral purpose and political character of global governance and transnational society, and sustains critical and radical conceptions of global politics as well as arguments which support current developments. Many critics of the contemporary global order fail to register the ideological diversity and complexity which has grown up around these issues.

Contesting global governance

The discourses associated with the new internationalism, such as globalization and universal human rights, have discomfited the left because internationalism has for a long time been treated as its preserve, while nationalism and realism have been central to the outlook of the right. This change has led to a flurry of writing aimed at attacking the new internationalism and seeking to discredit it. Some of this literature is powerful on polemic but weak in any historical or analytical understanding. But there are exceptions. Perry Anderson (2002a) has developed a striking, and provocative, account of the changing modalities of nationalism, its relationship to internationalism, and the different meanings which internationalism has had as a result for the political left. Pivotal within his historical conspectus is a switch in the relative positions of capital and labour in relation to nationalist and internationalist aspirations in the second half of the twentieth century. From the 1950s, nationalism was invoked by forces 'from below', beyond the affluent continents of Europe and in North America, in the form of a variety of anti-colonial and post-colonial movements. At roughly the same time, those who controlled and benefited from the prevailing modes of capital accumulation began to shift their mode of operation and political ambitions beyond the scope of the territorial nation-state. 'Internationalism', in the sense of support for the institutions which sustained a multilateral liberal world economic order, became the ambition and primary mode of operation of some of the largest economic enterprises and simultaneously the mission of sections of the political elites of the most powerful nations.

This turn-around, Anderson argues, has been carried forward with a quantum leap in the contemporary period. The processes of economic globalization, accelerated by the implosion of official communism and the end of the cold war at the end of the 1980s, represent an unprecedented phase in the configuration of the relationship between metropolitan capitalist interests and those opposed to their hegemony. It is the former who sweep all before them, deploying the logic of neo-liberalism and overseeing the ambitious remodelling of the legal and institutional architecture of the world economy. Projects like the formation of a currency union within Europe, the adoption of region-wide trade agreements and, most powerfully, the construction of an 'architecture' systematizing global economic governance are being driven forward with precious little opposition. Figures from the political left are being sucked into the vortex of this new global 'common sense', a worldview that permits internationalism to become synonymous with the interests of the United States. Leaders of other states who support US-led intervention in the name of universal human rights are merely helping perpetuate its status as the undisputed superpower (Anderson 2002a; 2002b).

Anderson's rather bleak account of the contemporary period is mitigated by his openness to the contingencies of historical development and the complex relationship between the politics of nationalism and internationalism that he suggests. But his characterization of the contemporary period as one in which political reformers and radicals of the left are reduced to passivity and uncertainty by the apparently polarized choices represented by national and international political struggle is extremely resonant of a great deal of contemporary left opinion. Certainly in relation to the communities of Anglo-American radicalism, he captures (and appears to endorse) the dominant mood of bitterness and disillusion, not least with centre-left governments which talk enthusiastically of acting in the name of the international community to defend and promote human rights, and then attempt to enforce this vision with the use of bombs and troops.

Central to Anderson's argument, and that of many other radicals, is the notion that a new interlocking political and economic elite has become established at the global level, reflecting the unchallenged hegemony of neo-liberalism (2002b). A similar classification is adopted within some 'radical' approaches to international relations in which critical theory is counterpoised to dominant liberal accounts of 'global civil society' (Macdonald 1994). This dualistic approach to ideological debate is apparent too in critiques of the new global liberalism from the right of the political spectrum, which emphasize the irreducibility of nation-states, national economies and national cultures, as well as the folly of imagining that a true universalism that was not a cloak for national interests was ever possible (Gray 1998).

Global governance and civil society: delineating ideological contours

Such an account is reinforced by the argument that talk of a global civil society necessarily involves perpetuating a particular account of Western values, consumer capitalism and the individualistic model of freedom rooted in Western democracies (Pasha and Blaney 1998). Collapsing all arguments into an all-encompassing neo-liberalism does scant justice, however, to the very different ways in which such notions as global civil society and governance are currently understood. There are a number of contending models in circulation, with their roots in earlier ideological narratives. Indeed, the adoption of grand accounts of global change which stress spatio-temporal transformation and historical discontinuity (Rosenberg 2001) has tended to deflect attention from assessment of the role of extant political traditions in shaping understandings of economic and political change. All contemporary ideologies face dilemmas in trying to come to terms with the far-reaching transformations represented by the trends towards a more global economy, the end of strategic bipolarity following the collapse of the Soviet Union, and the rise of a global civil society (on the nature of dilemmas for political traditions, see Bevir 2000). These dilemmas are centred upon how each ideological tradition should respond to the weakening of the power and legitimacy of nation-states in the contemporary period, the ending of the long period in the twentieth century when territorial conceptions of world order focused on nation-states and their associated empires were dominant. Each tradition has had to re-orient itself, re-evaluate the meaning of the national and the international and consider what kind of world order it endorses. This process does not necessarily mean the collapse of any particular ideology, but it often requires the re-ordering of particular elements of a tradition, and the rediscovery of older, neglected aspects within it. In the past, conceptualizing politics from an international perspective was central to certain forms of liberalism and socialism, but such ways of thinking became much less prominent during the twentieth century, and it is only now that they are beginning to revive. This process contains many paradoxes, not least the casting of the new internationalism in the form of 'globalization' as the enemy to be struggled against. More generally, the gradual shift of political and ethical debate to embrace spheres beyond the national often involves the projection of traditions that owe much to their national context on to new kinds of political spaces. Interpreters of these ideological traditions try to adjust them to take account of the new world that is emerging. What does not exist is a simple opposition between globalization and anti-globalization, or between liberalism and anti-liberalism.

Conservative neo-realism

What these simple oppositions do in particular is to overlook not only the diversity within liberalism but also the very different emphases of the conservative and liberal traditions, and the importance of the conservative tradition, therefore, in understanding the nature of ideological contestation in relation to global politics. The neglect of conservative thought by many contemporary radical anti-globalization critics in their characterizations of US hegemony is quite striking. The continuing impact of conservative ideas over key political actors within the United States, as well as the 'organic intellectuals' within the intelligence, strategic and defence communities of the US erodes the simplistic duality favoured by many critics. Those working within the institutions of the new global 'empire' are by no means all liberals. The elite levels of world politics are places where contending visions of an emergent global society and polity are becoming apparent, and the conflicts between these have very different implications for the way in which this global society and polity will develop.

Most strands of the conservative ideological tradition tend to make their adherents highly suspicious of the very notion of global governance, as an ideal that can never be realized, and which, if attempted, will lead to the destruction of whatever fragile order exists. But there are different ways in which this basic insight is expressed by contemporary conservatives. The starting point for conservative thinking about international relations has most often been the nation and national sovereignty, but this has been supplemented from time to time by arguments about competing civilizations, cultures and ideologies, which require broader cooperation to meet a current danger (Kissinger 1994). Conservatives are disposed to see the world as a threatening, dangerous and insecure place. International affairs is depicted as a Hobbesian state of nature, but in which no lasting agreement to cede powers to a global sovereign to impose order is considered either feasible or desirable (Waltz 1965).

From the realist standpoint, the primary duty of each state is to guard its own security, and pursue its own interests. In the classic nineteenth-century formulation of this doctrine, a state has no permanent friends and no permanent enemies. Alliances shift according to changes in circumstances and interests, and the order that is created is a fragile one, reflecting temporary accommodations and a provisional balance of power which can always be upset by new circumstances (Bull 1977). There is no global economy or global society; at most there is an international economy and an international society, both firmly rooted in the territorial jurisdiction and sovereignty of the nation-state and therefore based on relationships between governments. Whatever intergovernmental agreements are concluded, however, the order that results is intergovernmental rather than supranational, and whenever there is a crisis the world reverts to a competition between rival nation-states. Conservatives have as a result only given limited support to projects such as the League of Nations and the United Nations because they suspect the intent behind their creation, and dispute the right of such bodies to override the national interest of states, or to set limits to the ability of states to defend their interests in the way they see best. Liberal cosmopolitanism has always been derided and despised by conservatives because they see it as peddling illusions, and because they do not believe that supranational organizations can ever hope to replace the nation-state as a focus of legitimacy and identity (Scruton 1984). In order to do so, such organizations would need to suppress existing national identities and jurisdictions by creating a new state.

Realism may be the default position for conservatives in thinking about global governance, but few are capable of adopting an entirely consistent realist standpoint. Instead realism is supplemented by notions of civilizations, races, cultures and ideologies, which arrange nations into competing blocs. The world is still an insecure place, but beyond the basic division between nations there are certain communities of interest and identity which can bind nations together in a common cause. Most important among these for conservatives have been various racial, cultural and ideological bonds. Defining their nation as part of the white race, or of Christendom, or of the West, has long been part of conservative argument. Such broader attachments have been used to identify friends and enemies, and to justify interventions and limited wars. One of the most influential recent expressions of this has been Samuel Huntington's view that the world order which is succeeding the cold war order will be shaped by a clash of civilizations, based ultimately on the religions of Islam, Christianity and Confucianism (1998). The differences between the civilizations are irreducible and not to be overcome by a shallow liberal universalism; any feasible world order has to recognize the separateness of these civilizations and of the nation-states within them, and therefore of the impossibility of ever escaping conflict. All that world order can do is to manage conflict; it cannot eliminate it.

After the end of the cold war in 1991, in the wake of the disintegration of the Soviet Union, there was a brief period of conservative cosmopolitanism. So complete appeared the ideological triumph of the West that some conservatives believed that the world might now be unified through every country adopting the Western model of economic and social organization, and accepting voluntarily the ideological and cultural hegemony of the United States. The end of the cold war momentarily appeared to have resolved not just the ideological question but the security question as well, and removed the basis for fundamental conflicts. These ideas were widespread throughout the Western media, and were voiced by many conservative Western politicians, including Margaret Thatcher, Ronald Reagan, Helmut Kohl and George Bush, all of whom instantly recognized the profound significance of the events they were witnessing. This feeling of triumphalism and finality were perfectly caught in Francis Fukuyama's declaration that this at last was Hegel's 'end of history', the end of ideological evolution and contestation, and the final victory of liberalism and capitalism (1992). Fukuyama's view represents a (mis)appropriation of liberal ideas for largely conservative ends. The modern world could at last begin, and it would be a conservative world, although not the world of which the conservatives of the *ancien régimes* of Europe had dreamed.

But this phase proved short-lived, not least because conflicts based upon economic rivalry, strategic imperatives, and cultural difference re-emerged in international politics. Huntington raised the spectre of a clash between civilizations, with the conflict between Islam and Christianity being singled out as the new fault line in international politics. This became consolidated after 11 September 2001 with the identification of Islamic terrorist networks as the new enemy of the West and the main threat to the security of its states. Margaret Thatcher labelled these terrorist networks as the new Bolshevism, and argued that as concerted and long-lasting a campaign had to be waged against these new forms of terrorism as had been waged against Communism (2002). In this way the ideological and the security concerns of conservatives are united once again in a heady cocktail, after a brief period when some conservatives had seemed disoriented in a world threatened by an outbreak of universal peace.

The playing of the security card by the new realists of the Bush administration in the United States, such as Condoleeza Rice and Donald Rumsfeld, has dampened enthusiasm for transnational aspects of the neo-liberal agenda as well as sidelining the more cautious statecraft of the State Department. In particular, it assists those in the United States arguing for a more forceful assertion of the nation's interests, and strengthens opposition to any new political and institutional structures beyond the nation-state. A more effective governance of the global economy is not desirable for conservatives if it entrenches supranational institutions with powers to override national governments. The unwillingness of the Bush administration to be bound by any international treaties which might produce judgements unfavourable to American interests led to the withdrawal by the United States from key agreements in 2001 and 2002, including that signed at Kyoto and the agreement to set up an international court to prosecute war crimes.

Conservatives have had to balance this new security agenda against sustaining the institutions necessary for an expanding global economy. This has created numerous dilemmas, for example, over how far to go in supporting multilateral free trade or new forms of regional co-operation such as the European Union, as against pursuing a narrow protectionist agenda to satisfy domestic interests. For many conservatives, national interests and national sovereignty are paramount and must always be put first. Others, however, have emphasized the concessions that must be made to establish a true hegemony, transcending short-term national advantage. In the first two decades after the Second World War the United States followed the second course, but in the last two decades it has placed its own national interests first, and has increasingly relied on force rather than persuasion to get its way. This has fuelled opposition to the United States, some of it violent, and this in turn (especially since 11 September 2001) has provided the pretext for another major expansion of the US security budget, after its contraction in the 1990s.

Another strand of the conservative tradition is opposed to big government of any kind, and doubts whether the new security agenda will make the United States more secure. Some thinkers, like John Gray, believe that the United States is trying to pursue ends that are incompatible – protecting its own security, and maintaining a neo-liberal institutional order for the global economy (1998). Gray argues that the dream of a neo-liberal order is a delusion and that the attempt to impose neo-liberal solutions on the whole world has produced instability and economic collapse. A world order has to be based on stable national capitalisms, and these will vary depending on the national and cultural traditions of different societies. The implication for conservatives is that many of the international institutions which impose neo-liberal solutions, such as the World Bank and

WTO, should be disbanded or fundamentally reformed. To contain the threat to its security, a state like the United States needs to disengage from the rest of the world, and stop seeking to impose any particular form of capitalism upon other states, accepting instead the organization of the world as a varied set of capitalisms and political systems.

Even if such a disengagement were possible, Gray (2002) is pessimistic about the chances of promoting a viable world order because of the new collective threats posed by environmental risks and technological discoveries to the security of all states. Modern technology has shrunk the world, making all states interdependent to a greater extent than before. The solutions to these challenges are not to be found within the 'spontaneous' workings of the global economy but through a new emphasis on political authority and state capacity. The thrust of this kind of thinking is toward the revival of nation-states, and, failing that, the organization of strong regional political and economic arrangements, of which the European Union is a prototype. What commends the European Union to many conservatives is not that it is a vehicle for imposing neo-liberal policies on all its member countries or a step towards constructing a global economy, but that it is a large enough economic and political space to be self-sufficient and therefore self-determining.

Varieties of liberalism

Conservatism in various guises is a presence within both national and global politics. In contention with it are various liberal projects. These are not singular or homogenous. In particular, the goals of economic liberals and the requirements of political versions of liberalism are as much in tension as mutually reinforcing. A grasp of the internal tensions within liberal narratives is largely absent from the imagination of contemporary radicalism but is indispensable to understanding the character of the ideas that are guiding and framing developments in global politics.

The political ideas associated with the promotion of global civil society and with the justification of global governance through such institutions as the WTO, the IMF and the World Bank, are liberal in different respects. The project of establishing a space within which associational life can develop between individual, nation-state and global institutions, carries the flavour of the liberal heritage (Warren 2001). In more precise terms, sources of inspiration for the assumption that such a development is instrumental in the achievement of the liberty of the individual, and the belief that freedom of association is necessary for a stable economic order, include Adam Smith and John Locke (who can be called 'liberals' only anachronistically). The legacy of their ideas continues to pervade institutions such as the World Bank, where the American model of civil society provides the most likely blueprint of a democratic polity and 'good governance' (Albright 2000). Both of these are seen as intrinsically valuable to the prospects of a liberal international order as well. The influence of Smith and the nineteenth-century tradition of laissez faire was apparent within the powerful arguments for global free trade that gained ground among the political elites of leading nation-states and international economic institutions in the 1980s and 1990s (Rupert 2000). A number of historians have demonstrated the character and importance of this ideological shift, as the 'embedded liberalism' that emerged in the wake of Bretton Woods was replaced by an emphasis upon the economic benefits for the whole world that a more open trading system would bring (Ruggie 1996). This perspective informed the prevailing 'narrative' of strong or hyper-globalization that has percolated through the worlds of politics and the academy (for an account of which see Held *et al.* 1999). Globalization, it suggests, is both inexorable and a natural extension of the propensity for capital to move across artificial national boundaries. With increasing economic interdependence and exchange, these economic liberals suggest, there emerges the prospect of a more peaceful international order as various outlying states and illiberal political regimes find their populations drawn to the benefits of global capitalism and liberal democracy.

Doubts about the wisdom of this particular neo-liberal account of globalization have become widespread in the last five years. Some of these concerns arose particularly in the aftermath of the East Asian financial crises, leading powerful opinion-leaders such as George Soros (2002) to doubt the wisdom of financial deregulation in the context of rapid currency mobility and the opportunities for aggressive financial speculation. Soros has led the way in pointing to the importance of constructing regulatory mechanisms at the global level, a call that has been taken up by numerous critics of global capitalism. A good deal of commentary has focused on the legitimation deficit facing the new global economic elite and the central institutions of the international economy, such as the WTO. Some see a role here for the emerging networks of global governance. A liberal international order now requires a global political architecture, argue liberal intellectuals, who anticipate the construction of a global analogue of the democratic state (de Oliveira 1995). Much academic commentary upon the benefits of global governance and international civil society is informed by liberal aspirations as well. Within liberal philosophy it is the tradition of cosmopolitan ethical theory, inspired by the work of Immanuel Kant, that has shaped the idea of global civil society and the associated notion of global citizenship (Beitz 1979). Within the world of politics, however, arguments for global governance and a global economy remain couched within the discourse of national interests, though these are deemed to be compatible with the emergence of transnational association and an international legal order. Several commentators argue that neo-liberalism has been displaced as the prevailing perspective by a revised liberal stance which stresses the importance of progressive and incremental changes in international law and the benefits of a regulated global economy (Rupert 2000).

There is more than a hint of de Tocqueville's notion of a rich and dense group life as a means of sustaining the legitimacy of a political system in liberal claims that a global civil society is coming into being (Warren 2001). As John Keane (2001a; 2001b) puts it, in a sentiment that echoes the demands of many parts of the anti-globalization movement, global civil society poses the question: 'Who is in Charge

Here?', of an economic order in which human control and rational decision-making appear almost entirely absent. It does so, its advocates suggest, by bringing the public gaze to bear upon the tyrannical and corrupt behaviour of political and corporate elites, and by bringing alternative moralities and values to a global audience. Not all advocates of the new liberal international order are therefore unqualified supporters of economic liberalism. And many of those seeking to understand and criticize the existing pattern of development in these areas draw upon parts of the liberal heritage.

Within European and American liberalism, the status and meaning of democracy, and particularly representative democratic forms, have been continually debated. An influential body of political thought now argues that representative democracy no longer functions adequately at the level of the nation-state. The idea of a cosmopolitan democracy, encompassing a variety of political levels and representing a powerful constraint upon the abuse of political and economic power, is one important development of this idea (Archibugi and Held 1995; Held 1995). The case for cosmopolitan democracy is closely allied to republican arguments about constitutional arrangements and participation in public affairs (Onuf 1998). One of the most influential recent moves within the historical study of political ideas in the English-speaking world has been the excavation and reconsideration of the republican heritage, and its complex relationship with liberalism. This shift has spilled over into philosophical debates about the character of liberalism, and of liberal citizenship and freedom (Virilio and Shugaar 2002). Although republican arguments are often presented as antithetical to liberal goals, a potent strand of liberal republicanism has surfaced within recent political philosophy asking whether we can interpret the emergence of transnational alliances and operations among campaigning groups, social movements and lobbying organizations as contributing to the formation of a putative global civic culture. Keane detects the tentative and partial emergence of global 'public spaces' that are in some ways analogous to those that arose within nation-states (2001b). Other commentators explore the role of global systems of communication and the impact of the mass media in carving out and colonizing 'spaces' outside the scope of national cultures and borders (Morley and Robins 1999). Within these, the struggle between corporate control and citizens' 'voice' mimics the battles fought between the forces of instrumental reason and those defending the 'life-world' of citizens in the public spheres of democratic states (Cohen and Arato 1992).

The republican impulse is apparent as well in the efforts of such theorists as Jurgen Habermas (2001) to carry forward the project of liberal constitutionalism in a variety of transnational settings. Habermas's influence is widespread: the question of how to establish norms of dialogic interaction in spaces which allow for the encounter of different, and often hostile, cultural perspectives, carries a particular urgency following the attempt by terrorists to appropriate political Islam. The project of establishing a 'dialogue of civilizations' with a view to distilling minimal norms guiding international law and social provision in such areas as the education of girls, genital mutilation and abortion, flows from the republican approach to global civil society (Lynch 2000). It has, for instance, informed some of the path-breaking, and problematic, efforts of the United Nations to oversee informal assemblies bringing together representatives of states, social movements and cultural communities on such issues as gender and racism (Otto 1996). A liberal-republican agenda is immanent both within the perspectives of many of the most important non-state actors in global politics and in the assumptions behind the acceptance of the mandate of international law by many states. The next stage in the construction of a putative global republic is, as Martin Shaw suggests, to 'systematise the demands of global responsibility in a new conception of the roles, rights and duties of citizens, society, states, the system of states, and international institutions' (2000: 433).

A further element within the European and American liberal tradition has also exercised considerable influence on debate about the ethics of global society – the perspectives and themes associated with the social liberalism developed in the United States, Britain, Italy and Germany in the decades around the turn of the twentieth century (Freeden 1978). This is an internally rich and complex lineage, and one that has been extensively re-examined as one source of contemporary 'communitarian' thinking. Among its many themes and perspectives is an opposition to individualistic notions of the self, bequeathing a commitment to social solidarity and interdependence in the realm of ontology, and to social justice in political ethics. Today's campaigners against the social inequities and irresponsibility of unregulated global accumulation, and those calling for a more equitable settlement of planetary resources, are latter-day heirs to exactly these concerns. The moral and philosophical challenges posed by the problem of 'global justice' have become a major focus within academic political philosophy (Caney 2001). In these debates the work of John Rawls, a figure who picks up the tradition of social liberalism, is central. Again there are some interesting overlaps between philosophical speculation and political endeavour, for instance, in a figure like Amartya Sen. His argument that the development of a person's 'capabilities' rather than the absolute amount of their resources is the key to achieving autonomy and freedom has had a major impact on debates on economic development and global poverty, and has influenced a number of initiatives and programmes within the United Nations (Sen 2001; Nussbaum and Sen 1993).

Latterly there has emerged among liberal theorists a marked concern about the degree to which cultural difference ought to be affirmed, rather than merely tolerated within the terms of the rule of law. Some argue that liberalism's origins in the Reformation and its commitment, through figures such as Locke and Smith, to the idea of neutrality on the part of the state vis-à-vis contending religions, means that it alone offers a just constitutional basis for the co-existence of hostile cultures (Galston 1991; Larmore 1997). Other commentators seek inspiration in the thinking of nineteenth-century figures such as Mill in their attempts to present the allocation of special rights to cultural minorities as the logical outcome of liberal theory (Kymlicka 1995).

The concerns of this perspective are particularly resonant within contemporary debates about the character and limits of global civil society, as well as of conceptions of the international community proclaimed by Western politicians such as Tony Blair. They have moved to the forefront of political debate in the wake of the events of 11 September. Can the many different cultural, religious and moral perspectives by which nations live be reconciled with universal norms that are broadly perceived as legitimate and indeed just? Should the institutions at the heart of global governance tolerate local customs and cultures that appear beyond the pale of liberal decency? Does such a move require that we adopt a more relativistic conception of values, and avoid imposing 'our' values upon 'their' cultures? Does this disqualify Western campaigners from imposing universal conceptions of human rights in the face of political regimes which claim that these are colonial impositions and that civil and political rights are of secondary moral standing in local cultures (Bell 2000)?

The balance of these arguments is at a particularly precarious and significant stage, and is drawing upon the energies of activists and academics alike. Multiculturalist liberals have produced some powerful and hard-hitting criticisms of the foundations and consequences of liberal thought, but they have rarely rejected its fundamental commitments to some degree of moral universalism, the moral equality of persons, and the establishment of the rule of law (Parekh 2000). Equally, the demands for positive 'recognition' beyond the purchase of liberal tolerance that are associated with the myriad forms of identity politics in democratic states have a strong bearing upon conceptions of the global 'demos' (ibid.). What kinds of representative rights ought the United Nations give to religious groupings and minority cultures that are opposed to liberal norms in international forums? And what sorts of 'recognition' can be conferred upon states and communities in order to extend the boundaries of international community? Efforts to reconstruct liberalism around the problematic of 'recognition' carry a particular purchase for such issues (ibid.). All of them seek to reconfigure the public culture of democratic society, so that a variety of group and personal identities find themselves included within the constitutional framework of the community (Young 1990). Critics of the stereotypical depictions of Islamic culture in the mass media, of the orientalism of Western culture, and of the ethnocentrism of much liberal debate about global politics, are themselves part of a long tradition of liberal anti-imperialist reasoning.

Ideological contestation in global politics

There are good reasons, therefore, to regard liberalism as an ideological family rather than a single doctrine, confronting a number of established rival perspectives on the contemporary world order. Increasingly attention is being paid to the emergence of populist movements on the far right of the political spectrum which offer a powerful mixture of ethnic nationalism, hostility to immigrants and a critique of the global economy. Mark Rupert (2000) identifies the populist character and localized significance of this force within American politics in the 1990s, in the guise of a new hard-edged nationalist politics centred around such figures as Pat Buchanan and implacably opposed to NAFTA. Central to this populist conservatism is the conflation of the pernicious forces of globalization with cosmopolitanism in contrast to the security represented by ethnic forms of belonging. Similar ideological hybrids have recently come to the fore within several European democracies, most dramatically in the case of France during the Presidential elections of 2002. Located in the hinterland beyond mainstream conservatism, nationalism and neo-fascism, this kind of regressive identity politics is likely to emerge as a familiar part of the ideological scene in an era when many collective anxieties and insecurities are blamed upon an all-powerful liberal elite. In a context where political and ideological endeavour is shifting to scales beyond the national, the dream of returning to an ethnically pure nationhood is emerging as a powerful alternative to the liberal patriotism and globalism offered by political and economic elites. But other, non-Western ideological hybrids are equally significant as challengers to liberal ideas. Recent attempts to develop conceptions of Asian values, usually based on the precepts of Confucianism, as well as new versions of Islam, are especially significant in this regard. Benjamin Barber's (1996) apocalyptic duality between 'Jihad' and 'McWorld' does inadequate justice therefore to the plurality of ideological contestation beyond the reach of the nation-state, and the same is true of the new left fantasy of 'the Empire' which includes the terrorists who oppose it, and is arraigned against a diverse but ultimately unified opposition, 'the multitude' (Hardt and Negri 2000).

Equally, it is clear that internal differences within the family of liberal thought, and its various mutations from the eighteenth century onwards, continue to resonate within the Western political imagination. These traditions still afford invaluable resources for political actors and intellectuals struggling to provide an ethical account of the new global politics. Our focus has been upon the transfer of ideas and narratives that were once confidently applied to national political communities to debates about global politics and society. Yet it is also important to recall the arguments that continue among liberal theorists about whether such notions as citizenship, civil society and justice can be meaningfully applied beyond the boundaries of the nation (Rawls 1999; Miller 2001).

While philosophers continue to debate whether the criteria of rationality and logic permit the 'globalization' of liberal political ethics, it is significant that for those seeking to intervene within and offer a critique of developments in the world, the need to transfer familiar ethical traditions to these new levels has been overwhelming. Indeed this should come as no surprise in the wake of the recent appearance of several sophisticated interpretative models of ideology. These tend to suggest the inadequacy of the positivist divorce of action and ideas. Ideologies are not best understood simply as distorted or unnecessarily partisan beliefs, nor in the manner of some Marxists, as smokescreens arising from already formed interests (Freeden 1996). The hangover from this last conception is still with us. In particular, critics of globalization, global governance and Western civil society might do well to abandon the impulse to unmask all such talk as mere bourgeois ideology, concealing deep-laid plots by powerful interests to dominate the world. Instead, to achieve the radical critique they want, they need to come to a strategic understanding of the ideological field arising around these questions before making critical arguments and interventions. Together with other interpreters of recent developments in the realms of global politics, they need to be aware of the contribution of different parts of the liberal tradition in particular, and the modern cultural heritage in general, in shaping critical, counter-hegemonic conceptions of the architecture of the emerging global polity. It is only by coming to terms with the complexity and contingency of the ideological constructs shaping our understanding of these changes that critics can properly proceed with the tasks of critical engagement and transformation.

This brief sketch of some of the leading ideological positions shaping understanding of global developments is merely a start on the much more extensive mapping that is required. It reveals that some of the leading arguments of political actors within and beyond the processes and spheres being described here can be traced back to the development of the liberal heritage. It suggests too that the designation of a singular liberal outlook as the perspective of the metropolitan elite that figures in various radical narratives – both within the West and in parts of the Islamic world, leads to a fundamental misunderstanding of the ideologically contentious character of the construction of a global political order.

Conclusions

Our argument has a number of implications. First, the redeployment of a number of conservative and liberal 'narratives' in the context of international affairs shows that the view that political ideologies have ceased to play a role in ordering political ideas, and that ideologically driven conflicts are things of the past, is premature. The suggestion that with the declining significance of politics at the level of the nation-state (due to a combination of globalizing and localizing forces), political thought can escape its nationally grounded ideological moorings looks especially hollow.

The second intellectual and political implication of our argument is that critics have failed to engage with the specific character of the post-war hegemony exercised by the United States and its allies within the world order. This is a hegemony underpinned by a set of norms, broadly liberal in character, but some of which do not sit easily alongside one another. While hegemony generically implies domination and inequity, and the advancement of certain interests over others, hegemonies differ in their ideological character, as Antonio Gramsci (1971) sought to argue to his fellow Communists in Italy in the 1930s. The differences between a hegemony organized around broadly liberal precepts and one established around Stalinist, Fascistic or Theocratic principles needs to be grasped within the strategic and moral outlook of practitioners of radical politics. Liberal hegemonies offer particular kinds of openings and opportunities for leftists and democrats of various persuasions, as well as certain closures, silences and orthodoxies that require more overt challenge and opposition. A reconsideration of the heritage of Western radicalism would therefore be advantageous at this moment. In the period characterized by the fundamental reconstruction of the political, social and economic worlds of contemporary capitalism arising from the shift to a modern industrialized economy in the mid–late-nineteenth century, radicals and socialists saw themselves as the heirs to the democratic, republican and social revolutions that liberalism promised but was unable to complete. This produced an orientation towards critical, strategic and ideologically sensitive intervention that has few parallels today. There are, however, a number of disparate projects and ideas in circulation that possess some potential in this regard. One such example is the project of 'humane governance' skilfully and extensively advocated by Richard Falk (1995a). 'Globalization from below', he argues, results from the articulation of protest and complaint at the consequences of 'globalization from above' and is likely to result in the shaping of a new kind of global governance.

Critics from the left may well reply that even if liberalism does furnish some critical ideas about current developments, it does so in only limited and partial forms, and is in all its guises hampered by its neglect of political economy. This suggests an important and interesting question for our analysis, and is the third implication of the argument offered here: if liberalism and conservatism have been successfully reapplied on the global stage, is the same true of socialism, an ideology with such a strong internationalist heritage? Is there indeed any longer a distinctive socialist contribution to the debates on globalization other than a fatalistic condemnation of all contemporary forms of governance as irredeemably corrupt and subordinate to capitalist interests?

Some socialists believe that the current phase of world history, the triumph of neo-liberalism and the demise of apparent alternatives, means that socialism is temporarily dormant but will revive eventually as resistance to the new dispensation mounts (Anderson 2002a; 2002b). But this does not explain why socialism as a method of analysis has so far been so wanting in accounting for the new age of capital. The explanation may partly lie in the deficiencies of the socialist tradition itself, particularly in its insensitivity to questions of institutional and constitutional design, the rule of law, the need for civil rights, or multi-party democracy. The republican and democratic side of socialism has been relatively undeveloped, which is why the running has so often been made by liberals in these debates. Another deeper reason is a historic failure of socialists to renew their own tradition by taking Marx's project of dialectically transforming modernity seriously. Instead many radicals seem to prefer to reject modernity in its current manifestation altogether. If socialism is to renew its own internationalist tradition this will have to change.

Notes

1 The authors are grateful to Ian Bache, Michael Freeden and Randall Germain for their comments on an earlier draft of this chapter.

3 Intimations of a Gramscian approach to global civil society

Anne Showstack Sassoon

Introduction

The starting point for this chapter is considerable scepticism about the concept of global civil society and the way in which it is invoked. Such scepticism may seem misplaced given the emergence of a wide variety of non-governmental organizations, many based on voluntary support, which operate across national boundaries with increasing ease, or address global issues, or exert pressure on international institutions or a combination of all three (Scholte 2001). They appear to constitute the basis of an international or global civil society. Whatever the evaluation of the contents, forms, or strategies and tactics of these organizations, they exist, they have an impact on politics, and consequently they cannot be ignored. The concern about how civil society is invoked is no greater than scepticism about the usage of a range of concepts not only in academic debates but as they are deployed by policy-makers and politicians with implicit or explicit political agendas. Community, citizenship, globalization also come to mind.

The doubts here, however, focus on particular issues. These regard, first of all, the extent to which such a concept can be abstracted from its history and reference points from earlier historical periods and transposed and projected onto a very different moment and reality (Kumar 1993), most particularly from the 'national' to the 'global'. Secondly, much of the literature on global civil society is silent about or takes for granted the state and the rule of law. With a few exceptions, these are often implicitly reduced to the moment of coercion and the realm of necessity and are counterposed to the presumed freedom and ethical dimensions of civil society.[1]

Detaching civil society from the state obscures the fact that the former developed historically and conceptually hand in hand with the emergence of the modern state. Indeed civil society is a marker of its modernity and in turn the rule of law is the guarantor of civil society's conditions of existence. Separating civil society from the state leads to lack of attention to inevitably interrelated concerns. These are of the greatest relevance today and formed the background for the development of the concept and reality of both the modern state and civil society in their earlier incarnations: questions of security, authority, legitimacy and justice.

These 'traditional' questions are being posed anew at a global level, not least by 11 September 2001 whose roots can in part be found in groups which do not recognize the legitimacy and authority of existing regimes and institutions, whether in the Middle East or in North America (Halliday 2000: 40–1). They are also posed by international economic processes, environmental issues, and human rights agendas. It is not clear that the notion of governance can replace the protections and relative certainty of the rule of law and the accompanying need for institutions with sufficient legitimacy and authority to enforce it (Kenny 2001; Scholte 2000c; Shaw 2000: 88ff.). In a collection of essays published as a response to the events of 11 September, in the context of discussing global governance, Fred Halliday argues that the 'core of the system, the entities to which most people still look for legitimacy, identity and the provision of public goods, remains states. . . . Indeed, as some problems increase, states and inter-state cooperation may have more, not fewer, demands made on them' (Halliday 2000: 189). Nor can global civil society supplant states and inter-governmental institutions. He writes that although

> the special place given to NGOs and related social movements [is] . . . to a considerable degree justified, . . . the role and potential of these NGOs and of other elements in civil society should not be exaggerated. First of all, they cannot and should not supplant states and are in many ways dependent on the collaboration and, in the case of aid agencies, the funding of states. . . . Secondly, not all that is 'non-state' is liberal or benign. . . . Thirdly, in many semi- and non-democratic countries 'civil society' is controlled or suppressed . . . 'Civil society' operates where broader democratic and legal norms also operate and where these organizations themselves operate on the basis of good internal governance.
>
> (Halliday 2000: 190–1)

Martin Shaw's arguments are somewhat different. He maintains that 'Global statehood can be said to be coming into existence, to the extent that global state relations and forms are inclusive and constitutive of state relations and forms in general. However, the global state coexists and is in tension with other more particularistic forms of state' (Shaw 2000: 192). At the same time, he argues that

> The expansion of democracy, individual rights and an autonomous realm of civil society challenge the established modes of power in all state centres . . . The global revolution is rooted in society rather than in states, but its core process is a transformation of . . . the social relations surrounding state institutions . . . and it necessarily involves major changes in state forms. State elites are not the primary social forces transforming these relations, but they are active participants in the processes . . . States are paradoxically both obstacles to global transformation and central means through which change comes about.
>
> (Shaw 2000: 232 emphasis in original)

Civil society, then, may, or may not, contribute to democratic transformations, but it is not an independent variable. On the contrary, it relies on norms and processes which can only be guaranteed by law and hence by effective government. While organizations and activities associated with civil society may, or may not, contribute to the processes and cultures that make democratic legitimacy meaningful and effective, the sources of such legitimacy are not identical with or necessarily derived from civil society. In fact such organizations and activities can contribute to undermining what legitimacy exists. Indeed, anti-statist ambivalence towards government and law is a major factor contributing to low expectations of democracy and to cynicism about politics in general.[2] Hopes and expectations are often transposed onto civil society conceptualized as in some way detached and preserved from the negativity associated with the political sphere, splitting the 'good' from the 'bad'.[3]

Separating 'civil' from 'political' analytically and empirically is unhelpful, even when, as will be argued below, they must not be conflated. A real or perceived democratic deficit, the widely recognized inadequacies of traditional social democracy and other 'statist' politics (Shaw 2001; Stammers 2001), and the real constraints on what governments of whatever hue can deliver, all contribute to this silence on the state. On the one hand, while a 'global state' may as yet appear more as potential than actuality, we may be helped to conceptualize the emergence of a non-territorial 'global civil society' by thinking of it as an enabling and voluntary space (Kenny 2001), as made up not only of organizations which operate at a global level but of different communities, for example, scientists or economists in the conditions of the early twenty-first century. On the other hand, there is the argument that an imminent 'global state' is emerging with revolutionary implications both for politics and for conceptual frameworks (Shaw 2000). Certainly, questions concerning the extent to which 'global civil society' and national civil societies are influenced by the structures and policies of governmental institutions, together with strategic and practical questions concerning recognition and representation and how to shift power relations, mean that addressing the nature of politics and the state however conceptualized are unavoidable.[4] Indeed, in a field of very unequal power relations, the need for rules, order, fairness and justice is recognized, for example, by campaigns for fair trade or environmental protection or labour rights that address both national governments and international institutions (Richard Falk cited in Shaw 2000: 264). It is difficult, therefore, to separate 'civil' from 'political' analytically or empirically.

Lessons from the past

Framing these concerns is the paradox that, unless we simply reject all that has gone before and ignore the resources at our disposal, we have no choice – at least initially – to analyse the 'new' through concepts at hand, at the same time as historical change compels us to confront their limits and challenges us to develop new tools of analysis or to transform the old to help us to see the world differently. This paradox involves major philosophical issues that many people are grappling with today (Hoopes 1999; Scholte 1999; Shaw 2000: 25, 70ff.). In the 1930s Antonio Gramsci engaged with this very problem in struggling with similarly challenging questions (Sassoon 2000e). This parallel is one reason that Gramsci can help us to clarify some of what is at issue today even though he cannot provide all the answers. It is necessary, for example, to go beyond Gramsci to address many of the concerns posed at the beginning, certainly back to the liberal tradition or contract theory from Hobbes onwards, to consider questions of security and accountability, even if Gramsci's concept of hegemony can contribute to a broadening of discussions of legitimacy and authority. Nor can we expect ideas developed in such a different context to be applied *tout court* to the contemporary world. Of necessity they must be translated and developed as they are transposed.[5]

Gramsci's writings are therefore relevant not only because his concept of civil society is often invoked in recent debates about global civil society but because he developed and went beyond traditional concepts in order to reflect on major challenges to the received political 'wisdom' of his day. Furthermore, the major historical watersheds that stimulated the development of his ideas influenced the history that forms the backdrop to the contemporary situation. Above all, Gramsci is relevant today because his recognition of the significance of civil society is rooted in the study of the nature of political power as it evolved in the early twentieth century. Beyond the content of his ideas, the ways in which he engaged with these challenges to resurrect and reformulate old concepts, such as civil society, can help us to frame questions today. Thinking creatively and laterally, what would now be termed 'out of the box', making unexpected links inspired by unlikely sources, he attempted to capture the immanent trends and political potential in contemporary change in order to analyse precisely those aspects that did not fit easily into pre-constituted categories. The aim here, then, is to situate his writings on civil society in his historical period. It will be argued that his discussion of civil society must be connected to his concept of the state and hegemony. Gramsci's ideas cannot, of course, be reduced to his historical context but neither can they be fully understood without reference to it. However, only by understanding that they were developed as a response to specific challenges can their wider applicability as well as their limitations be evaluated.

Gramsci in historical context: war, the state and political power[6]

When Gramsci was writing in a fascist prison in the 1930s, the coercive power of the state was all too evident, and the expanded role of the state was a major international issue. The First World War had had a profound impact not just on the societies directly involved and beyond (Hobsbawm 1994: 22–36) but also, not surprisingly, on Gramsci's work. The war had demonstrated the capacity of states in exceptional circumstances to organize societies in unprecedented ways. The widespread social effects of the horrors and the destructiveness of the war had threatened to undermine political support for the governments involved. The consequences of the war forced political leaders to reach out to new constituencies and to make political promises, such as those by Lloyd George to the suffragettes, in order to consolidate support for the war effort. Consent was maintained through exchange or bargaining. Support the war and there will be votes for women and homes fit for heroes. An historically unprecedented dependence on mobilizing political consent and economic organization was the pre-condition for military success.

Writing only a few years later, Gramsci's reference to trenches as fortifications of the state therefore had more than metaphorical resonance. The war of movement, or frontal attack, might have succeeded in tsarist Russia, but the war of position, Gramsci argued, was the necessary metaphor for a strategy of fundamental change in complex Western societies. The latter derived from a reflection on the significance of the forms of modern warfare and from recognition of the connections between civil society, on the one hand, and political and military power, on the other (Gramsci 1971: 235, 238–9). The modern state, in one of Gramsci's famous formulations, had to be understood as force plus consent or as 'hegemony protected by the armour of coercion' (Gramsci 1971: 263). Moreover, hegemony had to be continually reconstructed in the context of ongoing historical change to protect existing power relations that, in turn, could only be supplanted through a struggle for widespread consent to a different social order. The expansion of support for a different project for society based on an alternative hegemony implied constructing an alternative historic bloc of diverse social forces won away from allegiance to the existing order (ibid.: 168, 418), bound together by a collective will (ibid.: 130, 133, 194, 195, 197). Such an alternative could only be established through addressing social needs and striking compromises in which widening sections of the population supported a different mode of social development. The legitimacy of political leadership rested on maintaining influence throughout civil society by guaranteeing social wellbeing and through winning people to an alternative vision of society. Political power also depended, as was obvious to the incarcerated Gramsci, on an ability if necessary to resort to force – although the deeper and wider the consent, the less the need for coercion. This is a long discussion but suffice it to say that the theoretical and analytical value that Gramsci placed on civil society was developed in the context of trying to understand the essential features of modern political power and modern societies and therefore the contours of the terrains of struggle to change power relations.

The extension of state activity and the mobilization not only of military forces through conscription but also of wider society brought with it several implications. Both in a modern war and in the maintenance of political power in modern societies broad consent was as essential as the productivity of the economy or social relations on the home front, however much military discipline or the capacity to resort to force internally continued to be fundamental. Secondly, differentiation between civil and political, or indeed civil and military, while useful methodologically and essential ethically, corresponded to only part of reality. Such distinctions, or indeed the either/or spatial metaphor implied, simply did not capture the new weave of threads connecting different parts or aspects of society, the nature of political power or social relations in the twentieth century. Civil society was a vital feature of modern states that could not be subtracted from politics. At the same time, however, as political power depended on civil society, or might be vulnerable because of challenges emanating from it, the possibility of the state employing coercion to back up the law and to maintain order remained an essential dimension of political power, not least to contain any violence which might erupt in civil society.

As the forms of state power were changing in the inter-war period, and political and civil society were increasingly interwoven, public and private spheres and the relationship between the two continued to be recomposed in the 1930s in countries as diverse as Italy, Germany, the USA and the USSR. These changes were taking place as responses to economic, political and social crisis. Attempts at social engineering and economic management and regulation, the creation of parks and garden cities, the building of dams and highways, the reclaiming of land and electrification, and the construction of monumental buildings with public finance were widespread (Ades *et al.* 1995). Public policy extended to addressing the development of mass cultural forms such as film and radio or, in some countries, the regulation of alcohol. Traditional social relationships, including gender relations, were challenged by the projects of building socialism in the Soviet Union, remaking and 'purifying' German and Italian society, and producing the kind of workers suited to a Taylorized assembly line. The family was the site of interventions – from Detroit to Rome to Berlin to Moscow – as traditional socialization no longer guaranteed desired outcomes and certainly not the noble women and men needed to construct new societies (De Grazia 1992). Changing values, controlling behaviour and motivating consent, both in economic organization and in maintaining allegiance to or at least passive acceptance of the state, entailed a range of practical policies, public or private, such as Henry Ford's attempts to control the private lives of his workers (Gramsci 1971: 303). Hegemony had roots in the workplace, the home, the school and the cinema.

This reconfiguration of major features of politics and society, involving changes in the roles of intellectuals, experts and politicians, meant that the nature of strategies to maintain hegemony could only in part be understood using traditional concepts. The words might remain the same, but their meaning was being transformed because of the effects on theory of profound economic, social and political change that was beyond the control of, but was also produced in part by the activities of political parties, social movements, and economic actors. Gramsci investigated these changed meanings as he attempted to take account of what we would now term the cutting edges of historical development (Sassoon 2000e).

Why civil society?

This is the context in which Gramsci resurrected and redefined a traditional concept, civil society, not notable at the time in left political discourse.[7] Why this concept? Because reformulated it helped him to comprehend several contemporary political developments: the resilience of capitalist regimes despite profound economic and political upheavals; the weakness of the post-Risorgimento Italian state and the success of fascism in Italy, based on a movement that arose outside 'normal' politics; and differences between Russia and the West. He noted that while the 1917 revolution could be successful in tsarist Russia, where an atrophied state, emptied of effective power, could be toppled by a frontal attack in the absence of civil society, such a revolution had failed in the West because the state was fortified by a complex civil society (Gramsci 1971: 235, 238).[8] Indeed, civil society was crucial not only in maintaining power relations but in transforming them. These required the development in the USSR of a modern civil society, which would be the real bulwark of the new system.

Hence Gramsci developed a set of analytical tools to help him to understand what most of his contemporaries in the working class movement and beyond did not – the complex nature of state power in the twentieth century and its intimate dependence on civil society. Gramsci quite consciously went back to a traditional term but then transformed it. When he writes that he *often* employs the concept of civil society (but implicitly *not only*) in the way that Hegel used it (Gramsci 1971: 208), he is referring above all to the ethical role of the state, to the structures, practices and ideas through which consent to the social order is achieved and to the roles of intellectuals. But going beyond Hegel, he neither reifies the state nor reduces civil society to a fractious realm of self-interest.[9] Effective political power in the modern world was not a one-way process of political management. Nor could it be understood without an adequate comprehension of the nature of civil society in the concrete. In its nationally and historically differentiated institutional forms and contents civil society conditioned state power and the activities of political parties, and was inevitably conditioned in turn.[10]

Gramsci was thus interested both in analysing contemporary reality and considering how state intervention might be changed from transformation from above for ends determined by the few, a mode of managing change he termed passive revolution (Gramsci 1971: 58–9, nn. 8–10, 106–20), into facilitating the liberation of human capacities. Gramsci's argument that the fulfilment of democracy and implicitly achievement of socialism implies the expansion of civil society and the shrinking of the state, in 'the narrow sense', as a lawmaking and enforcing body (ibid.: 261), as coercion can only be dismissed as dangerous utopianism (Keane 1988b) if it is subtracted from its historical context. Rather, it is important to understand how he reformulated the concept of civil society as he engaged in prison with several precise intellectual and political traditions: Catholicism, Italian idealism, economic liberalism, fascism, and Soviet socialism.

The parameters of debate

The unification of Italy ousted the Catholic Church from political control over central parts of the Italian peninsula. Having been forced out of a formal political role, the Church nonetheless retained enormous power and influence. Indeed it claimed to represent civil society, or what was termed 'Italia reale', which was contrasted to ' Italia legale' (Gramsci 1975: 2057–8). The Church refused to recognize the new Italian state, and did everything it could from its base in civil society to undermine the legitimacy of the political order.[11] As Gramsci analysed the unified state's limited hegemony, in part a manifestation of the opposition of the Church, he could not fail but be impressed by the political significance of the Church's role in civil society. While acknowledging the significance of its ideological and political influence and social power, and departing markedly from a long tradition in Italy of anti-clericalism,[12] Gramsci nonetheless disagreed with its claim to represent the whole of Italian civil society. Civil society, he maintained, could not be represented by any one institution, be it church, party, or state, but no one could doubt its political and strategic significance.

Gramsci's critique of the Italian idealist philosophers Benedetto Croce, Giovanni Gentile and Ugo Spirito, the latter two identifying closely with the fascist regime, is also relevant. Croce was part of the Southern Italian Hegelian tradition, a tradition that advocated a leading role for the state and for the stratum of intellectuals to which he belonged in modernizing and industrializing Italy. Despite his own role in politics, first serving in an early fascist government and then opposing the regime, Croce was little help in understanding the contemporary political and social roles of different kinds of intellectuals and experts or the complex weave of civil society which constituted such an important terrain of political struggle over what would be the dominant influences in that process of change (Gramsci 1975: 1302–3; Sassoon 2000c, 2000d).

Indeed, Italian fascism, Gramsci thought, had a much better understanding of the nature of modern mass society and the implications for state power. Yet, Gramsci is unambiguous when he argues against Gentile, Spirito and other fascist thinkers that, contrary to their positions, political and civil society should not be conflated. However interrelated, the latter could not be absorbed by the former in a developed modern state, and although tightly interconnected, conceptual differentiation was essential. Fascism aimed to unify society through a single party, associated bodies and the totalitarian state that, it was claimed, could represent all social forces eliminating the need for independent organizations in civil society. Gramsci argues, both analytically and strategically, against claims that political society should, or even could, absorb civil society (Gramsci 1971: 54, 264). Gramsci maintained that these ambitions were no more valid than the claims of the Catholic Church to represent all of civil society, or, significantly, those of any other intellectual elite, or political party or regime.

The implications are clear with regard to any regime, including the Soviet Union. A link that might at first appear unlikely is provided by Gramsci's critique of the assumptions of economic liberalism, another site of his discussion of civil society (Gramsci 1971: 263). The state was not the be all and end all (ibid.: 268–9). But could the state, defined as coercion, in fact wither away (ibid.: 267)? While confronted by the irrefutable statism of the 1930s reinforced by the Soviet model,[13] it is all the more significant that Gramsci nonetheless considered the terms in which the traditional Marxist question of the withering away of the state could be posed as a concrete political project. In his view, any notion of the state simply withdrawing and leaving a vacuum was unrealistic in modern society (ibid.. 261–3).

Consequently he disagreed that the liberal idea of a nightwatchman state, a state that does the bare minimum to protect society from danger (a metaphor that was adopted by parts of the social democratic movement), could serve as a model. A civil society which becomes more complex, as organizations within it articulate new needs and take on new tasks and responsibilities, had the potential to become the precondition, if not the guarantee, for the transformation of the state in which its ethical content expands; it increasingly reflects social needs, and its coercive role diminishes (Gramsci 1971: 261–3, 267, 283). This is a different perspective to claiming that the existing state could simply do less and less, providing minimal protection for society, with no more responsibility for its welfare than that of a nightwatchman. In the absence of the development of civil society, the state remains in Gramsci's terms backward, that is, predominately coercive, enjoying at best a highly restricted hegemony over society. To the extent that it can only depend on limited consent, it must consequently rely on force, and ultimately its authority is fragile.

The development of civil society, according to Gramsci, provides the context for the potential emergence of a *societá regolata* in which an ethical state regulates in the sense of guiding society rather than coercing it. This mode of governing – the Italian *regolare* is translated into English as 'to guide or regulate' – is no longer conceptualized as the Hegelian product of the knowing few or a political elite, but in relationship to an increasing capacity in the wider society for self-government. This is posed not as an utopian ideal but concretely and in all its extreme difficulty. The state, in another of Gramsci's formulations, is defined as civil-plus-political society, in which civil society potentially plays a role in the increase in the democratic and ethical content of politics and the decrease of coercion (Gramsci 1971: 263).

Therefore, the transformation of the state and politics in the conditions of modern society was a possibility. But it was by no means guaranteed. The development of the democratic potential of civil society would not be a spontaneous reflection of modernization. It could be facilitated or distorted not least by what Gramsci called bureaucratic centralism (Gramsci 1971: 189). A fully developed civil society was an ongoing political project. It would not be the automatic outcome of economic transformation and even less brought about by an identity between party and state. The qualities of this terrain would determine the qualities of a country's politics as much as the constitution or the political system.

Some implications for thinking about global civil society

Gramsci's objective was to provide the analytical tools adequate for a strategy to build a socialist society in a particular historical context. With a few exceptions (e.g. Haug 1999; Nielsen 1995), socialism is rarely on the political or intellectual agenda today. The world is very different from when Gramsci was writing. Rooted as it was in such a different context, can his approach still provide useful indications for discussions today? Is he any help in considering whether, in the absence of an easily recognizable if potentially emergent global state, there is any such thing as a global civil society? Or when contemporary civil societies are analysed as concrete terrains (e.g. Cohen 1997; Scholte 2001)? Or when deciding what the key questions are today?

One lesson that is still relevant is the need to analyse both the 'positive' and the 'negative' in really existing civil societies and to consider what potential and what dangers there are and might be in civil society for democratic politics, for example, with regard to what is now called the democratic deficit. Gramsci employed civil society in a self-conscious, reflective and analytical way. Civil society had to be valued as an aspect of society that had an impact on politics and was a measure of historical advance. But civil society itself had to be scrutinized rather than reified. For Gramsci civil society was above all an analytical concept rather than a normative one. Although marking historical advance, the outcome of a 'civilizing process', as a terrain with processes and relations inscribed in it and with reference to organizations inhabiting it, civil society could be far from civilized. It could throw up a fascist movement that would suppress much of civil society itself, or, Gramsci would argue, it could paradoxically also provide the basis of an increasing democratization of politics. Yet, both in Gramsci's work and now, there are normative and ethical implications. Turning to contemporary discussion, one implication is that the development of a 'good' civil society can be considered an ethical goal integral as it is to a well-functioning democracy and the overcoming of a democratic deficit – but a goal that is realistic only insofar as it is associated both with transformations in the functioning of the state (Shaw 2000: 264ff.) and more complex notions of state power in the global era. It can be argued that claims that this is a 'post-statist' world are founded on a simplistic notion of the state as 'an uncomplicated centre of state power, a singular sovereign . . . If we are looking for the uncomplicated singular world state, if we see only the diffusion of authority in a complex web of jurisdictions, we will miss the more complex global concentrations of state power that have actually come into existence' (ibid.: 95). Attempting to make local states accountable, responsible, and pluralistic, reinforcing the rule of law and transforming democratic political practice at both local and global levels is interrelated with enhancing civil society (ibid.: 266). What remains to be resolved is to what extent and in which terms responsibility lies at the feet of politicians to overcome the democratic deficit and hence to enhance the potential of civil society, and how and to what extent this responsibility is shared with civil society.

Just as in Gramsci's day, albeit in different terms, this is a period of re-evaluation of the role of the state within national borders, and especially in the post-cold war period, of rethinking the international order.[14] Urgent questions reasserting the need for the rule of law and for new forms of economic and other regulation are being posed. It is unlikely that concepts of state and civil society can simply be transferred from the national to the global. As in Gramsci's day, the very terms and the relationship between them are being redefined. Suitably translated and reformulated for different contexts, Gramsci's insights into the nature of political power, its reliance on what he called hegemony, and the positive potential of civil society are still relevant. The processes and cultures to make democratic legitimacy meaningful and the rule of law effective, to overcome democratic deficits, are the responsibility not only of politicians and policy-makers but also of civil society. There are no shortcuts in what is inevitably a difficult, long-term process.

Some tentative conclusions

What cannot be ignored is the need of national governments to maintain support, with different mixes of force and consent, within contemporary constraints of limited autonomy for economic management and a limited array of levers of power. This leads to the question of what programmes are likely to strengthen the authority and legitimacy of the rule of law for the greater the consent, the less the justification or need to resort to coercion. Implicated in what is inevitably an ongoing process is the potential constructive – albeit at times conflictive – role for civil society, aimed at the global as well as the local. What will not contribute to positive democratic political change is an oversimplified notion of politics. At the same time, there is ambivalence in the literature about the fact that governance or government, however ethical and democratic, and with it the rule of law, must be able to rely, in the last if not the first instance, on coercion as well as hegemony. The fantasy of a creative, fluid, 'free' civil society without the constraints of law and order may be attractive, but questions of responsibility and accountability remain however much responsibility and power is spread through society. Advocacy of civil society by policy-makers or social scientists cannot avoid the associated question of the role of the state. An effective civil society requires an effective state, and with this relationship comes the ethical and strategic goal of creating or recreating democratic bonds between politics and the people. In turn, what policy-makers, law-makers and politicians do, and whom they represent, what is created, enacted and enforced, has an impact on civil society. The two spheres are tightly intertwined and cannot be separated even if they can be differentiated. If the state is not always beneficent, neither is civil society always benign. The organizations that operate on the terrain of civil society may be anything but ethical as conceived within certain discourses, or they may combine ethical claims while exhibiting criminal attributes – the examples are not hard to find. As Martin Shaw suggests, the transformation of the state and military power and the implications for the whole repertoire of analytical concepts is too often ignored for a presumed promised land of governance and a non-statist civil society (Shaw 2000: 88ff.). Reconceptualizing and putting the state 'back in' and focusing on the processes underway in civil society, and in political systems which provide the basis of transforming politics in the sense of shaping and managing change to enhance rather than frustrate pluralism and democracy, are fundamental in creating a democratic social and political global environment.

Notes

1 A notable exception is the work of Martin Shaw (Shaw 1994: 648–50; Shaw 2000, especially Part III).
2 Shaw points to an implicit anarchism in the field of international relations (Shaw 2000: 263).
3 Splitting is a well-known psychological phenomenon that affects academics and politicians as well as other people.
4 April Carter, Kimberley Hutchings and Craig Murphy raised some of these points at the conference 'Global Civil Society: critical engagements and ethical encounters', 10–12 September 2001, Gregynog, Wales.
5 Shaw provides a good example of criticizing Gramsci's limitations while drawing on his perspective to consider political agency in a globalizing world (Shaw 2000: 96).
6 The following section draws on Sassoon (2000b) and Sassoon (2001).
7 For a fuller discussion see Sassoon (2000b).
8 In addition to the imagery from the First World War, Gramsci may have been affected by relatively progressive Vienna or Budapest confronted by their hinterlands.
9 With regard to the relationship with Hegel see the debate between Bobbio (1979) and Texier (1979).
10 Note Gramsci's interest in organizations in the United States such as the Lions or Rotary clubs (Gramsci 1971: 286), to a limited extent prefiguring Putnam's work (Putnam 1993; Putnam 2000).
11 For example, the Church threatened to excommunicate anyone (male) who voted in elections. This did not prevent the development of Catholic political movements culminating in the establishment of the Partito Popolare that gained a large parliamentary representation after the First World War. The mutual recognition of Church and State in the Lateran Pacts under Mussolini was therefore particularly noteworthy.
12 Gramsci argued that rather than attack its ideological influence directly, it was more important to bring about agrarian reform which would undermine the power of the Church and offer socio-economic alternatives to those most affected by it (Gramsci 1971: 101–2). People's religious beliefs could co-exist with progressive politics, a position widely acknowledged today but unusual in the period.
13 Isolated in prison, Gramsci kept in touch with significant aspects of Soviet development both from articles in journals and from new prisoners.
14 It could be argued that most of the literature on global civil society does not adequately acknowledge the significance of the end of the cold war. This is a fundamental parameter in Halliday (2001).

4 Late modern civil society

Nicholas Onuf

What makes any society civil is the subject of much confusion. Most observers hold that any society, as a (conventionally designated) totality of relations, has (may have, should have) a variously defined civil sphere – it has a civil society. This I shall call the liberal view of civil society. As an alternative, I hold that any society worthy of the title has an inclusive structure, a recursive pattern of ruled relations among agents and institutions – thanks to this structure, it is a civil society. This view has an ancient pedigree; I shall call it the republican view.

With Hegel's help, we can visualize this inclusive structure in the form of ascending levels and adjacent columns. Never fully articulated, the inclusive structure of any civil society depends on additional processes, or ongoing ruled practices, effectuating agency and activating institutional relations. These I take to be modes of structuration. Participation, representation and recognition constitute the primary modes of structuration through which agents and institutions are recursively related.

In the late modern world, many observers notice extensive connections among civil societies. Some observers, I among them, think that these connections constitute a totality of relations making them a society global in scope and scale. States have formed a distinctively structured society for two centuries or so, only partly displacing old regime societies. International society, in whatever form, has always had an inclusive structure, and thus the properties of a civil society. As modes of structuration have developed and institutional possibilities opened up, global society has achieved an inclusive structure in an unprecedented sense. Late modern civil society incorporates all other civil societies, and not just states as sovereign agents.

Two views of civil society

In early modern usage, the term 'civil society' was a synonym for '*civitas*' (Riedel 1984: 132–7; Onuf 1998: 60–70). At a time when 'state' was not a term used as it is today, this usage was inclusive. For Locke, civil society and political society were one and the same. For Kant (1991: 138–9), civil society and *civitas* were synonyms, and he translated the latter into the vernacular as state. In broad terms, this is a republican view of politics and society. As such it looks back to antiquity, and especially to Aristotle (Onuf 1998: ch. 2).

Even Hegel, writing in 1821, took this view. Nevertheless, Hegel identified civil society (*bürgerliche gesellschaft*) as a category clearly on a par with the family and the state. One can find these three categories in Aristotle's politics. There the *polis*, or state in most translations, and the *oikos*, or household, left space between them for the many associations enriching city life for the Greeks. In the liberal imagination, this space and the many activities taking place within it constitute civil society.

Aristotle had something else in mind. The polis is an association and thus a natural whole. Within this whole all other associations, including households, naturally fit. This is civil society, and, for Aristotle, it was an inclusive category. So it was for Hegel, and so it must be for any republican. To clarify the difference between these two views of civil society, we should also notice that neither Aristotle nor Hegel made a hard and fast distinction between public and private worlds.

If republicans generally make no such distinction, liberals insist on it. In the liberal view, families are conceptually privileged as a private world. The state is no less privileged as a public world. Between these two worlds, liberals locate private individuals performing all those roles that take them out of their households, involve them in diverse pursuits, including the production and exchange of goods and services, and allow them to engage, shape and buffer the state. Obviously these activities are public in different ways and degrees; private initiatives have public consequences, just as public undertakings have private implications. 'for if the sense of a shared public is constitutive of civil society, so is the very existence of the private' (Seligman 1995: 5–58, quoting 5).

For liberals, family and state exemplify private and public domains. As categories, they have a taken-for-granted reality. By contrast, liberals tend to treat civil society as a residual category containing whatever is left over in society once they have established family and state as categories and identified their contents. It might be suggested that community and cosmopolis constitute comparable categories for republicans. While both categories affirm the republican conviction that social space is always public, the community would seem to resemble the family in the density of its affective relations, and cosmopolis to resemble the state in its quest to realize universal principles. This is, I think, a liberal reconstruction of republican categories, separating precisely what civil society connects, to reflect disagreements among liberals on the values that autonomous agents should pursue (read Brown 2001 in this light).

Institutions

Both views of civil society start with a structural perspective. Observers see structure, or stable patterns in social relations to which they impute causal significance. Agents implicated in these relations may see nothing of the sort. As structures do come to agents' attention, they will take them into account when they act. Because they act in institutional settings, their actions have institutional effects; acting on observed structures institutionalizes at least some of their features. In this account of civil society, I shift from structural abstractions to institutional settings in order to keep agents and their intentions in full sight (see Onuf 2002).

Observers are disposed to talk about structure because societies acquire persistent institutional features. Two of the most persistent institutions of the modern world are family and state. As I suggested, liberals tend to take these institutions for granted even as they translate them into structural categories, as universal as they are abstract. Let me outline institutional features of the modern family and the modern state against which most observers are likely to evaluate late modern practices.

The model modern family depends on gender and age to determine agents' status as family members. Other status markers are likely to define the relevant conditions of agency even further – race and religion are obvious examples. Individuals having the appropriate status (man, woman) constitute the family by marrying. Marriage itself is a formal exchange of promises, making partners of agents, to which a presiding officer gives the force of law. Quite frequently it is also a ceremonial act calling for status-ratifying gifts, and it creates additional statuses for both partners in relation to the other partner's family.

Once married, the partners form a household. Organized as a site of (re)productive activity, the household always has a head. Status differences between partners typically reinforce the hierarchical structure of household arrangements. Children acquire that status by birth. Even after they leave the household or form their own partnerships, they remain family members caught up in a web of status relations they could not sever even if they wished to.

For all the limitations of this sketch, it should be clear that family is a persistent feature of our world because of the status distinctions that it calls upon and sharpens up. Yet many observers of the modern family present it to us as a partnership in the first instance, which free and equal agents enter (and exit) as they see fit. Many of modernity's critics present the family as an organization deeply implicated in a world economy itself organized to exploit human beings as productive assets. Both miss the larger point that families provide people with their first and probably their most important point of access to a world of status relations.

When clans and extended families featured prominently in societies, and where they still do, this proposition borders on the trivial. The advent of the nuclear family allegedly reduced the family's status relevance in a more general process in which status considerations declined in importance. It is not at all clear, at least to me, that the importance of status has declined in the modern world – I return to this claim later in the chapter. Instead status groups have shifted about, some gaining and others losing in societal salience, access to resources, members' sense of self-esteem and, of course, status.

As a more plausible generalization, we might say that status markers have become more subtle. Many, but not all, status markers have become less formal. If professional credentialing rules have become more formal and restrictive over time, intricately related, thoroughly internalized complexes of informal rules nevertheless pervade everyday life. Outsiders find them inscrutable but see their power, often better than insiders do. Starting with family life, these rules teach us how to carry on. Whether we think it a public world of extended families and systems of patronage, or a private world of family intimates and shared destinies, people always know where they stand.

For many late modern observers, talk about family status borders on bad taste. Incessant talk of sovereignty suggests the opposite: a commendable curiosity about the state and its future. Even if we want to qualify or dispute the claim that states are sovereign, we end up privileging the state for conceptual purposes. The principle of sovereignty confers on the state an exalted status distinguishing it from all other institutions – in effect, the principle of sovereignty constitutes the state as such (Onuf 1998: ch. 5).

We typically think of sovereignty as having internal and external aspects reflecting the territorial scope of activities undertaken on the state's behalf and in its name. This distinction took hold only gradually. Early modern discussions of sovereignty focused on the internal aspect of sovereignty. Discussions shifted to the external aspect in the mid-eighteenth century. Hegel (1991: 315–21, 359–60) may have been first to make the distinction expressly. Thereafter it has been a commonplace of international legal doctrine.

The internal aspect of sovereignty presupposes that the state must be organized to exercise control over some clearly demarcated set of activities. Over time, territorial boundaries became the primary criterion for demarcating the state's reach, or jurisdiction. As organizations, states are sovereign when some officer, over whom there is none higher, issues directives that subordinate officers proceed to carry out. Day by day, the state rarely operates as a singular, rationalized chain of command. Nevertheless, the state is potentially capable of monopolizing access to physical and social assets within its jurisdiction when the need arises.[1] Other states' officers are reluctant to protest these manifestations of internal sovereignty or intervene more substantially unless invited to do so.

By bringing states into association, sovereignty also makes international society an integral feature of the modern world (Onuf 1998: ch. 7). As a result, states have rights and duties making them legal persons in their relations. The rules of association constitute an indispensable framework for the relations of states. Under these rules, states are institutions acting as agents on behalf of (notionally) whole societies, these states having been equipped with officers acting on their behalf. In this respect, the twinned aspects of sovereignty make international society a transcending feature of the late modern world. States also function as frameworks, or arenas, within which whole societies function. In the process, they constitute the state as a pervasive presence in the late modern world, always there when looked for.

Hegel

Hegel defined civil society as a 'system of needs' – *human needs* (Hegel 1991: 226, emphasis in translation). We satisfy them by working, generally together, yet in 'the most diverse processes' (ibid.: 231; also see Plant 1980: 69–83; Waszek 1988: 146–57; Cohen and Arato 1992: 95–105; Onuf 1998: 263–73; Ehrenberg

1999: 121–32). Such a definition recalls Aristotle's conception of the polis, in which a functional division of activities – work, in Hegel's sense – fulfils human needs and nature's purpose. While for Aristotle, the polis complemented households in meeting needs, eighteenth-century German writers regularly identified the kingdom as a household writ large, and the king as duty-bound to provide for the needs that other householders could not (Tribe 1988: 28–34).

In the German way of thinking, the system of needs presupposed that 'society existed as a corpus of distinct social orders (the *stände*) and not simply as a human collectivity. The stability of this system required that each should act in a *standesmässig* manner – in a way fitting to his or her station in life' (Tribe 1988: 31). By Hegel's time, this might have been an apt description of the old regime societies of Europe, but not of the modern world. Human needs and their relation to the *stände* continued to provide Hegel with a frame of reference, but family and kingdom no longer functioned in this system as they had.

Where once was kingdom, Hegel put the state, and then he gave 'the right of the state' an importance unimaginable in the context of human needs: 'it is freedom in its most concrete shape, which is subordinate only to the supreme absolute truth of the world spirit' (Hegel 1991: 64). In this context, Hegel presented family, civil society and the state as 'stages in the development of the will which is free in and for itself' (ibid.: 62). On philosophical grounds, he presented these stages as complementary 'moments' immanent in the concept of freedom. While this concept 'develops out of itself', its 'moments of development' are concretely expressed in cultural advances. Hegel saw his own culture as having reached an 'advance stage' to which family, civil society and state must all contribute in relation to each other (ibid.: 61).

At this stage, Hegel conceptualized civil society from two points of view. Seen from the outside, civil society exists in its own terms, and so does the state. Moreover, states are plural. Just as families function as individuals in the system of needs, so do states function as individuals in their relations with other states.[2] Seen from the inside, however, civil society exhibits inclusive institutional tendencies. The state has its place in the system of needs that constitutes civil society.

On Hegel's account, 'mediation of need and the satisfaction of the individual' lead to 'the protection of property through the administration of justice' and 'care for the particular interest as a common interest, by means of the police and the corporation' (Hegel 1991: 226, emphases deleted). The need to protect property brings the state into civil society, very much in the way that liberals favour. Care for particular interests implicates the state more substantially. Hegel's used the term police (*polizei*) more broadly than we would use it today, either in German or English ('translator's preface' in Hegel 1991: xlii–xliii; Riedel 1984: 152–3; Tribe 1988/1995: 32–4; Waszek 1988: 197–8; Tribe 1988/1995: 11–12). 'The police should provide for street-lighting, bridge-building, the pricing of daily necessities, and public health' (Hegel 1991: 262; see generally 260–70). Today we would be inclined to call these diverse activities 'public administration', but even this underestimates their importance in stabilizing social arrangements (Tribe 1995: 19–22).

Corporations share in responsibility for the care of particular interests. According to Hegel, the corporation is an association whose members' skills are appropriate to 'the trade which is the corporation's proper business and interest' (Hegel 1991: 270). Under public supervision, the corporation adopts its own membership rules, and it provides members with the advantages of 'a second family' (ibid.: 270–1). Equipped with legal powers that take precedence over members' rights, the corporation is undoubtedly an organization and not a voluntary association (Heiman 1971: 124–7).

Corporations constitute one of three estates, or *stände*, through which all interests in a society are advanced. Corporations selected deputies to represent trade and industry in legislative bodies. The other two estates – agriculture and public service – also selected deputies to represent their constituent interests in the same legislative bodies. 'Viewed as a mediating organ, the estates stand between the government at large and the people in their division into particular spheres'. On the one hand, they prevent arbitrary rule. On the other hand, 'they ensure that individuals do not present themselves as a crowd or aggregate, unorganized in their opinions and volition, and do not become a massive power in opposition to the organic state' (Hegel 1991: 342).

It would be a mistake to think of the estates as incipient classes (this is Waszek's mistake, 1988: 171–9). In an old regime society dominated by status considerations, the estates consolidate rank at three broad levels (this is the conventional way to visualize status relations). Yet in Hegel's system, the estates also mediate between individuals and 'the organic state'. To perform this function, the three estates stand side by side. Conventionally visualized as columns, they give civil society an enduring institutional architecture responsive to unchanging human needs.

In this conception, corporations combine characteristics of associations and organizations because the corporate column has local associations at its base, upon which there are secondary associations, and upon them tertiary associations. Just as skilled individuals coordinate their relations by forming associations, second-level associations form associations that coordinate relations on behalf of members at a higher level. Given the mediating function and vertical organization of the three estates, they constitute chains of command that are vertically and horizontally linked. Aristotle is the classical source of this way of thinking; in the early modern period, it gave rise to federal republicanism and, more recently, to corporatist practices.

Modernization

Inclusively conceived, civil society is the whole of society. Yet this is the very property that Hegel's transcending vision of the state would seem to deny society. Progressive liberal advocates of civil society deny the state a world historical mission such as Hegel understood it. Quite to the contrary, they are committed to strengthening civil society as a bulwark against the Hegelian state.

With Hegel, liberals separate the state from civil society, and they see civil society in relation to the concrete needs of individuals. Again with Hegel, they make much of associations. Modern liberals have long held that a pluralist society is a necessary condition for the liberal democrat state. Late modern progressives hold that a civil society rich in voluntary associations fosters democratic practices and social justice. In both cases, associations are seen to arise autonomously, coexist in egalitarian terms, compete for private resources, form partnerships and rivalries depending on their goals, and apply pressure on state institutions to achieve those goals.

In the liberal imagination, it matters what these goals are. For progressives, associations that underwrite the state work to limit democracy. In contrast, associations that confront the state help in democratizing it. Most significant in this respect are popular social movements. As self-identified associations of the like-minded, movements respond to those deeply felt needs and concerns not met by the state or society's other institutions.

Social movements conceived in just these terms date from Hegel's time. Indicatively, romantic intellectuals were drawn into the cause of Greek independence in such numbers that the movement, and not the cause, is what we remember. Just as this movement depended on local voluntary associations, so must they all. Because the causes to which movements are dedicated tend not to be localized, additional, loosely linked associations take up the cause, thereby spreading the movement. Civil society has become a global phenomenon, only weakly segmented and rapidly articulating, because social movements know no boundaries.

For progressive liberals, movements define themselves against states, and the arena in which they do so is civil society. Most studies of globalization make their frame of reference just as clear. Expedited by spectacular technological developments, the production and exchange of material and cultural goods move freely across state boundaries, whether state officers like it or not. It seems that we are faced with an unspoken division of conceptual space – on the one side there are active civil societies and on the other autonomous global processes – where Hegel taught us to look for one space within which diverse processes are functionally related.

Late modern Europe offers just such a space. Longstanding corporatist practices and long developing functional arrangements effectively reproduce a Hegelian conception of civil society by giving the region an inclusive structure formed from ascending levels of association and side-by-side functional sectors of activity. As Franz Traxler and Philippe Schmitter have pointed out, levels and columns need not develop in such a way that 'territorial and functional competences would be coterminous or coincident with each other.' Insofar as they do not, 'there would be many europes' (1995: 196–7). Understood in these terms, this is not a prospective or counterfactual claim: there are many europes already.

Taken together, these many europes constitute an irregular structure that varies both on vertical and horizontal dimensions. Furthermore, they constitute a variable segment of an even more inclusive structure. At global and regional levels, institutions that have states as members – commonly known as international regimes – link public offices in administering the global system of needs. States occupy the next level in the structure, where their many functioning parts forge vertical links with institutions at other levels.

Obviously the administrative presence of territorially demarcated states introduces massive structural irregularities. Yet this presence is consistent with the Hegelian model of civil society, where public administration is prominently featured. While functional sectors need not line up neatly from level to level, stratified networks help to make the overall structure more regular than formal variations, invocations of sovereignty and state organization might suggest. Forming institutions into ascending levels and side-by-side functional sectors, however misshapen, this structure gives the late modern world a Hegelian character.

If civil society today has globalized, this is, for most observers, an inevitable consequence of modernization. Ever since the Enlightenment, discussion of civil society has been integral to the larger discussion of modernity's triumphs and discontents. In the first instance, modernization meant challenging, and eventually overcoming, the old regime, understood as any highly stratified society, saturated in rules that define and confer statuses. Normally of the highest formality and most exquisite detail, these rules tend to be frozen in place, and resistant to any but the most glacial change in manners. Dominating the old regime were a few clans, a network of extended families; they also were to be challenged – indeed vanquished if they resisted too fiercely.

Modernization also meant the rise of a new regime. Replacing the old, customary rules conferring status, and the dominance of the old families, were new sets of rules, typically legislated, rationalizing administration and enumerating individual rights and duties. In a virtuous circle, new rules strengthened those institutions responsible for these rules. Looking back from the 1860s, Henry Maine famously remarked on the 'movement from status to contract.'[3] Others have emphasized the movement from status to state, but almost all observers, including Marxists, have no doubt that modernization is movement away from the old regime of families, patronage, and pervasively stratified social relations.

As I have suggested earlier, I rather doubt that these twinned movements – the rise of the state and the organization of production and exchange, multiplying rights and duties and the proliferation of voluntary associations – ended up displacing status considerations. In the late modern world, stratification is perhaps more subtle than it used to be, and families continue to do their work behind a thin veil of privacy. Nevertheless, institutionalized status relations are so obviously important that observers comment on them endlessly. If we construe civil society inclusively, as Hegel did, then it will include institutions of every stripe.

Three modes of structuration

Hegel insisted that civil society is an inclusive set of functional relations, and that these relations are structured, vertically forming the functional sectors, or columns, of civil society and laterally forming into ascending levels of institutional development. Agents locate themselves in these crisscrossing arrangements by reference to the rules constituting them as agents. Yet this suffices neither to give civil society its structure nor to give agency the continuity that we generally see it as having. There are additional processes at work, which firm up civil society as an inclusive structure of functional relations by simultaneously actualizing agency and activating institutions in regular and predictable ways.

These processes are ongoing, rule-related practices – social processes are always this and nothing more. Taken together, processes of this sort approximate to what I think Giddens might mean when using the term structuration. Giddens has been maddeningly elusive on this subject. In his two most sustained statements of 'structuration theory' (1979: ch.2; 1984: ch.1), I find nothing even approaching an actual definition.

Free from any constraints that a definition might have imposed, I suggest that the terms participation, representation and recognition broadly describe the three ways that agency instantiates, in particular, human beings, institutions come to life, at least metaphorically, and society constitutes a structured totality of relations. I would be tempted to call these generic rule-related practices modalities of structuration except that Giddens himself (1979: 82) cryptically referred to interpretive scheme, facility and norm in just these terms.[4] Highly abstract and never developed in this context, these terms suggest that, for Giddens, structuration is as diffuse as it is pervasive. They also suggest that Giddens never adequately theorized the way that rules and institutions shape structuration as a manifold social process.

Participation

The term 'participation' peppers recent discussions of civil society. Its use is highly normative, almost always introduced to identify modernization with democratization or to make democratization more authentic by freeing it from organizational constraints. Inspired by Tocqueville, Jean Cohen and Anthony Arato linked 'active participation . . . in civil associations' and 'the democratic character of . . . political culture' (1992: 19). Carole Pateman's 'participatory theory of democracy', drawn from Jean-Jacques Rousseau, John Stuart Mill and G.D.H. Cole (1970: ch.2), is a more recent source of inspiration for many participants in these discussions. Lately the continuing exclusion of status groups broadly connoted by such terms as 'race', 'class' and 'gender' from participation in democratic processes has gained a good deal of attention (see Young 2000 for an exemplary instance).

The preoccupation with democracy masks those properties of participation that make it, for lack of a better term, a primary mode of structuration. Rules assigning statuses tell agents which strata of society they are free to participate in and, by the same token, which ones are not open to them. The extent to which agents take advantage of participatory opportunities is no doubt variable. Yet it is probably the case that being (for example, a noblewoman) and doing (as in acting on and therefore activating those statuses) are largely indistinguishable – at least in traditional societies. Where passive participation is an active form of agency, transgressive participation, by which I mean an active defiance of status markers, will normally prompt an active response from agents in the transgressed stratum. Even then participants will often feign passivity as they silence or exclude the offending agent. If they act as if nothing happened, nothing happens.

In this light, we can see why modernizers have always called for the dismantling of the old regime of status relations. Active passivity inhibits change; acting to change anything activates an off-setting response; deliberately changing everything is the only way to change anything, and changing everything means jettisoning the entire system of status relations, with its homeostatic tendencies and stratifying consequences. By abolishing status, modernizers open space for agents to assume offices and roles which they must then actively take up and not just hold, for the organizations and associations thus constituted would not otherwise function. Being there is not enough.

Perhaps understandably, but I think misleadingly, progressive liberals call this something more than being there 'participation'. Citizenship, for example, is an office and making citizenship more inclusive is a modernizing goal. Voting and other acts of citizenship are, broadly speaking, 'participatory', but failure to participate in this sense has the effect of removing, if only temporarily, that officer from her place in the organizational apparatus of the state. Joining an association but then becoming inactive is, by the same reasoning, to have exited the association, just as performing a market exchange ends a brief though quite possible recurring association. Participation does enter the picture when agents collectively find status implications in their offices and roles and, by doing so, buttress organizations and associations with stratified networks. When conscientious citizens identify with and affirm the conduct of other such citizens, they form a network in which they see themselves actively participating.

Abolishing statuses en masse is, at best, a temporary condition, perhaps necessary to effectuate social change on any scale. It is quite likely that agents must form organizations and associations to do so. Once they succeed, new rules assigning statuses will emerge to solidify the new regime. Nevertheless, we should remember that the new regime in question is specifically modern – it has large-scale institutional features, such as democratic procedures, intended to regularize the dynamics of social change. Consistent with this possibly novel development is the emergence of rules assigning status-changing statuses to some, indeed many, agents.

In the late modern world, self-appointed cultural provocateurs, fashion mavens, party animals, not-quite students and, with help from the internet, sexual predators and rumourmongers actively transgress established status markers. In doing so they may make existing strata more inclusive. More likely, their activities contribute additional strata to an ever denser structure of status relations. The proliferation of strata creates the impression that agents control the statuses available to them and that society more readily accommodates change than it once did.

It would be better to say that proliferating strata make it possible for agents to pick and choose among them and participate more actively in some than others.

Perhaps this is what we should mean by the term 'democratization'. Exercising these choices, agents swell some strata and make them more important in relation to other institutions, and they shrink others, which then seem to diminish in importance. The totality of these choices significantly adds to the mechanisms of change already institutionalized in the general process of modernization. With so many changes, participation has also changed as a primary mode of structuration. Democratization suggests that participation performs a broader function than it once did.

Representation

If participants in recent discussions of civil society speak of 'participation' with too casual abandon, then the term 'representation' is under-represented in these same discussions. Early modern modernizers made no such mistake. Hobbes is the key figure (1998: 73–4; 1991: 111–12; also see Pitkin 1967: ch. 2 and 6; Runciman 1997: ch. 2 and 11). His point of departure is the person. Either an actor speaking on behalf of someone else or an author speaking for herself, the person is not simply the biological isolate whom we typically describe as a human being.

Every person is a 'civil person' and a 'representative'; civil persons may be human individuals or they may be institutions. Civil society (*societas civilis*) is the largest body of civil persons. As such, it is indistinguishable from the body politic – a civil person consisting of many such persons, for whom someone (a representative) or some body (a representative institution) acts as 'the person of the body politique' (Hobbes 1991: 157). The latter person is an officer, or an institution organized to speak in a single voice, whose acts consist of binding directives issued on behalf of the body politic and carried out by subordinate officers. At the bottom of the chain of command are the most numerous of these officers, and they are the citizens.

For Hobbes, civil society must have the organization of a body politic, a sovereign head and citizens as subjects, if it is not to descend into civil war.[5] Someone (or thing) in charge, a head, represents the body by acting in its collective interests, and the body makes its interests known to the head through authorized channels. Directives move in both directions, up and down the chain of command. As we saw, Hegel made institutionalized representation an integral feature of civil society (1991: 346–52). For federal republicans, its relevance was obvious. Alexander Hamilton (1961: 51) called it one of a very few 'great improvements' in the 'science of politics' since ancient times.

As worked out by Montesquieu, Hume and the framers of the US constitution, a (con)federal body politic resembles the Aristotelian *polis*, an association of associations matched to a *politeia*, an arrangement of offices, and taken as a whole body (Onuf and Onuf 1993: ch. 1–3). These associations occupy levels by virtue of being organized, thus enabling directives to flow up and down, through levels. Institutionalized representation regulates the flow of directives, first, by assembling and fusing them at each level on the way up, and, second, by disaggregating them at each level and distributing them across organizational branches on the way down. Federal arrangements formalize levels, and levels function as platforms for additional institutional developments. As a primary mode of structuration, representation helps to stabilize civil society as an inclusive structure.

This is a modern development. For Aristotle, *polis* and *politeia* were directly connected in the *agora*. Office-holding was a restricted but intense activity; citizens spent a great deal of time representing themselves and their households. The *polis* could only function as an inclusive structure on a very small scale. The installation of a sovereign officer at the head of the body politic provided a Hobbesian solution to the Aristotelian size problem, but only for downward representation. With federal arrangements, the election of representatives readily solved the size problem for the upward direction, and gave the structure far greater stability than the vertical arrangement of offices, and downward movement of directives, could ever provide.

Representation in both directions makes states into democratic republics (even if they remain nominal monarchies), and it makes them more effective organizations. Modernizers were, or could be, persuaded that democracy meant the extension of the 'rights' of political 'participation' to more and more citizens, independent of status considerations. While I think the terminology is confusing, the idea is simple enough. If citizens cannot assemble, speak their minds, vote freely and stand for election, then they cannot represent themselves, and no other officer is likely to represent them to their satisfaction. The key to adequate representation, and thus to effective states, are procedures that make it possible for citizens to join together and decide on officers to represent them at the next level. At the citizen's level, voting procedures get most attention.

At higher levels, officers are more likely to send formal directives than elected officers to represent their interests at the next level. Voting will recede in importance as rules of assembly and debate shape the upward movement of directives. Procedural formalities aside, modern political practice emphasizes the connection between representation and group interests. We see this emphasis in both pluralist and corporatist theory (Onuf 1998: 252–9). Recent discussions of civil society devote much attention to the procedural requirements of democracy and, of course, to the associational milieu that makes these procedures effective. There is much hand-wringing about active citizenship.

In these discussions, the ways that officers represent their interests at the higher levels of association go relatively unnoticed. Thanks to pluralist and corporatist theory, we had, perhaps, a clear enough picture of these processes of interest mediation when the sovereign state occupied the highest level in the inclusive structure of civil society. In a late modern context, global and regional levels complicate this picture enormously. Refractory concepts, such as cosmopolitan citizenship, do little to help (see, for example, Hutchings and Dannreuther 1999: ch. 1–3, 8). Institutional vehicles for representing interests at higher levels are likely to be an informal consequence of bargains that officers strike out of public view. How well these bargains represent lower-level interests, and how well they work in shaping the upward flow of directives, is impossible to say, at least until observers learn more about the organization of global civil society at its highest levels. I, for one, am sceptical.

Recognition

If late modern discussions of civil society give short shrift to representation as a mode of structuration, these same discussions make recognition a favourite theme. Typically they do so by taking Hegel's brief remarks on recognition (*anerkennung*) in *The Phenomenology of Spirit* (1807) as a point of departure. The context for Hegel's remarks is self-consciousness and, more specifically, his claim that '[s]elf-consciousness attains its satisfaction only in another self-consciousness' (Williams 1997, quoting Hegel, emphasis deleted).[6] Such an achievement requires recognition of the other, and it implies reciprocity: the other must recognize her recognizing other in order for that other – the one initiating recognition – to be able to recognize herself. Hegel's demonstration that selves depend on mutual recognition leads to his famous analysis of forced recognition and failed self-consciousness in the relation of master and slave.

By combining a concern for self-consciousness and social reciprocities in a subjectivist philosophy, Hegel appealed to self-conscious, and thus self-consciously (post)modern, critics of modernity's objectivizing, instrumental tendencies. Indicatively, the extraordinary outburst of scholarly interest in the other has induced little if any public recognition that this is a meaningful way to think about others, much less oneself. There are obvious reasons, ranging from inaccessible prose to ideological posturing. Freed from a subjectivist preoccupation with self and other, Hegel's concept of recognition nonetheless points to the role of mutuality in commitment, agreement, rights and duties, and association.

In contemporary discussion of civil society, these themes are conspicuous. Others join together voluntarily – they associate – just as 'we' do. By associating with us, others obtain the same rights and duties that we have. Exercising our rights individually and collectively, we make commitments that others accept, and, when we make those commitments formal and reciprocal, we make contracts. In the absence of reciprocal commitments, we invite others to associate with us. These acts, normally in the form of declarations, elicit declarations in kind, and side-by-side declarations function as joint commitments – they constitute a voluntary association of formal equals (see Onuf 2001: 79–90).

As modernizers routinely observe, unilateral acts of recognition have displaced what Charles Taylor has called 'general recognition' and I call in these pages the old regime of status markers.[7] In the shift from general to unilateral acts of recognition, however multiplied these acts are, Taylor located a large, intractable and very contemporary problem of civil society: 'what has come about with the modern age is not the need for recognition but the conditions in which the attempt to be recognized can fail' (1992: 35). To put the problem somewhat differently, agents can withhold recognition, just as they can refuse to negotiate reciprocal commitments. When they do so, others are excluded from association. As the atrophy of old status relations increasingly limits some forms of participation, excluded agents cannot compensate by associating, except of course against those associations from which they are excluded.

Voluntary associations with exclusionary rules are clubs. When clubs reinforce existing social strata, often by supplying them with identifying slogans and insignia, we may commend them for the solidarity and self-esteem that they encourage, or criticize them for aggravating the sense of exclusiveness that stratified arrangements produce on their own. Social movements frequently form in response to exclusionary practices. In the late modern world, claims about universal rights foster a sensitivity to clubs and their particular practices, and yet these same claims enable agents associating in movements to avoid coming to terms with the exclusionary logic of a stratified society. As I have suggested, stratification is a pervasive institutional feature of any civil society.

Not all clubs are so exclusive that they incite movements to form against them. Yet many, if not most, associations are clubs because they have membership rules specifying status requirements. They also impose any number of other requirements on candidate members, such as sponsorship, membership fees, ceremonial expressions of commitment and probationary periods, all of which are intended to show that candidates recognize the goals that associations seek to fulfil. Admission to any club is an act of recognition, implying a reciprocal act of recognition. Agents not willing to reciprocate in this fashion are excluded by their own choice.

International society provides a compelling example of recognition at work. States join this society when they meet status requirements by exercising internal sovereignty and when other states recognize them, thereby acknowledging external sovereignty in their relations. As members of a club, a rather exclusive club at that, states (meaning, of course, their agents) may decline to recognize candidates. Yet they cannot easily prevent other states from doing so if status requirements are met and candidates evince a recognition of the club's rather limited but singularly important goals and a willingness to live by club rules.

In my opinion, it is no coincidence that Hegel began to write about recognition at the very time that states took on their fully modern character and formed themselves into a club. They did so by formalizing recognition as a ruled practice (see Alexandrowicz (1958) on early developments). At this time, states' agents systematically began to invoke the rights and duties of states in their mutual relations – more systematically, I might add, than any so-called liberal society did for its members until quite recently. Once in the club, states are free to associate as they wish and to undertake reciprocal commitments, formal and informal.

Over time, club members have committed themselves collectively to the organization of sectors of activity more or less corresponding to the usual branches of governmental organization. Another of Hamilton's 'great improvements' was the 'distribution of power into distinct departments' (1961: 51). Widely mimicked, this improvement carried over to international society, and it now provides global civil society with its vertical structuring. Not only do functional sectors define tasks for officers at every level, but they give associations a basis for common action (Onuf 1998: 156–62).

Acts of recognition in all degrees of formality normalize relations among associations at every level. Collectively they confirm and support functional differentiation along existing lines. Vertical boundaries are the product of many agreements and cumulative recognition. Without them, global civil society would barely exist and agency, as we have come to know it, would be severely curtailed. A primary mode of structuration in the late modern world, recognition has an institutional significance that few discussions of the 'problem' of recognition ever come close to recognizing.

Conclusion

Readers of a volume devoted to global civil society may be surprised, and perhaps amused, that one of its contributors prefers not to use this locution at all. Instead I have substituted 'late modern' for 'global'. In my view, civil society has taken on global dimensions because a general, multi-faceted process called modernization (for lack of a better term) has substantially succeeded in imposing a kind of order, at least indirectly, on the totality of human relations. In these pages, I have tried to indicate what kind of order this inclusive social arrangement is, how it differs from the liberal conception of social relations on a global scale and, more briefly and impressionistically, where it came from.

Embedded in contemporary discussions of civil society and global change are a number of related assumptions about the general process of modernization over the last several centuries. Let me summarize these assumptions. (1) Modernization depends on ideologies and moral systems emphasizing individual autonomy, aspirations and achievements. (2) Modernity provides people with the personal security and material support that they need to fulfil their individual potential. (3) Modernity cultivates instrumental rationality and organizational efficiency. (4) Modernity displaces the old regime of stratified social relations and strips away stultifying status markers. (5) Modernity demystifies nature and reins-in identification with clan, tribe, nation, or any other allegedly natural social arrangement. (6) Modernization produces long-term moral and material improvement as people outgrow their atavistic tendencies and pre-modern prejudices. (7) Nevertheless, modernization is slow and uneven because of the continuing resistance of pre-modern social formations, tensions inherent in the process itself, and the scepticism, dissatisfaction or alienation of its presumed beneficiaries.

The liberal conception of civil society makes it a spatially conceived zone, neutral and unstratified. In this zone, the tensions inherent in the process of modernization work themselves out. Most obvious are the tensions between individual choice and productive activity on the one hand, and mandated behaviour and collective need on the other. The generally good results that follow from the existence and proper functioning of this zone have additional, unintended consequences. They reinforce the recognized boundaries between individuals, households, markets, productive enterprises and states, and they support the coextensive development of these autonomous entities within their respective spheres of competence.

At the same time, reinforced boundaries perpetuate civil society as a notionally empty zone. Within this zone, concerned citizens and social movements address the ever-shifting agenda of problems brought forward by the process of modernization. With the globalization of markets, productive enterprises, and organizations constituted by states to serve their collective needs, not to mention the development of space-reducing communication and transportation systems, multiple civil societies have transcended state boundaries and merged to form a space that is, as I observed earlier, no more than weakly segmented. Liberals would have us visualize this space as a global playing field, cordoned off, level and open to view, as any well-formed civil society must be.

I reject this conception of recent developments for two reasons. First, it seems like a fanciful exercise in liberal logic to claim that modernization produces a huge variety of institutional features yet manages to leave an empty zone called civil society. I maintain instead that the general process of modernization calls on processes of structuration. As sketched in these pages, these processes order the institutional products of modernization in a discernible pattern – or structure – characterizing any society as a totality of human relations. Structuration operates everywhere and at all levels; as a totality of relations, the late modern world exhibits a generically familiar structure.

My second reason for rejecting the liberal conception of civil society has to do with the enlightenment disposition to think schematically of modernization as a two-step process. First modernization requires that the status-ordering of the old regime be dismantled. Then it requires that a new regime based on some combination of Lockean rights and Hobbesian offices be installed in its place. Whether the process is gradual or abrupt, or indeed the steps reversed (new institutions simply overwhelm the old ones), it is presumed to eliminate status and stratification as the basic means for ordering the totality of relations in a society.

The enlightenment campaign against inherited privilege and for equality of treatment is, of course, something that most of us members of the late modern world admire a great deal. Yet it is naive to think that, once dispatched, status ordering and stratification will never return, or that they can never matter very much in a society where modern institutions are fully functional. Indeed, I would suggest that we conceptualize modernization in three steps. First, the old regime of status is dispatched, and then modern institutions are put in place. Finally, status markers are adapted to new circumstances, rules for participating in modern society are selectively broadened, and stratification resumes its place in giving society its structural integrity.

In the world today, valued skills confer status, rules for participation continue to operate selectively, and stratification yields a relatively impermeable boundary between those with skills and those in need. This division is a general, globally manifest property of late modern civil society. Reinforced by enduring status markers associated with gender and race, it anchors the social arrangements of modernity in material conditions that are only marginally susceptible to change. Wealth and poverty are not just convenient ways of describing these conditions. Wealth and poverty are the primary status markers of the late modern world.

Notes

1 This model of the state is famously Weber's (1978 I: 217–23, 311–50). Hans Kelsen's discussion (1961: 21–30) of the monopolization of the use of force inspired my emphasis on potentiality.

2 'The family disintegrates . . . into a plurality of families whose relation to one another is in general that of self-sufficient concrete persons and consequently of an external kind' (Hegel 1991: 219, emphasis deleted; also see Cohen and Arato 1992: 628–31 n. 48). As for the state: 'The outward orientation of the state derives from the fact that it is an individual subject. Its relation with other states therefore comes under the power of the sovereign' (Hegel 199: 365; emphasis deleted; also see 366–71).

3 'All the forms of Status taken notice of in the [Roman] Law of Persons were derived from, and to some extent are still coloured by, the powers and privileges anciently residing in the Family. If then we employ Status, agreeably with the usage of the best writers, to signify these personal conditions only, and avoid applying the term to such conditions as are the immediate or remote result of agreement, we may say that the movement of the progressive societies has hitherto been a movement *from Status to Contract*' (Maine 1970: 164–5, emphasis in original).

4 'The modalities of structuration are drawn upon by actors in the production of interaction but at the same time are the media of the reproduction of the structural components of systems of interaction' (Giddens 1979: 81). We are never told what distinguishes each modality/medium in performing a dual function common to all three of them.

5 'Each of the *citizens*, and every *subordinate civil person*, is called a subject of him who holds the sovereign power' (Hobbes 1998: 74).

6 Williams's is the most systematic treatment of Hegel's conceptualization of recognition available in English; it is especially valuable for tracing the concept through all of Hegel's work, including the *Philosophy of Right*. There is a substantial German literature, largely untranslated. But see Honneth (1995) for an influential exception.

7 'But in the earlier age recognition never arose as a problem. General recognition was built into the socially derived identity by virtue of the very fact that it was based on social categories that everyone took for granted' (Taylor 1992: 34).

Part II

Citizenship and global civil society

5 Media, cultural citizenship and the global public sphere

Nick Stevenson

The development of the media of mass communication over the course of the nineteenth and twentieth centuries ensured the construction of one-way forms of communication within national public spheres. The arrival of the press, radio and television all developed a specifically national basis as elites utilized various media to promote a sense of loyalty and obligation towards individual states. Notably these developments became the source of a popular cultural citizenship which involved certain rights of communication, participation within the cultural life of the nation, and a sense of community with others. Media had a democratizing effect upon public life by the extent to which it allowed more inclusive definitions of the public. Whether listening to a sports event, the voices of political leaders or the daily weather report, the nation is symbolically constructed as 'home'. The media communicates collective identities as ongoing events. Historically the core message of national broadcasting has been the dominant tone, language and style of national life (Schlesinger 1991). Media across the globe has been responsible for giving people a taste for the meanings, gestures and tone of nationality (Martin-Barbero 1993). Hence a diversity of media become a key focus for claims to citizenship and for developing a sense of solidarity amongst strangers.

However, there is a growing concern that through a number of key transformations these identifications are being restructured by economic, technological and cultural developments. The arrival of new forms of electronic communication has partially deconstructed the assumed links between media, culture and citizenship. Here two developments are central. The first has been the emergence of transnational media organizations whose power and reach are more significant than that of any single nation-state. The new media order is characterized by vast conglomerates like Time Warner and News International who have become international players across a range of different media (including books, television, films, etc.) and whose webs of power stretch across different parts of the world. Secondly, the intensification of globalization processes has meant the world is now a more interconnected place. The global trade in information and entertainment, the capacity of technology to compress time and space, and the enhanced traffic of peoples and symbols have all sought to develop a different communications environment beyond that of the nation. However, what is not currently clear is what kind of mediated public sphere is emerging? Some have argued that a global public would need to be constructed at the planetary level in an attempt to mirror the development of a global political economy (Garnham 1992). Others have suggested that a global public sphere will be necessarily elitist given only a tiny minority of the world's population have access to the different levels of cosmopolitan information necessary to make sense of a global polity (Sparks 1998). Other commentators continue to resist the idea that a public sphere could ever exist beyond the nation given its continuing power to shape citizens' loyalties and identities (Smith 1995). My argument is that we should resist these constructions, and try to understand more carefully some of the evident ambivalences, complexities and indeed possibilities of the current situation. Here I want to trace briefly some of the arguments in respect of citizenship that have emerged at the level of the nation-state. This will include a consideration of the idea of a national public sphere and the fears that it is currently threatened by more global flows and governance. From here I want to propose a different understanding of global and cultural citizenship, in respect of the media, to the one that has emerged at the national level.

The attempt by many commentators to search for the replication of a national media politics at the global level has meant that the idea of a global public sphere has been prematurely rejected. In this respect, I want to build upon some of Geoff Mulgan's (1997) ideas of 'connexity' – that is, the capacity of media technologies within a global world to enhance a cosmopolitan mentality. My analysis then will seek to tie the possible emergence of a global public sphere into the ordinary ability of citizens to be able to forge ethical links, solidarities and connections with others who are distant in time and space. The development of communication that is not dependent upon face-to-face interactions on the surface seems to allow for the possibility of cooperative forms of human conduct that transgresses national boundaries. However, my analysis, unlike that of Mulgan's, will be alive to some of the less utopian and generative political consequences of these transformations. Further, and as we shall see, such reflections are not intended to substitute for the necessity of developing a substantial public sphere at the level of the nation. Yet the emergence of a cosmopolitan/global public sphere is dependent upon an active civil society that has been able to deconstruct oppositions between the national and the international. In such a view civil society acts not only as the realm of voluntary organizations, legal rights and elections but also encompasses the realm of symbolic communication.

The media of mass communication in modern societies is an important resource in the development of diverse civil societies. It constructs public narratives, symbols and identities, and provides the ground for a number of imagined communities (Alexander and Jacobs 1998). Hence the construction of cosmopolitan civil societies depend on an intersubjective framework of human rights, political activism, and common symbols and markers; that might be stretched to include common rituals and media events that help raise questions of solidarity and identity across a number of divides (Sreberny 1998). Such a view of civil society would take us beyond the usual distinctions between information and entertainment, and quality and commercial broadcasting to encompass the normative and cultural horizons of everyday life. Within such contexts an inclusive cultural citizenship or public sphere depends not only upon our shared attempts to critique official politics rationally, but also involves symbolic attempts to construct boundaries between 'insiders' and 'outsiders' through a variety of mediated cultural forms (Stevenson 1999). If the construction of a cosmopolitan civil society is not exclusively focused upon oppositions between civil life and pleasure, or upon the local as opposed to the international, how might we understand the current contours of our communicative universe? This is what I aim to explore.

Media, citizenship and cultural power

The idea of a genuinely public, as opposed to private or commercial, system of communication usually makes reference to Jürgen Habermas's (1989) seminal study of the public sphere. Here Habermas famously traces the historical emergence of a critical domain that upheld the principle of open public discussion on matters of universal concern. Across seventeenth- and eighteenth-century Europe there emerged coffee houses and salons where male members of the bourgeoisie met to discuss works of literature. Despite the exclusive character of these debates, Habermas argues that they continue to have a normative relevance. That is, we can judge contemporary media by the extent to which they facilitate free and open debate. The tragedy of the bourgeois public sphere however was that the very social forces that brought it into being would eventually lead to its decline and destruction. The instituted dialogue of the salons and coffee houses would give way as communication became increasingly organized through large commercial concerns. The progressive institutional elimination of private communicative individuals coming into conversation emphasized an increasing separation between public and private life.

From this point on, commercial culture was consumed in private, requiring no further debate or discussion. Unlike the print culture of the discursive bourgeois salons, much of the new media (television, film and radio) disallows the possibility of talking back and taking part. Just as modern mass culture is received in atomized contexts, so the technical development of new cultural forms promoted privatism. Along with the 'privatization' of culture, Habermas adds, there has also been a corresponding trivialization of cultural products in order to gain a larger share of the market. For Habermas, the operation of the market is best seen as a dual and contradictory process that has both emancipatory and dominatory effects and implications. For example, the video market provides a small strata of viewers with access to high quality films. However, the lowering of entrance requirements has meant that film has had to be accommodated to a mass leisure culture that encourages passive relaxation and ease of reception. Modern cultural forms integrate subjects into a depoliticized culture, which bypasses the public sphere where claims related to rightness could be discussed. This has led to what Habermas has called the refeudalization of the public sphere.

Habermas's model has attracted a good deal of critical dialogue.[1] Yet, despite the numerous criticisms, many media scholars have sought to develop Habermas's model of the public sphere as a means of defending public systems of communication (Stevenson 2002). The idea of the public sphere has proved to be important as it offers a model of democratic communication. This model however has taken on a different set of meanings depending upon the spatial context to which it is applied. For example, some commentators have argued that Western Europe has a tradition of public service broadcasting that needs to be defended against market penetration (Weymouth and Lamizet 1997). Within Britain, the tradition of public service broadcasting has aimed to provide licence fee payers access to quality information, universal reception and a diversity of entertainment. From the 1960s and beyond, cultural critics like Raymond Williams (1962) and Richard Hoggart (1995) have sought to defend and revise this model. This has been primarily through calls to make public service broadcasting representative of the wider society, and to enhance its autonomy in respect of the state. In America, Daniel Hallin (1994) has argued that while there is no tradition of the public sphere to point back to, Habermas's views continue to display a critical purchase. Whereas the press has always been defined by commercial interests (linking partisan political views to elites from their inception in the eighteenth century) the media has become progressively depoliticized. News media journalists in this respect have come to view themselves as professionals who search for objective facts. The consequence of this is that most news media tends to value objectivity over discussion. Whereas the early newspapers had a built-in expectation that the audience would respond, contemporary news media assumes the passivity of the audience. Hence the problem with American news media is not the quality of the product, but that it is offered as a form of privatized consumption that disallows the participation of the public.

In this respect, intellectuals such as Douglas Kellner (1995) regard the Internet and new communications media as providing new possibilities for critical citizens who are largely excluded from dominant media institutions. New computer technology has critical possibilities as it is less hierarchical and more dialogic than traditional media. Building on Habermas's theory of the public sphere, the problem with commercially orientated and centrally organized media is that it disallows the possibility of dialogue. Yet, and despite the impact of Internet, most of the media we consume disallows the possibility of directly participating within its construction. It is a fundamental feature of most forms of mediated communication that it is essentially one-way communication. My argument is that this need not be a problem. I think we should accept in a global culture that dialogue is neither necessarily just nor practical. John Durham Peters (1999) has recently argued that the search for the kinds of reciprocity implicit in the public sphere model need not necessarily be democratic. The need to be reciprocal within a mediated culture should not be allowed to overshadow other principles such as responsibility, imagination and the capacity to voice our solidarity with others. Rather than the search for consensus that is implicit in the Habermasian model it is perhaps better to imagine communication 'as a dance in which we sometimes touch' (ibid.: 268). Further, as J.B. Thompson (1995) has argued, it is no longer clear what practical relevance discourse ethics has for global media cultures. Practically, discourse ethics applies to those who share a common social location and who are able to have dialogue directly with one another. But under global conditions where the media is able to recontextualize imagery into local contexts, what would an all-inclusive conversation look like? How could the millions of spatially diverse people, whose lives are affected by issues from poverty to pollution and from AIDS to the proliferation of nuclear weapons, make their voices heard? The media of mass communication has fostered a non-localized and non-dialogic form of publicness operating across national contexts. Taking the points about the one-way nature of most mediated flows and the lack of practicality evident within the model of the public sphere, a more sustainable model of communications would seek to institute a framework that sought to mediate a diversity of views and where the powerful could be challenged.

In these terms, Graham Murdock (1992, 1994, 1999) has argued that public systems of communication need to be both conserved and extended in order to defend a common idea of citizenship. For Murdock public service broadcasting is part of an ambivalent heritage that has provided a publicly funded forum where viewers, listeners and contributors are addressed as though they are citizens in a national community. Hence, whereas public systems have a responsibility to the public as broadcasters, commercial media institutions are primarily concerned with either the selling of air time to advertisers or subscriptions to fee payers. Public broadcasting then is a relatively decommodified public realm that needs to be defended against the market. Murdock maintains this position despite his recognition that public broadcasters such as the BBC have often displayed elitist dispositions towards certain forms of popular culture and a hegemonic version of Englishness that excluded many on the grounds of class, ethnicity, age and gender. Public systems of broadcasting need to be extended to become less exclusive, while protecting people's rights to participate within a shared cultural space. Here Murdock identifies four basic cultural rights that should be commonly shared within a national community. These include rights to information, knowledge, experience and participation, all of which require public protection from commercial interests. That these rights require explicit protection is largely due to the enhanced role of the market within communications. Pierre Bourdieu (1996) has recently argued that where public broadcasters aimed to civilize the general public in the 1950s, by the 1990s the aim was to gain the largest possible audience. For Bourdieu it is market competition (rather than, say, questions of ownership and control) that ensure the dominance of tried and tested formula and the communication of banality. The media, like education, health, welfare and other social goods, requires common forms of protection from a neo-liberal agenda.

In the American context there have been calls to develop a system of publicly funded communication systems as a means of strengthening civil society (Giroux 1999). The dominance of commercial organizations over the communicative structures of society serves to promote excessive consumerism and undermine the possibility of public forms of reflection. Here the struggle for public dialogue becomes the struggle against commercially run media.

The primary effect of the new media age in this reading has been the deregulation and privatization of public media. The commodification of public space has led to increasing numbers of channels and communications services and has pushed 'public' media into commercial ventures of their own (Herman and McChesney 1997). The development of digital broadcasting will improve picture quality, lower production costs and increase the available number of channels. The neo-liberal agenda has directly determined the communications agenda in the interests of global corporations such as Time Warner, Disney and News International, all of whom are likely to profit from an increasingly commercial culture based upon cross-selling, cross-promotion and conglomerate merger. In this analysis, globalization and trade liberalization are rendered equivalent as commercial competition progressively seeks to undermine the operation of public media. Such is the connection between the freedom to communicate and the free market that the operating logic of the market and communications policy becomes 'Let people watch what they want' (Mattelart 2001).

Further, if national public broadcasting is being eroded from above by globalization processes, it is also being eroded from below by sub-national developments. Morley (2000) reports that whereas in 1995 only 4 per cent of the French population subscribed to satellite television, 21 per cent of Arabic-speaking households had access to these new channels. In other words, new channels of communication are not only popular because they talk in the popular language of consumption, but because they allow minorities to escape from the perceived restrictions of national media systems. Diasporic communities are able to maintain a sense of ongoing connection to an absent homeland through the transportability of videos, films and television programmes (Gillespie 2000; Sreberny 2000). Arguably these features question the ability of public systems to fully 'represent' overlapping communities within an increasingly post-national age.

Cultural citizenship in a global mediated culture

So far I have argued that public systems of broadcasting need to be repositioned in terms of both global and sub-national developments. Yet we also need to be aware that many cultural theorists have pointed to the media's ability to enhance international dialogue, empower minorities and potentially construct solidarity at a distance. These features are poorly appreciated by a tradition that seeks to preserve 'authentic' forms of communication against the corruption of the popular and the market. The media's ability to be able to move texts and images through time and space opens the possibility of what J.B. Thompson (1995) has described as 'intimacy at a distance'. The audience's relation with celebrities, media events and politicians differs from that with persons who are co-present. A non-reciprocal relationship of intimacy depends upon the scrutiny of the celebrity or news event by the audience and not the other way round. For many, the media's capacity to enhance *connexity* holds out the possibility of enhancing surface forms of cosmopolitanism. It is the capacity of media cultures to move perspectives and images through time and space that contributes to the making of 'fuzzy' cultures (Hannerz 1992). The globalization of the media means that we are likely to become more tolerant of the 'other', or that our capacity for reflexivity will become enhanced, or even finally that such developments will help foster a society of 'clever' people who are no longer bound by parochial geographies (Mulgan 1997; Giddens 1994; Urry 2000a).

These projections hold out the possibility of a form of citizenship that is no longer contained by the nation-state. The main problem with the way that citizenship has been constructed thus far is that it is inattentive to the ways in which social movements, events, lifestyles, consumer products, human rights abuses, religious ideas, risks and hazards and ethical beliefs all struggle for visibility within a global media culture. Here we might follow John Urry (2000b) by making a distinction between a citizenship of stasis and a citizenship of flows. With a citizenship of stasis the desire to defend and deepen the culture of public service broadcasting can be linked to a membership of certain nation-states (not all nations/states have such traditions). Alternatively, a citizenship of flows is more concerned with the capacity of mediated material to cross borders. That is, the movement of refugees, viruses, images and symbolic material all involves questions of rights and responsibilities that take us beyond specific national societies. Yet while we cannot escape our symbolic inclusion in a media culture that multiplies the possible worlds of our experience, there remains a diversity of personal and collective reactions to these new contexts. If in the twentieth century the cultural bonds of the nation were maintained by communication technology we can no longer assume this to be the case. The cultural connexity of technological society is constructed through networks that are discontinuous (Lash 2001). This holds out the prospect, as we shall see, of a complex dialectic of identification and disindentification. Hence, returning to Mulgan's (1997) idea of connexity, we need to study the complex circuits of information that the new media order makes commonly available. This will mean abandoning any simple idea (evident in Mulgan's original formulation) that new forms of technology necessarily enhance cosmopolitan mentalities. Instead, along with others, I prefer the metaphor of the network where circuits of information simultaneously promote connection and disconnection (van Dijk 1999; Castells 1997). For example, the new media order has rapidly expanded the amount of information made commonly available while enhancing the capacity of citizens to choose their own level of interaction. Yet we can equally argue that the commercialization of the media has exaggerated the divisions between a global information rich and a global information poor (Schiller 1996). As we shall see, what remains crucial in respect of these dimensions is not the global construction of public systems of broadcasting or the need to return to more dialogic forms of communication. A more globally orientated cultural citizenship should be more concerned to explore the ambivalent connections, disconnections, miscommunications and possibilities global systems make commonly available.

For the remainder of this chapter I want to investigate these questions. I shall briefly examine the ways in which the global flows of the media of mass communication can be connected to questions of cultural citizenship in respect of: (1) the global struggle for human rights; (2) the impact of new media; (3) the enhanced speed of modern communications; and (4) the fostering of indifference and cosmopolitan connection.

Human rights, social movements and global media

One of the most significant moral and political achievements of humanity remains the 1948 Universal Declaration of Human Rights. The principles laid down in this document recognize that everyone irrespective of national boundaries is entitled to the rights and freedoms held out in the Charter. The Charter has provided the basis for international law setting out common standards that might reasonably be expected by all peoples (Falk 1995b). The Charter, in Article 19, contains a defence of the freedom of information and rights of expression, that includes the right to impart and receive information irrespective of frontiers. These universal rights to communication have provided the inspiration behind attempts by Third World nations in the 1970s to challenge Western media dominance, and a series of commissions and reports that issued declarations on the rights of peoples and the responsibilities of the global media. More recently Cees Hamelink (1994, 1995) has argued that the globalization of mass communication has led to the disempowering of ordinary people when it comes to exerting power and control over their communicative environments. Globalization processes have increased the power of large-scale media conglomerates and flooded the world with cheap standardized media products. These processes can only be reversed through a human rights initiative that enables participation within cultural and political life by providing peoples with access to information so that they might make autonomous decisions. Thus whereas global media empires are disempowering in that they infringe upon local cultural space and privatize access to information, human rights approaches treat knowledge as a collectively owned common good to be shared, debated and contributed to by equal citizens. The reduction in cultural space enables the West to control the flow of information and disempower 'other' peoples from developing their own sense of identity.

Starting from local networks, the world's peoples are encouraged to search for alternative sources of information exchange that emerge from under the disciplinary power of the state and the commercial imperatives which govern global media empires. The development of a genuine people's media through community radio and newspapers and the burgeoning of a people's community network over the Internet could form the beginning of local and global sources of information that provide alternative sources of communication. Politically we can afford to be optimistic about such movements due to the revolt of civil society. By this Hamelink means that alternative networks of communication will arise along with social movements such as ecology and feminism. The emergence of a 'double citizenship', or what Albrow (1996) has termed 'performative citizenship', means that such movements point to a new form of politics that seeks to link national internal struggles to more global levels of interconnection. As a first step in building upon these civic initiatives, Hamelink proposes the worldwide adoption of what he calls a 'People's Communication Charter'. The main aim of the charter is to raise the awareness of individuals and social movements to the shared importance of securing both human and cultural rights. The charter then builds upon Article 19 of the 1948 declaration by granting people the right of freedom to form an opinion, gain information, enter into public discussion, distribute knowledge, protect their cultural identity and participate in a shared public culture. The idea then is to make this both a movement of non-governmental forces (groups such as Amnesty, CND, Greenpeace, etc.) and to have the charter adopted by the United Nations.

The most obvious and immediate objections to such arguments are that the Declaration of Human Rights is not legally enforceable, and without the reform of the United Nations itself such charters have historically had little impact. The 'People's Communication Charter', from this cynical viewpoint, merely ends up adding to the meaningless pieces of paper that are produced by the United Nations' bureaucracy. These proposals could be further criticized in that they are unlikely to have any lasting impact on the dominant rationale and structures of the global media.

The first point to make is that the widespread acceptance of a 'People's Communication Charter' is not solely dependent upon its ability to produce legal effects. Like other human rights that are widely accepted amongst non-governmental organizations, its 'cultural' existence gives groups something to appeal to and build a social struggle around. It is undeniable that, in terms of its perceived moral legitimacy, such a process would be greatly enhanced if the charter were accepted by the United Nations. This would give social movements a platform on which to perform a form of immanent critique whereby signatories could be embarrassed by their refusal to uphold the principles they had formally agreed. Human rights documents in this respect are important in that they help create a set of general political and cultural expectations which – when violated – potentially attract the attention of the media and political movements alike.

There are of course no guarantees in this respect, but, if movements for social change are able to point to international treaties or other collectively agreed documents, it will aid them in making interventions in the global televisual arena. The argument being proposed here is that the economic (wealth and resources), political (influence over public policy) and cultural (modelling stocks of discourses and concepts) power of the new media order is such that an international recognition of people's rights in respect of information exchange could indeed have an empowering effect upon the interrelation between local, national and more global public spheres.

Yet it is likely that Hamelink presses the case of the colonizing effect of media conglomerates too far. As J.B. Thompson (1994: 94) notes, currently global media cultures subject the world's nation-states to a form of *global scrutiny*. By this he means that the exercise of political power increasingly takes place upon a visible world stage. The medium of mass communication makes the actions of despotic states visible to the globe's citizens. This process can also be coupled to the global re-mooring of images and perspectives that give individuals some idea of forms of life different from their own. This surface knowledge of other cultures, Thompson (1995) argues, gives individuals a social resource, enabling them to distance themselves from more official state-driven viewpoints. To claim that the globalization of the media places restrictions on the activities of nation-states is undoubtedly correct, but this remains dependent on social context, as states still have considerable powers to isolate themselves from the internal impacts of global criticism, no matter how self-defeating this might prove over the longer term. That is, more globally orientated forms of mediated citizenship need to challenge agendas which seek to move against the formation of international law, ensure the development of peaceful dialogue free of damaging stereotypes, and seek to affirm other principles such as self-determination and a commitment to human rights more generally. Further, and perhaps more crucially, there is a considerable amount of evidence that post-colonial media cultures continue to promote ideologies of superiority and dominance (Bhabha 1992). This is not of course to adopt a mode of theorizing that points toward a progressive Americanization of world media cultures. Post-colonial thinkers have questioned such images in the name of hybridity, multiple identity and diaspora. Popular culture considered along these lines cannot be contained within the frameworks of Americanization or nationalism. With these features in mind, Pieterse and Parekh (1995) have called for the 'decolonization of the Western imagination'. While such a view dispenses with a one-dimensional view (like those advanced by Hamelink) that media cultures promote Westernization, this does not mean they are free from ideologies of dominance. Much media culture, as my own research on the televisation of the Rwandan genocide revealed, makes binary distinctions between the civilized West and the barbarism of the 'other' (Stevenson 1999). While 'official' media cultures continue to trade in these terms, they serve to mask more complex sets of narratives of exile, travel and intercultural dialogue. In mediated terms then, a cosmopolitan media is one which has deconstructed a host of stereotypes which remain the common fare of journalism.

Finally, the faith that we might have in the 'People's Communication Charter' is undermined not so much by the trust it places in institutions as in people's initiatives generally. Civil society is currently made up of organizations which aim to reinstate patriarchy, ethnic nationalists, religious fundamentalists and all kinds of other causes that Hamelink would find himself out of sympathy with. This begs the question as to whether a charter that emphasizes the 'right' to be heard can really solve the communicative crisis within civil society today. However, the politics of mediated human rights remains a key area for contestation and debate within a global arena where citizens are able to appeal for help, publicize suffering, make terrorist- and state-driven acts of violence visible, thereby seeking to attract the attention of a 'global community'. While a globally mediated human rights culture can enhance post-national forms of interconnection, we should be aware that such agendas continue to be subject to the power of transnational media empires and the nation-state.

Technocultures, media and community

Current debates in respect of the development of new media technologies have a strong overlap with the nature of connexity. The media of mass communication is rapidly diversifying just at the point when old communal relations are increasingly open to question. Are new media technologies responsible for undermining a sense of community by robbing people of participatory public spaces or are they the sites where more diversified relations of solidarity can be made? Crudely, we can divide arguments in respect of the effects and transformations brought about by new media into opposing optimistic and pessimistic schools of thought. The pessimists propose that the development of new media technologies can be coupled with the continuation of modernity and the destruction of communal forms of identification and the progressive privatization and commodification of public life. On the other hand, more postmodern frames see the emergence of the net, video, mobile phones and portable stereos as opening out new possibilities for voices that have been traditionally excluded from public cultures. New, more affective attachments can be formed through underground networks, fan magazines, MUD sites and phone chat lines. Unlike traditional communities in which individuals are born into co-present local relations, so-called postmodern communities are more likely to be the result of 'individual' choice and the product of mediation. Whereas one set of critics views the global triumph of capital as destroying the communal identifications that allow people to resist capitalism, the other views community as a more fluid site and a potential place of radical politics. To overstate the point, where one set of critics is mournful at the passing of old ties, the other is celebratory in the hope that new ones might be made. The central debate concerns the ways in which people are connected and disconnected from a spatially complex media culture.

The pessimists' camp houses a wide spectrum of political viewpoints from old style radicals to cultural conservatives. For instance, Julian Stallabrass (1996) argues that the super information highway and cyber space will not offer a utopian domain of free communication, but the perfect market place which can operate through space and time at the flick of a switch. Those who are currently excited about the future possibilities of the Internet are failing to ask who will control the information, work out to whom it is going to be made available and in whose interests it is likely to be run. The answers to these questions are all traceable back to the needs of global capital. For instance, so-called virtual communities are places built upon irony and play, whereas real communities are places of obligation and responsibility. If within cyberspace we are able to disguise our identities, this effectively denies the possibility of a genuinely democratic communicative exchange where the particularity of the 'other' has to be engaged. Instead, it creates a 'kingdom of information, whose palatial halls we may wander without fear, free from chaos, dirt and obscurity' (Stallabrass 1996: 67). Cyberspace becomes a zone of irresponsible consumption where the poor will never appear as subjects in their own right and only very occasionally as 'objects' for discussion. Indeed the desire to create 'virtual' communities over the Web both points to the disappearance of 'real' communal relations being trampled under the atomizing effect of commodity capital, and to the fact that humans desperately need a sense of belonging and will create it with whatever tools they currently have to hand.

Further, according to Robins (1997), new media technologies are invested in omnipotent fantasies and feelings. Cyborg relations promise to melt the distinctions between humans and technology while offering the 'thrill of escape'. In the new media universe we are invited to choose disguises and assume new identities thereby distancing ourselves from 'real' human relations. The capacity of technology to magically solve human predicaments offers us an 'instant' solution to the problems of self and community. That is, the Net can both promote the warm feelings of community while we are being atomized and deliver us the fantasy of self-creation free of actual social encounters. In cyberspace we become blind to questions of difference as we only encounter the privileged, retreat from the brutal realities of late capitalism and escape from the burden of geography. On the Net there are few real surprises and little that is unfamiliar. Rather than dealing with the otherness of the Other, cyberspace is based on the governance of corporate capitalism (Robins and Webster 1999).

Significantly, the development of new communications technologies has been read differently by writers who occupy less traditional frames of reference. Maffesoli (1996) questions the pessimistic projections of those who are concerned with the fragmentation and privatization of the modern subject. He does this by articulating a notion of the subject that is continually searching for emotional connection with intersubjectively related others. Maffesoli rejects the idea of the isolated individual split away from others through the operation of mass culture, and points to what he calls the 'tribalisation' of the social. By this he means that through the creation of football teams, self-help groups, friendship networks, Internet sites and religious associations, individuals are increasingly likely to belong to a number of diverse and contradictory communities. What we are currently witnessing therefore is the de-individualization of modernity and the growth of more affective communities based less on utilitarian notions of self-interest than on sociality. The new tribes are based upon shared sentiments, whether they are regular visitors of an Internet site, members of international human rights forums or even occasional viewers of a soap opera. These new emotional communities are constructed more upon fleeting identification and periodic warmth than the stability of traditional ties. Hence the argument here is not so much to bemoan the ways in which capitalism has destroyed traditional forms of association as to investigate the creative ways in which social solidarity might be reimagined in the late modern age.

Yet, as these remarks suggest, we need to be able to view new media beyond the binaries of utopian possibility and sociological nightmare. The development of global cultural citizenships are likely to be formed through the power of technology to connect and disconnect the globe's citizens in a multitude of ways

(Featherstone 1999; Stevenson 1999). These questions will undoubtedly be driven by questions of symbolic power, representation and disconnection. However, within this we should be careful not to assume that access to technology automatically makes for cosmopolitan horizons or that a 'rootedness' to locality invariably spells parochialism. Alternatively, we should also be careful not to unproblematically assume that the Internet can be read exclusively through the prism of connection or disconnection. Rather the Internet is likely to play an important part in the social construction of social movements. The progressive shift away from a print culture within modernity can be linked to the pluralization of voices and the popularization of a wide range of perspectives. The Internet has already played an important role in a range of globally oriented civil actions including the international ban on landmines. Here NGOs targeted the globe's media with emotive images of children in wheelchairs and truck loads of crutches while also setting up influential websites (Warkentin and Mingst 2000). The Internet was part of a media strategy designed to establish a global network between NGOs and sympathetic states helping to promote a momentum for social change. However, we could equally point to the very real problems of Internet and technological access that will inevitably be encountered within a global context. Again it is the Internet's ability to foster complex circuits of engagement and silence, and interaction and exclusion that holds the key to understanding its considerable power.

Speed and communication

The temporal dimensions of media cultures have strong connections to processes of globalization. For instance, in the mid-eighteenth century it used to take letters approximately 40 days to cross from Europe to the United States. Today, through the intervention of telephones, World Wide Web and live broadcasts we have entered the age of instantaneous and immediate communication. The experience of what Giddens (1990) has called 'time-space' compression has meant that the increasingly 'event'-driven nature of media reporting has become exaggerated in correspondence with its global spread. Newspaper stories, television news items and radio programmes are no longer determined by their immediate proximity to the location of their production. The linear and sequential nature of time that according to Benedict Anderson (1983) allowed the nation to imagine itself collectively progressing through history is being displaced by a global time of immediate and instantaneous transmission. The idea of historical progress through time by a hermetically sealed nation-state has been undermined by simultaneous global happenings and the blurring of strict boundaries between past, present and future. This new structure of feeling is propelled by a media culture of nostalgic revivals and pastiche where firmly distinct historical periods and sensations are difficult to maintain in an increasingly mongrel world (Baudrillard 1994). The displacement of temporal frames associated with the linear and sequential time frames of modernity by the speeded up and disorganized dimensions of postmodernity has important consequences for the way we understand global media cultures. Hence, the compression of the temporal flow of the media can lead to a situation where the rational forms of reflection necessary for participatory citizenship are undermined by the formation of immediate opinions, collective forms of forgetting and a wider culture of uncertainty.

Paul Virilio (1997, 2000a, 2000b, 2000c) has argued over a number of publications that the impact of new technologies of communication on the human senses is mostly negative. The 'real-time' of modern media communications has fundamentally altered and distorted the subject's conception of reality. What Virilio (2000a: 57) calls the 'industrialization of vision' has not so much added new realities, but has displaced our sensitivity towards different temporalities within modernity. The real-time of television has come to dominate our shared definitions of reality. The showing of events 'as they happen' has meant that a society of images and spectacles has come to replace public forms of dialogue. Within this the linear time, patterns of modernity have become displaced by the hegemony of instantaneous communication. Speed destroys thought and the possibility of democratic deliberation. Ideas concerning the possibility of using technology to enhance democracy are mistaken in that what is more likely is a culture of conditioning where communications are used to condition the responses of the public (Virilio 2000b). The quickening of the time allowed for opinion formation can lead to the production of superficial perspectives in place of those which should have taken a deeper and more substantial view of the subject. We might be in a position to receive more information more quickly than ever before, but we are denied the interpretative opportunities to make the world more meaningful.

Yet it is a mistake to proceed as if the media only colonize society's shared capacity to construct meaningful relations with others. For instance, the culture of immediacy and speed can also feed the idea that we, the nation or international alliance, in a time of crisis ought to do something. This can be invaluable if, say, we are considering offering immediate humanitarian aid to the victims of a disaster, but can also have other perhaps more negative consequences, given that speed can be used to displace the necessary labour of democratic discussion. The rapidity at which these decisions are made might mean that a wide-ranging public discussion has not yet taken place and that not enough 'quality' information has been made available to make a judgement. Here I am struck by a basic ambivalence between the need to receive information quickly and the consequences this might have for human reasoning. The wider point is that the temporal bias introduced by media cultures disrupts our capacity for critical reflection as well as providing a necessary service and influence on contemporary political culture. The issue here is to hold an intellectual concern regarding the lack of slowness in our culture against an appreciation of the political necessity of speeding up information exchange.

Moral indifference and cosmopolitanism

We have already seen that the interconnectivity of the media can have ambiguous effects in respect of the connections between media and politics. A different way of exploring these questions is to ask what effects the visualization of suffering has upon our shared moral landscape. We might argue that practices of time–space compression make it increasingly difficult to ignore the plight of the 'Other'. The daily screening of images of suffering on our television sets means that it has become increasingly difficult to shrug off our responsibilities towards others in a shared world (Adam 1997). Through televised appeals on behalf of peoples we will never meet we become aware that a donation 'right now' could have an immediate impact upon the well-being of distanciated others across the planet's surface. Television and new media technologies arguably make cosmopolitan compassion and moral solidarity more possible. This is especially the case when such concerns become connected to the emergence of a cosmopolitan civil society which includes the global spread of human rights, charitable agencies like Oxfam, and the globalization of communication networks. However there are a growing number of more sceptical voices in this respect. Keith Tester (1995: 475) argues that television cannot actually create moral solidarity, but it can provide a cultural resource for those who have a predisposition towards 'moral leaps of the imagination'. The images and perspectives of the media do not have any automatic moral consequences: the representation of murder, war and suffering seen on television has no necessary connection to the development of cosmopolitan solidarity. Tester (1995) continues that a world that is awash with images helps to foster a blasé attitude amongst the audience whereby they repeatedly fail to be shocked by the pictures of horror and distress that are the daily diet of the television news. Television images are too fast and fleeting to leave any lasting moral trace of their presence. The box presents the moral issues and problems of living in an interconnected world as crumbs that can be easily swept off the collective table. The television screen, in this regard, can be seen as a 'door' which we stand behind, rather than a 'bridge' directly connecting the viewer to the sufferings of others. In this, the screen is not really a 'window on the world', but can literally be seen as both a barrier between the viewer and those whose lives are represented. If the media is a door rather than a bridge we can then keep it shut in order to maintain our social and moral distance from the sufferings of others (Tester 1999). Indeed, in this scenario the act of giving is largely a means of maintaining rather than closing social distance. Tester (2001), along with Devereux (1996), argues that global news, telethons and documentaries are more often concerned with the cleansing of suffering and the sanitization of the 'Other'.

However, I think that these arguments, while asking important moral questions, are also in danger of being overstated. Images of suffering still have the capacity to move some of the people some of the time into political concern, expressions of sympathy and care. As Stanley Cohen (2001) has argued it is not so much information overload or a pervasive culture of indifference that affects relatively privileged populations, but demand overload. If we take the estimates that 46 per cent of the world do not have access to clean water, that 8.5 million African children by 2010 are likely to be orphaned due to AIDS, and the current estimate of 16 million refugees worldwide, the question is often where to start? Such statistics do not so much induce indifference as the impossibility of knowing how to act. For instance, Tester's example of television cultures' ability to foster a blasé attitude is misleading. Like most people, I find that I respond to some appeals for help but not to others. That people do not respond to every appeal for help does not necessarily mean that the public is indifferent.

The sheer fact of actual moral distance is difficult to close. A better metaphor than either blankness or engagement is suggested by Jose Saramago's novel *Blindness.* The novel tells the story of humanity's panic when it learns that 'blindness' is contagious. Blindness is an ordinary human ailment that is passed on much like the common cold. As the story unfolds, the state attempts to limit the spread of the disease by placing the blind in guarded prisons where the afflicted battle against one another for survival. The novel suggests that we are all blind people (whether sighted or not) who have the capacity to 'see' the sufferings of 'others' if we attend to the voice of the other. Saramago suggests that the 'visibility' of suffering has a deep connection with the moral and ethical capacities and engagements of modernity's citizens. The ambivalence within this account suggests that a global civil society remains both less and more possible than considerations that exclusively point to global connections or disconections routinely think. Our capacity to be able to 'experience' the pain and grief of another will ultimately depend upon the ethical resources of the self and the community.

The concern expressed here has been to plot a course between a modernist emphasis based upon giving people access to 'correct' information, and more postmodern accounts that mournfully trace the impossibility of knowing the other in a media age. Instead, I would like to emphasize that media cultures are capable of contributing towards what Peter Dahlgren (1998) calls 'civic confidence'. That is, television and media cultures, despite their many limitations, continue to have a role in reminding us of our obligations towards others in a globally shared society. However the 'effect' of those images cannot be dealt with through blanket assumptions of either interconnection or disconnection. Instead our capacities to respond to the visualization of suffering are likely to be the result of personal and political agencies which seek to interpret and interrupt the global circulation of images.

Mediated citizenship

This chapter warns against attempting to read the diverse impacts of media cultures as either fostering more cosmopolitan tendencies or as the arrival of new forms of domination and colonization. The possibility of the media's ability to be able to shift information through time and space is dependent upon a range of agencies which include the construction of cosmopolitan forms of virtue within the horizons of citizens, the regulation of media cultures, new spaces of dialogic exchange and the uncertain intersubjective development of a global civil society based upon human rights. Yet, as I have stressed throughout, we also need to recognize that the media simultaneously reinforces the dominant centres of global cultural power. Further, my argument has been that we need to reconsider the way that global information and entertainment flows are restructuring what we take to be mediated citizenship. While this is not intended to displace the concerns of those who wish to defend 'national' public service broadcasting, it does connect questions of public space and citizenship to more global concerns. We may indeed be persuaded that neo-liberal economics makes the need for inclusive forms of national public broadcasting more pressing. However, we also need to consider the ways in which the transformation of the media is informing new citizenship agendas, and that as we begin the task of understanding these new co-ordinates we would do well to occupy an ambivalent language that recognizes the media's ability to frustrate and engage the political ambitions of those who wish to gain our attention (if just for a moment) within this new global society.

Notes

1 For a more extensive discussion of Habermas's writing on the public sphere, see Stevenson (1999 and 2002).

6 Subjects, citizens or pilgrims?

Citizenship and civil society in a global context

Kimberley Hutchings

Introduction

The title of this chapter refers to three modes of conceptualizing the political position of individuals.[1] As *subjects*, individuals are affected by the power exercised by state and non-state actors and institutions. This power ranges from the straightforwardly coercive authority of rulers or employers over individuals, to the effects of what Susan Strange terms 'structural power', which shapes the opportunities and agendas of particular individuals in ways over which they have little control (Strange 1988). As *citizens*, individuals are bearers of rights which both provide protection from their abuse as subjects and enable them to play a part in shaping the forces of subjection through various kinds of political participation, though always within the parameters set by a certain institutional context. As *pilgrims*, individuals act on their faith in a world beyond existing parameters in order to transform the conditions of both subjection and citizenship. Traditionally the transformation of the political position of individuals within liberal Western societies has been envisaged as one in which individuals draw on the ideal visions of *pilgrimage* (of perfect freedom and justice for all) in order to argue for the shift from *subjection* to *citizenship*. Citizenship is the middle term which holds the moments of both subjection and pilgrimage within it, but also keeps them at bay, so that as a citizen one is neither a passive victim nor an entirely autonomous agent. To be a citizen is to hold a particular status and role, to act as a citizen is to act according to the entitlements inherent in that status and role, whatever the normative vision that motivates that action. The paradigm of subjection as opposed to citizenship is the condition of serfdom, in which individuals' rights over themselves and external property are limited to the point of non-existence. Ideals of autonomy and equality are crucial to modern liberal notions of citizenship, but so also is the concept of legitimate authority located within the state. The latter underpins the institution of citizenship in practice, locating citizenship rights within a specific jurisdiction in contradiction to the universalistic language of liberal ideals. States, including those embodying legitimate authority, and the state system affect individuals (both citizens and non-citizens) in ways which those individuals cannot easily protect themselves against or alter. However, although liberalism is grounded in concern about the power of government to oppress those within its jurisdiction, the idea that a territorially and demographically limited political jurisdiction in itself could be an aspect of subjection has only recently registered within liberal political theory. At the current time, the interplay between the conceptions of individuals politically as subjects, citizens or pilgrims is being revisited in a series of arguments about the possible emergence of global citizenship.

Notions of 'cosmopolitan' or 'world' citizenship are not new. As is frequently mentioned, they have a history going back to the stoic's identification of himself as a citizen of the cosmos and not simply of polis or empire. Within the modern period, the idea of universal (cosmopolitan or world) citizenship has been associated with the enlightenment cosmopolitan 'man of the world', with the putative member of a Kantian kingdom of ends, and with a range of movements for world peace and cross-cultural understanding (Heater 2000). In its most recent reinvention, however, the notion of world citizenship has taken on a meaning which differentiates it from the ideal significance that it has heretofore enjoyed. The use of the word 'global' as one of the ways to express the notion of cosmopolitan citizenship is significant of this shift in meaning (Dower and Williams 2002). The term 'global' is firmly linked to processes of economic, social and political change which are held to characterize the last quarter of the twentieth century. These changes have, it is argued, made a world which is more clearly shared by all inhabitants of the earth and which is already subject to socio-economic forces and processes of governance beyond the sovereignty of states (subjection). At the same time, these forces have pushed the generalization of ideals of universal justice and freedom (pilgrimage) across the globe, ideals that are necessarily linked to the transformation of global subjection into global citizenship. The conditions of possibility for a genuinely global politics, it is claimed, are coming into place. As might be expected, within the tradition of Western political theory, global citizenship emerges as the product of a combination of global subjection (in which all individuals are commonly affected by coercive global forces) and global pilgrimage (in which individuals envisage a world in which the forces of globalization are transformed in terms of universal ideals of autonomy and equality). An important part of this process is the transformation of the coercive powers of subjection inherent in unaccountable agencies of global governance (state and non-state) into some new form of legitimate authority (Falk 1995a, 2002; Held 1995, 2002).[2]

The purpose of this chapter is to examine some of the arguments for the idea of global citizenship and to demonstrate that they rely on a mistaken understanding of the politics inherent in the position of individuals as subjects, citizens and pilgrims in the contemporary global context. It will be argued that the result of this mistaken understanding is an oversimplified and over-optimistic account of the political actualities and possibilities of global citizenship. I will begin by looking at the ways in which notions of cosmopolitan or global citizenship have been articulated by thinkers such as Linklater and Falk (Linklater 1998, 1999; Falk 1995a, 2002). In both cases, their argument for global citizenship is supported by the invocation of a particular conception of civil society which operates as the vehicle for individuals' pursuit of ideals of freedom and justice (pilgrimage) and thereby for the transformation of coercive power into legitimate authority. This move is echoed in two other recent contributions to the debate over global citizenship which draw on a version of the 'civil society argument'. The first argument is that of Iris Marion Young in *Inclusion and Democracy* (Young 2000). Young's argument suggests a version of global citizenship sustained by global civil society, on the one hand, and by cosmopolitan political authority, on the other. This argument is similar to that offered by Kaldor in her critical appraisal of the normative and practical significance of transnational civil society in post-cold war Europe in the 1980s and 1990s (Kaldor 1999a; 1999b). Kaldor's argument is more empirically specific than Young's, but it too presses for a conception of global citizenship which is nourished by the commitment to 'civility' inherent in civil society, on the one hand, and by transnational legal and political institutions, on the other.

It will be my contention that ultimately all of the above arguments suffer from an under-appreciation of the conditions of possibility of political agency which in practice link subjection, citizenship and pilgrimage together as recognizable aspects of individuals' actual political positions in the contemporary world. At the root of this under-appreciation is an over-moralized conception of the nature of both pilgrimage and citizenship that is particularly manifested in the highly normative use of the idea of global civil society, and that neglects the extent to which both pilgrims and citizens are conditioned (enabled and limited) by the forces of subjection to which they are opposed. This moralization of the political positions of pilgrims and citizens is necessitated in the arguments for global citizenship by the lack of a global polity to underpin citizenship with a universal legitimate authority. However, it comes to substitute for this authority in a way which is highly misleading, both structurally, in terms of the kind of status and practice that global citizenship represents, and substantively, in terms of the kinds of political agendas with which global citizenship is associated. Part of what has been forgotten in the debates on global citizenship is the fact that citizenship has always been a privilege, even where it is also a right, and has always had to be underpinned by coercive powers (legitimate or otherwise) which exclude and limit as well as protect and enable. The other part of what has been forgotten is that the link between both pilgrimage and citizenship and any particular normative agenda is contingent rather than necessary. This does not render the concepts of global citizenship or of global civil society meaningless, but it does make them much more ambiguous in terms of their political implications.

Citizenship – going global

Linklater and Falk both want to utilize the notion of global citizenship[3] as a meaningful concept which grasps certain contemporary global political actualities as well as possibilities. At the same time, they are both aware of the problems of translating the concept of citizenship to the global sphere. They recognize that the conditions underpinning citizenship, as it is familiar to us within the context of the nation-state, are absent or underdeveloped beyond the boundaries of the nation-state. There is no global polity, no cosmopolitan positive law, no universally shared global identity or solidarity which underpins mutual obligation between all inhabitants of the earth (Linklater 1998, 1999; Falk 1995a, 2002). In acknowledging the differences between state citizenship and global citizenship, Linklater and Falk are conceding ground to critics of global citizenship such as Miller (1999: 70–9). Miller dismisses the idea of global citizenship as, at best, a highly attenuated form of moral obligation which carries little if any political weight in terms of the activation of the rights and obligations standardly associated with what citizenship means. In contrast to the cosmopolitan theorists, Miller argues for the dependence of citizenship in its fullest, republican sense, on the existence of 'bounded' political community and the dependence of bounded community in turn on national identity (Miller 1995, 1999: 61–70).

Linklater and Falk respond rather differently to the type of criticism made by Miller and other communitarian thinkers such as Walzer (1994). Linklater's response involves putting citizenship within states into a broader historical context and making an argument for the rational implications of liberal universalism as it becomes institutionalized within the modern state and state system (Linklater 1982, 1999). At the same time, the conception of global citizenship which Linklater argues for is a complex and many-layered one in which multiple identities and loyalties may co-exist in a way very different from Miller's single polity, republican model (Linklater 1998: 198–204). For Linklater, global citizenship is an aspect of a historical but also logical process which is inherently linked to the universal values of enlightenment. This process is one in which an outcome sympathetic to the global inclusiveness of enlightenment values is implicit, even if it is not assured. Linklater's argument involves the application of Habermas's theory of communicative rationality to the understanding of political developments both within and beyond states (Linklater 1998: 87–108). For Linklater, the emergence of global citizenship, or something like it, is a product of the collective moral learning which Habermas claims is the phylogenetic effect of communicative reason (Habermas 1990b: 105–6). Linklater builds on Habermas's view that the Enlightenment, and the emergence of deliberative public spheres with which it is associated, is the equivalent on the collective level of the development of capacities to judge in terms of universal moral principles in Kohlberg's account of moral maturation at the level of the individual (Kohlberg 1984). In other words, for Linklater, the public recognition of the moral arbitrariness of non-universalist thinking which is implicit in the Enlightenment commitment to universal rights itself provides the impetus for the translation of the lessons of the enlightened liberal polity into ever more comprehensive spheres (Linklater 1998: 184–9, 1999). Linklater argues that it is the contradiction between liberalism's supposed universality and its actual exclusiveness which pushes the extension of citizenship rights and recognition within the state and which cannot or ought not consistently to stop at the boundaries of the state. This process is what explains the gradual accommodation of liberal states to the demands of their subjects for universal citizenship rights within them and also explains the development of nascent institutions and identities which support notions of citizenship beyond the state. The latter include developments such as the Universal Declaration of Human Rights (UNDHR), the growth in protection of individuals in international law and the emergence of political experiments in transnational citizenship such as that of the European Union (Linklater 1999).

In summary, Linklater responds to Miller by arguing for a different understanding of the meaning of citizenship within a liberal state. Both thinkers stress the importance of public deliberation within democratic politics and see the individual's capacity to participate within that deliberation as crucial to citizenship. Nevertheless they disagree on the question of what makes the 'civil' process of deliberation possible. For Miller, deliberation is made possible by a recognition of shared identity and fellowship which is inherently particularist; for Linklater, it is made possible by a rational capacity which is universally shared and has become explicitly recognized and institutionalized both within states and within inter-state and trans-state political relations. The power of this universalism, according to Linklater, fuels struggles for political inclusion within and beyond states. It therefore explains global civil society movements for human rights, peace and justice as much as it does intra-state civil society movements which struggle, and have struggled, for inclusion in the rights and obligations of citizenship. In Miller's eyes the reason why 'bounded' citizenship is necessary is in order to shore up the weak foundations for collective action which are inherent in individual rationality (Miller 1995: 49–80). For this reason, the individual's capacity for moral reason within the world at large cannot be an adequate substitute for full-blooded political identity within the settled norms of a community. But Linklater's response to this is to argue that the capacity for moral reason can run through a more flexible version of political identity and loyalty, which is closer to the complexities of global political realities. He does not deny the importance of local solidarities or the possibility of conflicts between them and individual identification with broader constituencies. However, his response to this is to suggest that we need far more complex institutional arrangements to enable recognition of and negotiation between different levels of solidarity, not that we need to return to a Rousseauian conception of the polity and politics.

> Political transformation would involve the divorce of citizenship from the state, just as it was uncoupled earlier from the medieval town and the Renaissance city . . . Citizenship would have to be reworked in the light of multiple allegiances and authorities . . . This project is immanent within the concept of citizenship itself, and one of the primary objectives of societies which are moved by its normative commitments should be to reconstruct citizenship with a view to expanding the boundaries of interaction which are governed by dialogue and consent.
>
> (Linklater 1998: 197)

Falk's response to the claim that citizenship is only meaningful within the context of a nation-state is less rationalistic and less secular than that of Linklater, and therefore to some extent less optimistic. It is also more firmly linked to the idea that the archetypal global citizen is a member of a transnational social movement which pursues an ethical goal (Falk 1995a: 207–12). Falk's account of global citizenship is premised on an account of globalization as a dual process in which tendencies towards oppression, exploitation and inequality are being countered by the development of pressures from 'below', from grass roots social movements which push for a non-oppressive, non-exploitative and egalitarian global political agenda (Falk 1995a: 209). Falk is contemptuous of claims to global citizenship made by the global elite, in which group he would include both the bourgeois traveller and the higher echelons of multinational or transnational corporations (Falk 2002: 26). In this respect, he echoes Miller in linking citizenship to an active political engagement in which the ends of action are to do with the common good as opposed to individual interest. Nevertheless, he acknowledges that the sense of identity and solidarity engendered by participation in global social movements and commitment to goals such as gender equality, sustainable development, peace, etc. is not equivalent to 'the idea of being a member of a comprehensive political community, which is the core meaning of 'citizenship' (Falk 2002: 26). Instead he argues:

> the only kind of visionary citizenship that can be taken seriously will have to be grounded in what is occurring on the level of fact, norm and value as both trend and potentiality. It must be rooted in the future, the not yet, rather than unconvincingly affirm as 'real' such a reconfiguring of political allegiance as is so unconvincingly claimed by secular minded 'world citizens'.
>
> (Falk 2002: 27)

Falk's analysis, therefore, suggests a more significant gap between citizenship, as traditionally conceived in liberal states, and global citizenship than does Linklater. The latter concedes states and formal juridical and political institutions a major role in the historical development of the moral potential of enlightenment rationality towards universal political inclusion, though only to the extent that those institutions embody the principles of enlightenment rationality in the first place. Falk is more inclined to link the state to the project of geo-governance from above, and find the source of global citizenship in the sphere of global civil society, though he acknowledges that strong democratic states might also have a role to play (Falk 1995a: 207–9). Global civil society is understood by Falk as the 'visionary' sphere of grass roots voluntary and oppositional political action. It is something which is not yet fully actualized, but which can be seen as implicit within the political agendas of the global social movements mentioned above. In their accounts of global citizenship, Linklater's emphasis is on the significance of the moral values inherent in modernity, which work through both state and civil society; whereas Falk's emphasis, in contrast, is on the significance of political commitment on the part or behalf of the excluded and oppressed or of the world/species in general. Falk's account does not rely on the universalizability of the implications of communicative reason to carry history forward in the same way as Linklater's, but like Linklater's his argument does rely on making a link between certain kinds of political activity and a universalist normative agenda. In this sense, both Linklater and Falk share an account of the logic of historical transformation in which pilgrimage (the commitment to universal values) transforms the conditions of political subjection into a globalized version of citizenship.

Both Linklater and Falk are advocates for the strengthening of democratic political institutions at the global level (though not for world government), which is clearly one way to address the 'not yet' of global citizenship. However, in neither case does the project of cosmopolitan democracy carry much of the weight of the conception of global citizenship which is being put forward. For both thinkers, citizenship is not reducible to a purely juridical identity. Instead, they tend to stress the normative and what Falk refers to as the 'psycho-political' dimension of global citizenship, in which individuals identify themselves as global citizens and with their fellows in terms of a universal moral goal (Falk 2002: 21). Both thinkers are, however, aware that the norms endorsed by their own theories are the product of Western culture and history and that psycho-political identity may be nourished by alternative universalist projects or by 'atavistic tribalisms'. For both, the answer to this problem is the promotion of inter-civilizational dialogue within the global public sphere (Linklater 1998: 209–12; Falk 2002: 27–8). In Linklater's case this dialogue is conditioned by the possibilities of communicative reason, in Falk's it is a quasi-religious commitment to transcend the 'shadow side of post-Westphalian struggle' represented by Huntington's clash of civilizations thesis (Falk 2002: 27–8). In both cases, however, a key potential source of the psycho-political conditions of global citizenship is located in the sphere of voluntary political commitment and action or the sphere of civil society. Global civil society comes to do the work of both state and nation as an enabling condition of global citizenship. On the one hand, it substitutes for the state by underpinning the active, deliberative engagement of individuals with political issues for the sake of a greater good. At the same time, it substitutes for the nation as a source of political solidarity. The values which underpin voluntary action and political commitment within civil society are treated as necessarily linked to ideals of universal rights and justice which provide the reasons why all inhabitants of the earth should figure as fellow citizens.

The civil society argument – going global

The arguments of both Linklater and Falk rely on the identification of voluntary political commitment in global civil society with a set of universal values. On this account both pilgrims (the activists of civil society) and citizens are understood primarily in terms of normative commitments which are generalizable across space and time. This moralization of the concept of civil society is not confined to Linklater and Falk, but has become a standard element in liberal democratic theory, and in particular in democratic theory which seeks to extend democracy in a cosmopolitan direction. The rediscovery of the importance of civil society for democracy was partly due to the experience of the emergence from authoritarianism of ex-Soviet bloc states in the 1980s and 1990s (Walzer 1992; Young 2000). For citizens of states emerging from years of authoritarian rule, civil society was experienced to be a key factor in political change and an effective counterweight to centralized state power. For democratic theorists within liberal states, this 'civil society argument' resonated with an ongoing dissatisfaction with both liberal democracy and welfarist social democracy as the available normative models for how democracy should be (Mouffe 1992; Hirst 1994; Cohen and Rogers 1995; Habermas 1996). As has been made clear in earlier chapters in this book, civil society is a complex concept. However, within the realms of recent democratic theory it tends to figure in quite straightforward terms as that sphere of public deliberation and action which is defined, largely in opposition to the state, as the sphere of voluntary, uncoerced activity, of pluralism and free association. As such it embodies the universal values of pilgrimage and is the antithesis of subjection in all of its forms (Young 2000: 157–64).[4]

The key theme of Young's democratic theory is inclusion and the inseparability of the value of autonomy from that of equality. In *Inclusion and Democracy*, Young bases her arguments for a particular kind of democracy on the importance for individuals of two central values: self-determination and self-development. Self-determination refers to the individual's capacity to determine how they live their own lives and, for Young, necessarily implies having an input into the mechanisms and principles according to which society is governed and regulated. Self-development refers to the individual's capacity to fulfil their potential and flourish as a person, and implies the requirement to meet material, social and cultural needs. Young relates each of these values to a correlative evil, 'domination' on the one hand and 'oppression' on the other. For Young, whilst domination is very largely to do with political power which stifles individual autonomy, oppression is largely, though by no means wholly, to do with economic power, which stifles self-development for many in its unresponsiveness to needs (Young 2000: 31–2).

In her definition of civil society, Young eschews the spatial metaphors which have characterized both sociological and normative definitions of civil society in the past. Rather than seeing civil society as a kind of 'space' between or beyond the spheres of family, economy or state, Young concentrates in her definition on distinguishing civil society as referring to a certain kind of activity, one characterized by voluntary association and by, following Habermas, communicative rather than instrumental/functional rationality (Young 2000: 160). Civil society, according to Young, is particularly important because it works as a counter to tendencies towards domination which are an inevitable feature of the concentration of state power in complex societies. Voluntary political association and activity in civil society are essential to self-determination, particularly for those groups who are marginalized in mainstream politics. Moreover, civil society activities are crucial to public discourses which connect 'people and power' within complex societies and enable oppositional voices to be articulated against dominant groups and interests.

However, although Young is insistent on the value of civil society activity to self-determination and making connections between citizens and the state, she is less certain as to its value in relation to self-development. It is in this respect that she claims that the civil society argument has limits. Although she does argue that political association and activity in civil society may aid self-development, Young acknowledges that civil society may also either be unable to provide such aid to all or may even actively impede it. This is because civil society lacks the capacity to ensure that the needs of citizens as a whole are met, either in terms of material equality or recognition and respect. In particular, Young suggests that civil society is not able to counter economic power, partly because of its inherent diffuseness, but also because of the lack of universal guarantees of inclusion in the membership or aims of civil society movements. Civil society is the realm of particularity and difference, in which citizens may organize around private, civic and political activities and goals, but in which there will clearly be alternative and sometimes contradictory positions (Young 2000: 167, 190). Here, Young argues, state power is necessary to counteract not only the inegalitarian and anti-democratic effects of economic power, but also the potential for exclusions within the voluntary associations of civil society. Young's assessment of civil society is that it is necessary to democracy but is also politically ambivalent. She ends up arguing for both a healthy civil society and a democratic state as the key to maximizing self-determination and self-development for citizens.

The ambivalence of Young's assessment of civil society reflects a certain ambivalence in her definition of it. At some points in her analysis, it seems that civil society activity is defined in terms of communicative rationality and therefore in terms of universal norms of justice. At other points, civil society is defined in terms which acknowledge the partiality of interest and identity in civil society activity and therefore the fact that it is not 'necessarily good', either in terms of its internal organization or its aims (Young 2000: 167). In this respect, Young's work reflects the dualities already identified within arguments about global citizenship, in which a 'republican' emphasis on voluntary political commitment and a 'liberal' emphasis on certain universal values coincide rather uneasily. Young invokes the state in order to address the tensions she articulates. In a quasi-Hegelian fashion, the state is necessary not only to ensure material distributive justice but to counter the potentially divisive politics of civil society. Young makes it clear in her analysis that state power operates differently to that of civil society. She identifies the liberal state with the power of legitimate coercion, in contrast to the uncoerced communicative power which emerges from civil society activity (ibid.: 158–60). The coercive power of the state is necessary to enable the uncoerced power of civil society to flourish, just as the uncoerced power of civil society activity ensures that the state does not overstep the legitimate limits of its coercive activity. This suggestion of a need for balance between institutionalized power and the power generated by voluntary association, however, clearly depends on the existence of strong, legitimate formal political institutions. This is something which is clearly not available when, in the final chapter of *Inclusion and Democracy*, Young transfers the location of her arguments about the proper form of democracy from the liberal democratic state to the global level.

> In Chapter 5 I discussed the important function of civil society in fostering independent public spheres through which individuals and groups expose the activities of powerful state and economic actors, express their opposition to or criticism of some of those activities, and hold powerful actors accountable. Global democratic processes could not be very strong without such public spheres that in principle included all the world's peoples. Already the possibilities of transportation and communication in the world today see the formation of incipient public spheres composed of active citizens in global civil society.
>
> (Young 2000: 197)

Young's interest in concepts of global civil society and citizenship is developed from her democratic theory, which is grounded in the institutional context of the modern, capitalist, multicultural, liberal state. Her ideas self-consciously trace the same path as thinkers such as Held, in which a particular model of democracy is found to be unworkable if the analysis is limited to domestic politics within the context of globalization. However, Young finds the same difficulties in addressing the democratic deficits within the global context as Linklater and Falk and, like them, articulates a twin solution. According to this solution, the establishment of democratically accountable, legitimate institutionalized power at a global level is presaged by the development of global public spheres, global civil society and global citizenship. Whereas in her analysis of the liberal state, state and civil society encompass parallel, co-dependent forms of political activity, in the case of global politics, Young suggests that civil society activity comes first, potentially to be followed in time by institutional reform (Young 2000: 271–5). As with Linklater, Young's guarded optimism about this possibility is inseparable from a Habermasian view of the power of communicative reason. Both Linklater and Young identify the transformative potential of global civil society with the way in which it embodies norms of communicative reason which work against arbitrary exclusion of individuals from both rights and political participation. In the global context, Young like Linklater, uses global civil society as a substitute for the institutional and normative conditions of possibility for political agency embodied in state and nation.

Kaldor's interest in civil society and citizenship beyond the sphere of the state arises in a different context from Young's. In Kaldor's case, it arises directly in relation to the phenomenon of the cross-border role of civil society movements (in the West as well as the East) in the break up of the old Soviet bloc in Eastern Europe, followed by the emergence of violent nationalist and ethnic conflict in the former Yugoslavia (Kaldor 1999a; 1999b). Her concern is with the way in which the civil society movements within Bosnia were not in the end capable of resisting a turn to the 'uncivil' politics of nationalism and ethnic hatred. Kaldor's conception of civil society, puts emphasis on the term 'civil' and lacks the ambivalence which emerges in Young's argument. For Kaldor, the history of civil society is the history of movements arguing for the conditions of a civil politics, it is therefore by definition to be distinguished from an 'uncivil' politics, such as that of grass-roots political movements with exclusionary (ethnic nationalist or religious fundamentalist) aims. For Kaldor, transnational civil society stands for the values of democracy, non-violence, multiculturalism and secularity (Kaldor 1999a: 206). Like Young and many other contemporary democratic theorists, however, Kaldor makes a strong link between grass-roots civil society activity and the notion of citizenship. Kaldor's essay on transnational civil society is part of an edited volume on human rights in global politics (Dunne and Wheeler 1999). Kaldor suggests that the idea of international human rights is virtually the same as the ethos of civil society as she has defined it. However, she argues that 'the advantage of the language of civil society is precisely its *political* content, its implications for participation and citizenship'. Kaldor wants to shift from a moral to a political language in international politics in order to keep in view the need for political action and political institutions to fulfil the aims implicit in such documents as the UNDHR. Like Falk, she sees the transformative possibilities within contemporary world politics located in the realm of citizen-pilgrims, pursuing a civil vision in a uncivil world. In Kaldor's case, however, it is not the power of communicative reason as such but of political commitment to ethical goals which will bring about progress. As with all of the theorists considered, however, Kaldor also finds that global civil society is not in itself enough to guarantee global citizenship. Global civil society must be succeeded by legitimate global political authority.

> The lessons of the 1980s were that civil society has to be built from below through the efforts of self-organized groups of citizens working together across national boundaries. The lessons of the 1990s are that such groups cannot succeed in a globalized uncivil world without responsive institutions at both local and transnational levels.
>
> (Kaldor 1999a: 210)

Young and Kaldor both argue that civil society is a necessary but not a sufficient condition for sustaining democratic citizenship either at the local or global level. In arguing about the importance of global civil society and citizenship, they both give civil society a crucial normative significance which lies in the virtues of political commitment, participation and self-determination which it nourishes. At the same time they also argue for the supplementation of civil society movements by global political institutions and authority. The pattern of their arguments follows that discernible in Linklater's and Falk's accounts of global citizenship. Here, too, a great deal of weight rests on civil society as the necessary underpinning to democratic politics, but at the same time the arguments look forward to the establishment of cosmopolitan political authority.

In the conceptions of citizenship drawn on by the four theorists there is a combination of two different modes of theorizing citizenship, both of which have a long tradition within Western thought and which reflect rather different values. Citizenship is understood by all the thinkers, in both liberal and republican terms, as a matter simultaneously of individual rights and protection, and of civic virtue and participation. It is a truism within democratic theory, however, that there is a tension between a conception of citizenship which takes universal equality of right as its normative model for citizenship and a conception of citizenship which takes active, collective self-determination as its model. On the one hand, as Linklater insists, liberal rights are conceptually all-inclusive, they provide no grounds for a distinction between 'human' and 'citizen'. On the other hand, as Miller insists, republican conceptions of citizenship are tied to the notion of an exclusive collective and imply a link between particularist solidarities and active citizenship. In theorizing citizenship within the state, as Young's work illustrates, democratic theorists hover between an institutional and a normative response to the tensions between inclusion and exclusion in the liberal and republican ideals of citizenship. Institutionally, it is dealt with through the enabling and constraining power of legitimate political authority (often embodied in a constitution) which deals with 'uncivil' society and permits citizenship in the republican participatory sense to manifest itself only in certain ways, constrained by liberal universalism. Normatively, it is dealt with through the power of certain norms over the realms of both civil society and state, which ensures that citizenship is nourished and exercised within civil and political realms in accordance with liberal principles that are grounded in universal morality. Whether one is sympathetic to the above argument in relation to citizenship within states or not, it is clearly not straightforwardly translatable to the global sphere. This is both because of the absence of political authority at a global level (clearly something which Young, Kaldor, Linklater and Falk would want to address) and because there is no normative consensus amongst the 'citizen-pilgrims' of world politics which could be depended upon to counteract the potential for incivility at work in the sphere of civil society. Neither the political nor the moral prerequisites of citizenship appear to be in place. Yet the response of the theorists we have been considering to this claim is not to backtrack on the claim as to the saliency of notions of global citizenship in the contemporary world, but to put ever greater emphasis on the positive role of global civil society. This is in spite of an acknowledgement, in particular in Young's work, that civil society should by no means be understood as an unambiguous force for good.

A key tension within the concept of civil society, as it operates in the arguments we have been considering, is between its definition in terms of a particular sphere or form of action (voluntary, uncoerced, politically committed activity) and its definition in terms of a particular set of values (universal rights). As we have seen, this is evident in Young's work and she deals with it partly by linking 'civil' activity with Habermas's notion of communicative reason, and partly by acknowledging the normative ambivalence of civil society as the sphere of voluntary association. By identifying civil society with communicative reason, Young suggests a necessary link between civil society activity and fundamental principles of right. So that, for instance, notions of fundamental human rights which ground the terms of engagement of debate within the public sphere are themselves inherent in civil society activity. At the same time, in her acknowledgement that all forms of activity in civil society are not necessarily good, Young suggests that civil society activists do not necessarily realize, in Habermasian terms, the presuppositions of the communicative activity in which they are engaging. This is a tendency which is compounded by unequal access to resources for voluntary association and deliberation in the public sphere by different civil society activists. For this reason Young argues for the state as a necessary balance not only to economic power but also to the exclusive and divisive politics which may characterize civil society left to its own devices. Yet, in the context of global politics and the absence of legitimate political authority, Young is forced to rely on the Habermasian aspect of her argument to carry the possibilities of global citizenship forward. This is in spite of the fact that on the basis of her own analysis, it is unclear how far the power of communicative reason may extend given the forces of subjection inherent not only of the systemic power of hegemonic state and capitalist market, but also in the potential for incivility of civil society itself. As with Linklater, when it comes to the stage of global politics, Young's analysis relies on an implicit philosophy of history, in which the values inherent in communicative reason govern the development of world politics.

In Kaldor's case the ambivalent possibilities of civil society identified by Young are dealt with by definitional fiat in relation to both domestic and transnational politics. Kaldor takes the term 'civil' as crucial, and opposes it to 'uncivil' politics as well as to the external powers of state and market. In this, she is following the precedent set by Falk, who identifies global civil society with human rights, peace, environmental and feminist movements – campaigning on non-exclusionary, universal grounds. The ethical ambiguities of state, economy and civil society within existing states, which is reflected in Young's democratic theory within state borders becomes a Manichaean story in which the forces of civility and incivility and of 'geo-governance' from above and 'humane governance' from below do battle. Kaldor's removal of ambiguity from the concept of civil society does not therefore resolve the tension identified by Young as located within civil society activity, but reinvents it in a simpler form as a struggle between good and evil on the stage of world history. Kaldor's analysis, like Falk's, lacks the optimism of Linklater and Young, even as it embraces a cosmopolitan politics (Kaldor 1999b: 112–37; 149–52). The implicit philosophy of history working through Linklater's and Young's analyses relies on the idea that there are common universalist implications bound up in communicative activity in which all persons engage. Falk and Kaldor, in contrast, understand politics as essentially a matter of normative commitment or choice rather than communicative reason. Either the good or the evil path is embraced. Nevertheless, all four thinkers share the view that the key to the development of global civil society and to the meaning of global citizenship is the engagement of individuals in a politics motivated by the moral ideal of universal inclusiveness.

Conclusion – subjects, citizens or pilgrims?

Linklater, Falk, Young and Kaldor use notions of cosmopolitan, transnational, global or world citizenship to capture the existing reality and ethical promise of certain kinds of political activity in the context of world politics. In doing this, they suggest a significant relation between global citizenship and global civil society. In all cases, however, their analysis demonstrates the uneasiness of the link between these two in the context of globalization. This is partly because of the pressures of what Falk has termed 'geo-governance' from above, namely, the forces of state and market which work to counter the rights and potentiality of political action of individuals and grass-roots movements in the contemporary world (Falk 1995a: 9–46). The second source of uneasiness, however, is located precisely in the realm of grass-roots voluntary association which is held to be the key characteristic of civil society itself. The influence of Habermas is important here, because it is he, above all, of contemporary political theorists who has suggested a necessary, as opposed to contingent, link between certain kinds of activity in the public sphere, the reasoning upon which these activities are premised, and a universal conception of the parameters of justice (Habermas 1990a; 1990b; 1996). As we have seen, all of the thinkers considered above depend in their arguments for global citizenship on something like the Habermasian view that global citizenship implies a coincidence between grass-roots political action and an essentially liberal moral agenda. This moral agenda both substitutes for the institutional prerequisites of citizenship and for what Falk calls the 'psycho-political' aspects, in which citizens find the solidarities and commitments which motivate and sustain political action.

Do the problems inherent in the above account of global citizenship render the notion meaningless? To a large extent, it seems to me that they do. Nevertheless, it may be that the notion of global citizenship is not entirely redundant, since it provides a means of conceptualizing developments in global politics which are real and which may have significant political implications for the future. These developments are not fully captured in a vocabulary of either subjection or pilgrimage. They include the increasing legitimation of the political activism of individuals within and in relation to state and non-state actors in the international context. The most obvious example of this is the institutionalization of interaction between NGOs and international organizations in policy formation and delivery. They also include the development of trans- and super-state juridical and institutional frameworks within which individuals may lay claim to status and rights beyond the state – from the European Union to international law. However, as these examples make clear, access to global citizenship is radically unequal between different individuals. Moreover, that inequality is non-arbitrary in the sense that the capacity to identify oneself, be recognized as, and act as a global citizen is parasitic on the dramatically undemocratic and inegalitarian nature of the global order in general, both institutionally and normatively. Global citizens are able to be global citizens because, crudely speaking, they are rich and mobile and because they share the conceptual frameworks that dominate the global order. There is therefore a strong tension between global citizenship as it currently exists and the egalitarian, universalist rights-based version of citizenship which most advocates of global citizenship put forward.

To the extent that the notion of global citizenship has meaning, it is more closely linked to pre- or early-modern republican conceptions of citizenship than to the idea of the universality of rights characteristic of enlightenment thinking. In this more machiavellian worldview, citizenship is a privilege that belongs to a restricted caste. This privilege is, in principle, inseparable from obligations to the polity, but it is also entwined with political actualities that enable the exercise of considerable discretion as to how those obligations are to be identified and acted upon. A citizen may be a bad citizen and yet still be a citizen, since citizenship is a political rather than a moral status. This is not an exact parallel – in the early modern city state citizens knew who they were and the polity to which they belonged. In the case of global citizenship, it is a status that is acquired, recognized and acted upon contingently and intermittently in relation to a polity that is as much imagined as real and which the citizen is actively oriented to *making* rather than *protecting*. For a great many individuals in the world the prerequisites for global citizenship are entirely lacking. In those parts of the world where it is open to individuals to act as global citizens, it remains largely a matter of choice as to whether and how they will do so. Even where the identification of oneself as a member of global civil society or a global citizen is possible, this does not automatically mean identification with the normative agenda with which most theorists of global citizenship wish to associate these terms. Falk has coined the term 'citizen-pilgrim' to express the available realities of global citizenship, but he is also well aware that there are a variety of 'new Jerusalems' on offer in the current era and there are no guarantees that the normative agenda of 'citizen-pilgrims' rather than that of 'atavistic tribalisms' will come to dominate (Falk 1995a: 211–12). This raises the fundamentally political question of how, in the absence of an overarching juridical or political authority, ideological commitments emerge from or are conditioned by actual, lived experience and solidarities with others. This is a question which, I suggest, is taken insufficiently seriously by the proponents of global citizenship, and which poses problems for the highly moralized versions of the meaning of 'civil society' and 'citizenship' upon which their arguments rely.

Notes

1 My usage of the terms 'subject' and 'citizen' is a standard one and captures a familiar contrast. I have adopted the terms 'pilgrim' and 'pilgrimage' following Falk's coining of the term 'citizen-pilgrim', which uses 'pilgrim' to signify political actors seeking to transform the world according to an ideal universal vision of how it ought to be (Falk 1995a: 211–12).

2 This is not to suggest that globalization is a straightforwardly unifying process. Even the most optimistic accounts of the positive political potential of globalization acknowledge that it is a set of processes which includes fragmenting as well as unifying tendencies (see Camilleri and Falk 1992; Falk 1995a; McGrew 1997).

3 From now on I will stick to the formulation 'global' citizenship as a shorthand for the various terms which are used (cosmopolitan, world, transnational, international). 'Global citizenship' should be taken to encompass any account of citizenship as a status which is not wholly authorized and exercised within the confines of the nation-state.

4 There are many different versions of the civil society argument within democratic theory. At one end of the spectrum associative democrats argue for investing increasing power and authority within civil society associations and reducing the role of the state to that of a distant guarantor and referee of the democratic process (Hirst 1994; Carter 2002). At the other end of the spectrum, theorists such as Walzer, whilst insisting on the importance of civil society as the sphere of voluntary activity and plurality, are equally insistent that the democratic state is as necessary to civility in civil society as civility is to the state (Walzer 1992). Another strand of democratic theory which has embraced a version of the 'civil society argument' is one which makes necessary connections between democracy and public deliberation and links the concept of civil society to that of the 'public sphere'. Broadly speaking, the ideal of deliberative democracy is one in which citizens are granted the opportunity to deliberate about political choices and decisions by which they will be affected (Benhabib 1996b; Elster 1998). Some versions of this argument put the emphasis on formal forums for deliberation within a structure of government (Cohen 1996b); others see civil society as a crucial arena for democratic deliberation, which supports and sustains deliberative mechanisms at the more formal level (Fraser 1993). An influential voice, in relation to both lines of argument, is that of Habermas, whose democratic theory insists on the need for public communication and debate as the necessary complement to more formal structures if democracy is to flourish (Habermas 1996: 359–87). As with the rediscovery of civil society, the emphasis on deliberation in democratic theory is designed to introduce into the 'passive' citizenship characteristic of liberal models of democracy some active republican elements, given the context of large-scale complex societies and the difficulties of reinventing a Rousseauean polity. In this sense, Habermas's democratic theory exemplifies a whole range of work in the way in which it seeks to reconcile the ideals of popular sovereignty and universal rights. Young is an example of a democratic theorist making and combining arguments for both civil society and deliberation in her ideal of democracy within contemporary liberal states. Young draws critically on a variety of sources in her democratic theory, including Habermas. But she also criticizes theorists such as Habermas and Cohen for having too formal and rationalistic an understanding of communicative reason, which is thereby exclusive (Young 1996).

7 Situating global citizenship

Nigel Dower

Introduction

The purpose of this chapter is to defend the claim that the idea of global citizenship has application in the modern world,[1] and more generally by implication the claim that there is a transnational social space within which individuals can act and indeed do act appropriately as agents with global objectives and remits. This transnational social space can also be referred to as global civil society. Many, though not all, parts of global civil society, in the form of networks and associations, constitute part – and as the world is now the major part – of the embodiment of global citizenship. Other discourses have also become popular such as global democracy and global governance, which also point to or presuppose the existence of this transnational social space and, in so far as 'active' global citizens can be seen as participating in deliberative activities which contribute towards our collective management of global issues, global citizenship is also linked to these two ideas. Put another way, we are right to recognize that various discourses such as global civil society, global democracy, global governance, as well as global citizenship, all point to a reality about global relationships which is transforming our understanding of the relations between states and the position of citizens within states. These ideas may or may not pick out quite the same reality. As we shall see, there may be tensions between what each presupposes. They certainly pick out different *aspects* of whatever this emerging reality is. On the interpretations which I offer they complement each other, and can in summary be related in the following schematic way: individuals (global citizens) are members of a global society (primarily global civil society) a function of which is to contribute to the management and shaping of public affairs (global governance) through a particular process or manner of participation (global democracy). Apart from defending a particular interpretation of the relationship between these concepts, this chapter is partly programmatic, in setting out a large network of possible relationships that are or might be suggested.

Of course, the main driver of such changes is globalization, but we have to be clear that the relationship which globalization has to what these discourses all point to is quite different to the relationships between them.[2] Whereas these discourses all point to a changing role of ordinary individuals in playing an active part in global affairs, and they stress a normative dimension to this process, globalization as such indicates a process of increasing global connectedness and interdependence, or increasing deterritorialization of social relations (Scholte 2000c). This leaves rather open whether these changes include the emergence of global civil society, and so on, and whether they have significant normative consequences. The differences are not absolute. With the above discourses, the normative interest is usually, though not always, significant, if not uppermost, whereas with globalization the primary interest is either descriptive of the process which is going on or explanatory of why it is happening. Nevertheless, one's interest can be about what kinds of globalization are to be regarded as desirable and worth promoting (see for example, Scholte 2000c). Such interest presupposes what may not always be granted about globalization, namely that its general direction can be controlled, whereas the earlier discourses all presuppose the possibility that the deliberate decisions of people can make a significant difference. Furthermore, although globalization is of course itself a contested concept, there appears to be far more agreement about the reality of the process than there is about the reality of global civil society, the applicability of global citizenship, and so on, as aspects or consequences of it.

The main part of this chapter then is on the relationship between the various discourses that I have mentioned. Whilst, as I have said, there is likely to be a high level of convergence amongst those who use these discourses, there may also be significant areas of disagreement as well, and it will be useful to produce first a kind of conceptual mapping. The chapter then focuses more specifically on global citizenship and why I believe it to be a particularly important concept to work with.

Convergences

The convergence, I believe, stems from the following features, which can be separated roughly into the empirical and the normative.

Empirical commonalities

First, there is the empirical claim that the so-called Westphalian model of the world divided into autonomous nation-states, which between them determine or regulate broadly the way things go at a global level, is now seriously challenged by developments of various kinds (for example, Linklater 1998 and 1999; Falk 2002; Rosenau 2000). This is a way of indicating of course the facts of globalization. Second, the challenge does not just come from economic globalization (in which the key actors are financial and commercial institutions), but from the roles and status of ordinary individuals. Increasingly individuals act, whether through organizations, through informal networks or on their own, in ways that engage with the world and its problems. Of course, small numbers of individuals have done this sort of thing over many centuries, but the scale of such involvement, especially in the last thirty years, has been such that it has become a third force in world affairs 'in addition to states and corporate economic power' (Nerfin 1987). Thus many individuals join in organizations which express cosmopolitan solidarities such as Oxfam, Amnesty International or Greenpeace, or engage in 'particularist solidarities', as Scholte (2000c) calls them, such as transworld concerns of particular groups of people united by class, gender, ethnic or religious identities (though these are often implicitly cosmopolitan as well, in so far as they are appealing to universal conceptions of justice or rights in defence of their group positions). We are increasingly involved in transworld economic relations as consumers and producers of goods transported to and from anywhere in the world, and again, in so far as we have ethical concerns as consumers or investors about the production of such goods, a dimension of active engagement with the world is shown (for example, Ethical Consumer 2002).

Although it would be foolish of me to claim that *anyone* using the discourses of global civil society, global citizenship, global democracy or global governance would assert *all* these empirical claims, I do think that by and large these claims are made by those using them, at least by those who are in some sense advocating these discourses as ways of thinking about world affairs.

Thus advocates of global citizenship could play down or ignore the current state of transboundary social relations and either focus on global responsibilities which we ought to recognize (even if most do not) or additionally focus on the importance of future developments (like the aspiration to create future institutions like a world state), but generally they acknowledge and indeed stress the existence already of various forms of transnational co-operation and engagement, and see themselves as engaged in forms of it.

Likewise an advocate of global democracy could point to the desirability of the development of formalized cosmopolitan participation or cosmopolitan democracy (Archibugi and Held 1995; Held 1995), for example, in a second UN assembly, and see the current world as still essentially (if regrettably) an inter-national world, but is rather more likely to make much of the emergence already of new patterns of decision-making in the world in which individuals have a significant role.

Global governance, as the generic term for ways of ordering our public affairs (of which government as a system of coercive regulation is one species, albeit currently the dominant species), could of course be advocated in such a way as either to endorse the current international system as the best way to organize and regulate the world, or to advocate another level of formal government in the form of world government (which would simply replicate the current form of coercion at another level). Many of those who use the discourse, however, have in mind (as the Commission on Global Governance's Report of 1995 made clear) other forms of governance involving new roles for individuals in global civil society alongside forms of government – even if that report's internationalism did not go as far as other cosmopolitan theories go in questioning the current international system (Commission on Global Governance 1995; see Isin and Wood 1999 for critical comment).

Of the four discourses, that of global civil society seems the most unambiguously committed to the view that the reality in the world is one in which there already exists elements of transnational society which are incompatible with the Westphalian model. But users of all four discourses are generally in agreement about the empirical analysis I have indicated.

Normative commonalities

Further commonalities emerge when we turn to the normative dimension.

(i) The fundamental orientation is one of a global ethic. By a global ethic I mean a set of norms and values with the following two characteristics: (a) they are endorsed by someone who accepts a global ethic because he has reason to maintain that there are certain universal human values (i.e. universally applicable, not universally accepted), but more importantly that these values *matter* from a global perspective and therefore there is collectively a responsibility to so act that these values are not thwarted and indeed are positively promoted; (b) they are (or are taken to be by the person who accepts a global ethic) widely accepted or shared across the world (roughly what Frost, in this volume, calls embedded 'ethicality') and reflected in agreed statements and declarations, such as the *Universal Declaration of Human Rights* (1948), the *Declaration Toward a Global Ethic* (1993) of the Parliament of the World's Religions (see Küng and Kuschel 1993), or the *Earth Charter* (2000). By a 'global ethic' here, however, I do not mean either of two other things that may be implied by the phrase: namely, either a universally agreed ethic or an ethic which combines certain universal values and norms with a particular worldview, theory or source story, such as a Christian global ethic or a Kantian global ethic (though Christians or Kantians may well have reason to support a global ethic in my sense).

First, no ethic is *universally* accepted or ever likely to be; indeed, what is striking about the modern world is precisely the conflict between different global ethics as defined above. It is important to stress that the advocate of these discourses is not subscribing to *any* possible global ethic. Those who use the discourses of global citizenship, and so on, are likely to have ethical views which fall within a certain range, but not beyond. Neither a fundamentalist ethic which advocated a particular ethical or religious ideal and was intolerant of cultural or religious difference, nor a libertarian ethic which stresses liberty and downgraded responsibility, would be likely to be advocated – though they are both forms of a global ethic. What generally the advocates of these discourses have in mind is the ethical importance of combating poverty, protecting human rights, creating the conditions of peace, or protecting the environment. This is because poverty, war, environmental damage and the violation of rights all undermine the conditions of human well-being anywhere in the world.

Second, whilst there may be widespread convergence on the general ethical approach, there may be disagreements about the theoretical nature of global ethics and how to justify one's ethical position (for example, over subjectivism and objectivism, or Kantianism and Utilitarianism). These disagreements, however, are not as important as the agreements on values and norms which each party has reason to endorse from his or her theoretical perspective. Mutual acceptance of each other's differences of starting points is part of the wider acceptance of respect for diversity, and marks out this kind of global ethic as different from older kinds of cosmopolitan thinking which were often culturally imperialistic or proselytizing in character (Dower 1998; Edwards 1999).

Not all advocates of these discourses would agree with my general characterization of this common core. Whilst those concerned with global governance would generally accept certain common ethically justified goals of governance (justice, peace, environmental protection) (Halliday 2000) and those who advocate global democracy clearly subscribe to the universal norms of democracy, it is not obvious that those who believe in global civil society have to accept a global ethic in the sense I have used. Even though the word 'society' might seem to imply some common ethical core which makes it a *society*, this point might be ignored or marginalized if one stresses the diversity of ethical agendas of members of global civil society, so that one either says that there are many global ethics *including* the kinds I have rejected, or says that really there is no global ethic, just conflicting ethical particularities (ibid. 2000). The advocates of global citizenship might well reject the relevance of widely accepted norms and values or of statement and declarations, and simply rely on their own ethical theory and assert their global responsibilities on this basis. Nevertheless, my sense is that for the most part the advocates of these four discourses do have a broadly similar ethical agenda and see the importance and relevance of accepting and developing areas of convergence.

From this global ethics perspective a number of corollaries follow.

(ii) There is a common critical stance vis-à-vis nation-states. There is general rejection of both sceptical realism which questions the relevance of ethics for international relations, and that form of internationalism which tries to insulate the morality of states from global criticism by making it autonomous and validated by what states agree amongst themselves (for example, Beitz 1979). States can be, and are, critically evaluated if their foreign policies are not ethical enough. Recommendations on what states ought to do are appropriate; that is, not merely are individuals entitled to make or voice these criticisms, but government ought to listen to such criticism. Such recommendations are in fact often made by organizations acting as pressure groups and by individuals acting in various ways, such as writing letters to Members of Parliament. But the point at this stage is that states are subject to moral assessment from a global perspective (for example, Dower 1998). The protests by the so-called 'anti-globalization' protesters against the G8 and their deliberations about aid, debt relief and the world economy in Genoa in July 2001 (and at early meetings) illustrate what I am saying in the following way. Many of the protesters had a very strong view that Third World Debt should be cancelled or at least substantially reduced, but at the same time they also had a view that governments ought to listen to such protests or be more generally responsive to what individuals concerned about global issues are saying. Such active criticism is also part of the ethical agenda and part of what the critique of states involves. That critique is not just about what states do substantively in their foreign policies vis-à-vis poverty, the environment, arms trade, and so on, but also about a certain way states conceive of themselves as the dominant players on the world stage: states need to accept a changing political environment in which decisions are not always made in the ways the international community has been accustomed to.

Dissent from this general characterization might come from several quarters, particularly those who are concerned with global citizenship and global governance. Not all global citizens would necessarily see *political* engagement as the right way to express one's global responsibilities. Working through non-political charities or through other forms of service, for instance in one's church, might be preferred and advocated. Someone interested in global governance might think that the ethical goals of global ethics mentioned above are best served by a robust form of inter-state governance in which the other three discourses have neither a significant part to play now nor should be encouraged. Nevertheless these attitudes are the exception rather than the rule.

(iii) The ethical stance is not merely one of having views about what states ought to do, but also one in which the individual has a role to play in advancing global goals. In other words, the acceptance of the global ethic underlying these discourses involves an acceptance of personal responsibility to play one's part in creating a better world. How much responsibility one has and in which ways it is to be exercised are matters of great debate (within each discourse and not just between them).[3] Also at issue is whether, from the point of view of someone advocating these discourses, everyone – whether or not they accept these discourses – has global responsibilities, or only those who accept the discourses. But at least it is generally the case that those who do use one or more of the discourses do accept some personal responsibility to play their part.

Again there will be exceptions; it is not inconceivable that someone who accepts that global civil society actually exists and also thinks it is good thing that it exists, nevertheless does not feel any obligation to do anything himself. I accept also that someone could engage in these discourses with a view to attacking them – using a discourse does not automatically imply co-option to its agenda – but apart from the explicit critics or sceptics, who would never have had reason to consider it if others had not developed a discourse with an agenda in mind, there is a general normative thrust which includes the engagement of individuals.

(iv) The developments actually occurring in the world (already indicated in the earlier section on empirical commonalities) are generally perceived to be a good thing or desirable, in that they make it more possible for various global concerns to be effectively realized. By the same token, further developments of institutions, networks and other modes of cooperation that strengthen transnational engagement by individuals and groups (other than companies or governments) are seen as a good thing and something to be worked for. That is, there is generally a significant aspirational element in these discourses in that advocacy of them is not merely about saying that the world is already different from what the old inter-state model presented, or about asserting the need to accept global obligations, but about developing and strengthening appropriate embodiments of global responsibility. Of course there is a lot of disagreement about what those embodiments should be, as we note shortly, but here the key point is that the picture is generally one of an emerging reality, along with a commitment to work for its further emergence.

This fourth feature goes beyond the two ethical features mentioned already and in effect connects the ethical component with the empirical–descriptive component by normatively assessing certain features of the globalization process. Certainly, the acceptance of a global ethic, and along with it a critique of states and an acceptance of global responsibility, does not entail either a belief in the existence of any transnational social reality, or of its emergence, or even the desirability of its existence or emergence. Thus, one could conceive of oneself as an isolated moral agent and write letters to MPs about what governments ought to do from a global perspective, or give money for poverty relief or recycle to help save the environment and not have much interest in or awareness of changing global realities (or even be sceptical about the claims of globalization). Nevertheless, if one both accepts the global ethical perspective and the facts about transnational reality (current and emerging), then it is very likely that one will not fail to connect the two and will have views about supporting and strengthening what is there.

Congruence and its critics

If I am right that there is congruence in these areas between the four discourses, then at least some case is made for saying that though different people prefer different discourses, they complement each other, certainly in a broad normative agenda. If I am right, there is plenty of ground for critical engagement with these common assumptions of the whole approach, rather than with particular features of any one of them. It is clear that there are critics and sceptics who will question both the empirical claims as being misleading or exaggerated, the ethical claims as being mistaken, unrealistic or not grounded in social reality, and the aspirational claims that we ought to be trying to develop such transnational structures as being misguided. It may turn out that when critics criticize any one of the discourses, they are criticizing all the discourses because the object of criticism is a shared feature. Thus, if global citizenship is criticized because it is incompatible with a communitarian conception of community, then the same criticism will apply *pari passu* to global civil society, global democracy and global governance (if the latter proposes a level of global community needed for certain forms of governance).

I shall not pursue these general criticisms much further because my task now is to bring out some differences between the four discourses. Their broad agendas may be similar, but there are also areas in which advocates of each may be saying something different about the facts (current and prospective), about the norms involved and about what to aim for in the future.

Differences between the approaches

I will start by considering the relationship between global citizenship and global civil society.[4] One might think that it was straightforward: if global civil society exists, then it exists in virtue of agents who through their actions and participation in social relations (organizations, movements, and networks) are global citizens. Conversely, we are global citizens because we are members of a global society which is civil in respect of its members' participation in public affairs at the global level. But this immediately runs into objections. On the one hand, global citizenship seems to imply rather more than global civil society, and, on the other hand, rather less.

Global citizenship requires more than global civil society

If citizenship in 'global citizenship' is meant to entail something analogous to what citizenship entails at the level of ordinary citizenship, then the conditions necessary for global citizenship to exist are going to be rather more complex than what is necessary for global civil society to exist.[5] If global civil society is at all analogous to civil society, then what needs to be in place is rather less than what is needed for citizenship to be in place. As Frost suggests (in this volume), the status of 'civilian' in global civil society is distinct from that of 'citizen' in a political community. What people do, the relationships which they form, the associations which they join, may all constitute civil society without these activities being the activities of citizens qua citizens. Even though an important aspect of civil society relates to the pursuit of political goals and thus to what engaged 'citizens' do, such activities are not formally constitutive of what citizens do (since resident aliens could do all of these things and be part of civil society). It is in virtue of this wider character of civil society that makes it natural to see similar patterns at the global level and hence global civil society. Scepticism about global citizenship on the grounds that we simply are not (as yet) citizens of a world state or of an analogous world democratic order would be no basis – even if such scepticism were right – for scepticism about global civil society. The truth conditions for their existence are simply different.

However, there are other ways of marking this difference. There are several other ways in which global citizenship may be understood that are more fruitful. First, there are two other aspects of global citizenship – the ethical and the aspirational – which in some ways between them make up a reasonably rich conception. Second, if we do insist that global citizenship also needs grounding in certain currently existing institutions, this institutional aspect can and should be interpreted in such a way that it is intimately linked with global civil society as it currently exists.

Global citizenship requires less than global civil society

A claim that we are global citizens may take one of two forms: an ethical claim about responsibilities and no more, and an aspirational claim that we ought to work to create certain institutions in the future (for example, global democracy or a world state, see Dower 2003). In either of these forms, the claim that we are global citizens need not have any formal implications for the existence of global civil society or, if it does exist, for the conceptual necessity to use its institutions and practices.

(i) The ethical sense

In the former sense – the ethical sense – a person might have been a global citizen long before what is now thought of as global civil society emerged. The Stoics' conception of *cosmopolis* was really an ethical-cum-metaphysical conception that stood in direct contrast to any merely contingent or human-created association, whether that was city-state, nation-state or empire (Brown 1992). For thinkers in the Enlightenment, such as Kant, cosmopolitanism was primarily about membership of the universal moral community, or what Kant called the 'kingdom of ends'.[6] Likewise, in the modern world global citizens can choose whether to act through the institutions and networks that make up global civil society to further their global concerns or they can choose not to. They might engage in prayer for world peace, do their bit for the environment by recycling or not using their cars (reasoning on universalizability principles rather than on the basis of pre-existing solidarities of practice) or send aid to families on the other side of the world whom they have got to know about through personal happenstance, and in none of these cases are they acting through global civil society. The chances are that almost all global citizens nowadays do pursue their concerns though global civil society, but if they do so this is a contingent matter to do with effectiveness of action rather than something essential to the nature of global citizenship. In other words, global civil society is merely a means to the expression of global citizenship, not its essential embodiment.

(ii) The aspirational sense

In the latter aspirational sense, global citizenship is a more complex concept and makes something of the 'citizenship' component. It is essentially a two-stage conception involving (a) an idea of what the world would have to be like for us all – people generally – actually to be global citizens analogous to our being citizens of states as at present, and (b) a commitment by those who want us to become global citizens in the first sense and who thus work towards achieving this. Such agents because of their moral commitment to create such a world can now be described in an aspirational sense, by a kind of extension, as 'global citizens'. (In this sense only some of us are now global citizens.) Of course there will be a number of views about what being a global citizen in sense (a) would involve. One possibility is membership of a world state under world government, and this itself could be conceived as being more hierarchical and authoritarian or more federalist and democratic (Heater 1996). Another possibility (more popular these days) is some form of cosmopolitan democracy based on formal institutions – for example, the UN made more democratic – and a global legal framework of 'cosmopolitan law' which is less formally 'international' and more 'cosmopolitan' in the relationship which individuals have with such law (that is, an alternative to the predominant conception at present of a two-tier system of law, with domestic law within states and international law between states) (Held 1995; Archibugi 1995). To some extent the development of human rights law reflects this and for some this shows that we are perhaps already partly global citizens in a formal sense (Heater 2000).

The main point I want to make arising from this reflection is this: if global citizenship is conceived of in this robust institutional sense, then again, as with the ethical sense, the connection with global civil society is a contingent one (for example, Van den Anker 2002). If global civil society currently exists, it is certainly not in the form of some formal democratic order and a fortiori not in the form of a world political community appropriate to a world state. To be sure, many of the organizations, movements and networks that constitute global civil society aspire to be democratic, transparent and so on, but these internal features do not make global civil society democratic overall. Indeed many of its critics are precisely worried about the disproportionate power and influence that active bodies within global civil society such as NGOs have. For instance, the Northern bias in the membership and leadership of such bodies, for all their good intentions, can reinforce rather than challenge the Northern bias of formal international bodies (Scholte 2000c; Axtmann 2002).

Anyone who wanted us to move towards a new world order in which we were in some formal sense global citizens would of course become involved in global civil society as it is now. It is no doubt generally believed that the route by which such an order is to be achieved is the strengthening of global civil society, with more people becoming actively involved in more organizations and networks with global remits. But this can be conceived of as an empirical connection: global citizens are involved in global civil society because this is the effective way of advancing this agenda. Being a global citizen is not defined in terms of participation in global civil society. Global citizens in the aspirational sense now merely use and develop global civil society because it is a stepping stone to something rather different from global civil society – a world democratic order, for instance, in which we can all be said to be citizens.

The above analysis presupposes a fairly sharp contrast between global civil society and being a citizen of a global political community of some kind. Is this justified? There are other possible ways of conceptualizing the relationship. Someone who is active in global civil society may or may not have a vision of a future world in which a new kind of global political community has emerged. If not, he may be happy with or prefer the continuation of the international system as we know it, albeit improved in the way it works by the contributions of globally concerned individuals. Strengthening global civil society does not mean transforming it into something else. Global civil society complements the global political order by making it more effective, democratic and so on. On this interpretation, global civil society – or rather that section of it concerned with political issues – is itself part of global political community.

In a way there is an analogy with domestic civil society. A more active civil society is no doubt a very good thing, but it is to be seen as a complement to the political order, not an alternative to it, and as improving its working. It may be replied that within many countries there already is a democratic order so civil society only complements the political order because we are *already* citizens of that political community, and that is precisely what we are not at the global level. This is true, but it does not undermine the point that many of those who work within global civil society may see its role as complementing and improving the international political order (which they may hold to be the best bet at the global level).

Even so it might be thought that there is some kind of tension between the two in the sense that if a future global democracy became established then, to the extent that it was, there would be less need for global civil society, which in some sense stands proxy for other forms of governance. So even for someone who saw global civil society leading to the latter, the latter would in a sense replace the former or reduce its importance. On this view it is because the world has such a 'democratic deficit' that global civil society develops. Because of the forces of globalization, the crucial determinants of the life-prospects of people increasingly lie outside democratic political control within any particular country, so global civil society can be seen as a response to this 'deficit' in democratic power.[7] This response from global civil society is not *formally* democratic; rather it provides a limited alternative route to express their global concerns for those who would be active global democrats if only they could be.

Again this way of putting it overdraws the contrast. First, global civil society is not to be seen as an alien substitute for the democratic deficit but a way of making up the deficit itself. Second, a future more formally democratic cosmopolitan order, if this emerged, would need to be sustained and strengthened by an active global civil society. Formal democracy functions better with an active civil society; it does not dispense with the need for it.

A third way of conceiving global citizenship and global democracy

There is then a rather different route that can be taken (which the discussion in the last few paragraphs has led us up to) and that is to see what goes on in global civil society as already an expression of democracy and as already the right kind of framework within which global citizenship can be expressed – not merely as a convenient means toward something rather different, but as constituting as valid an expression of 'participation in global affairs' as more formal possibilities. We need, that is, rather more open-ended conceptions of both democracy (for example: Scholte 2000c; Shapiro and Hacker-Corden 1999) and citizenship (for example, Isin and Wood 1999; Young 2000).

Before explaining this, there is one other point I need to note about global civil society and its essence. It may be thought I am unduly politicizing and globalizing it in the sense that I assume that the main function of global civil society is to promote global values and express global responsibilities. This might be challenged on the grounds that global civil society does not need to have this interpretation any more than civil society itself does. If we look at the range of cultural activities which may be included under civil society, we may recognize that participation with a view to the public good of the whole unit is only a small and perhaps contingent feature of it, and that even amongst those who do pursue public social concerns, there are those who reject the 'political' as alien to them – some social movements and organizations may be quite explicit about this.[8] Furthermore many organizations are simply concerned with the private interests of their members, whilst some may have objectives which are actually anti-social, such as crime rings or sex rings. However, whilst it may be accepted, both at the global level and at local levels, that many of the forms of social and cultural cooperation that might be part of civil society are neither political nor directed to the overall good of the whole community (or the good of particular groups justified by appeal to common principles of justice or human rights), it would be strange not to see an essential part of the activities of civil society as being so directed. Indeed, part of the function of the word 'civil' is to point to an aspect of being a citizen, and arguably point to those aspects of being a citizen which go beyond formal membership of a political community and the bearing of formal rights and duties which that entails – namely, active participation in the public good of the whole community.[9]

This leads to the issue I raised earlier about how citizenship and global democracy are to be defined. If citizenship and democracy are defined rather formally in terms of membership of a nation-state and procedures for making decisions based on all being equally counted (either directly or via the election of representatives), then much of what happens in global civil society is neither the activities of people acting as citizens nor, from a global point of view, democratic.

But if the 'participation' aspect of citizenship is disconnected from the formal 'membership of a state' condition, we are free to recognize a wide range of cooperative activities as the activities of citizens. What is being retained is the element of deliberative engagement with others in the pursuit of the overall good of some community or other. That community might or might not be the state. Many of those who talk of environmental or ecological citizenship have in mind ecological communities which are at once both narrower and broader than ordinary political communities (van Steenbergen 1994). Much of recent discussions about identity politics – whether by feminists or by those concerned with the position of racial, religious or ethnic minorities – involves redefinition of what citizenship is about in terms of deliberative processes though which the rights of groups are advanced, rather than procedures through which the formal equality of individuals is guaranteed (Isin and Wood 1999).

In like fashion, a view of democracy can be developed which stresses not so much formal voting procedures as the public space in which individuals can deliberate – that is, make their contributions about what is to be done in the spirit of rational persuasion. Here I follow Scholte's broad definition of democracy as 'prevailing when the members of a polity determine – collectively, equally and without arbitrarily imposed constraints – the policies that shape their destinies' (Scholte 2000c: 262). A properly functioning democracy is one in which that space is guaranteed by law and political will. On the other hand, those who exercise their democratic powers (generally understood as a pre-legal basic right) may do so in the absence of such a guaranteed public space, for example, in oppressive or non-democratic states. On this model of democracy, the fact that organizations, including NGOs, engage in lobbying, or the fact that individuals who do engage in political activities such as writing letters to MPs, exercise influence quite out of proportion to their numbers is not to be decried as undemocratic, but to be asserted as democracy's very essence. (Where lobbying becomes dubious is where bribery and extraneous factors become levers of persuasion.)

An illustration of this issue was the protest, already referred to, in Genoa in July 2002. Were the protesters being undemocratic (because not democratically elected and because they belonged to various pressure groups) or could one see them as democratic precisely because they were trying (apart from those committed to violence) to make their position felt through reasoned argument? They were certainly exercising their democratic right to participate in public affairs, if we allow that such a right exists in some pre-legal sense as one of the bases for having a democratic political order within a state in which this right is legally guaranteed. Only if one thought that the right to participate in public deliberation was something that was *created* within some political communities (but not others), would one have reason to deny that the protesters were exercising a democratic right of participation – albeit one that was not recognized by the leaders of the G8 countries. Likewise, one would have no difficulty is seeing the protesters as acting as global citizens given that their concerns about Third World Debt, and so on, show a driving concern for the global common good.

If something like this view of citizenship and democracy is right, then what happens in global civil society can be represented as being the exercise of global citizenship and the expression of global democracy, even before any formalized citizenship or democracy at the global level has emerged, and we can see much more therefore of a continuum from what we already have in the world today to what might emerge in the future. I have in effect defended a form of global democracy which falls short of a fully institutional form such as Held and Archibugi's 'cosmopolitan democracy'.[10]

I have in effect coupled global citizenship and global democracy in the last account. Are they that close? The short answer is: yes and no. If a rights story is central to global citizenship, then they are not, or at least may not be; if the participation story is central, then they are. But the longer answer is more complex and nuanced. What is at issue here is partly whether the central normative feature of citizenship is the existence of rights guaranteed by law or whether the central feature is the duty of active participation in the public life of the community. This is sometimes seen as the conflict between the liberal and republican conceptions of citizenship (Miller 1999; Hutchings 1999). Whilst this labelling of the contrast may be misleadingly simple, there does remain a substantive issue concerning what is important about citizenship.

Marshall was influential in seeing citizenship in terms of rights – political, civil and social – and with his argument that in the twentieth century social rights – rights that are guaranteed by positive provision of benefits by the state – became important (Marshall 1973). On this basis, the important core of global citizenship is the assertion of a certain moral and legal status of all human beings through human rights law.

On the other hand, there is a tradition that goes back to Aristotle, and is powerfully reinforced in the writings of Rousseau, which sees political participation as the hallmark of citizenship. On this basis, the important thing about global citizenship is that there exists the opportunities for participation in global affairs and individuals do get involved as active citizens. Here the link with global democracy is apparent, either through the claim that informally democratic processes already exist or through the claim that we ought to develop institutions in which rights to global democracy can be formally exercised.

Even if we stress the importance of rights for global citizenship, it is worth noting that this does not really favour a 'passive' role for citizens (only needing compliance to law) without the need for global civil society and global democracy. First, political rights are rights which if they are to be properly realized require something like a democratic political order, or, as things stand in the international arena, at least an order which does not suppress or ignore the inputs of those who engage in activism at the global level. Second, *any* rights, if they are to be secured, require a public culture in which active defence of those rights (on one's own behalf or on behalf of others) is not only permitted but given proper channels for expression, the most natural forms of which will be democratic arrangements of various kinds.

In terms of the challenge Onuf raises (in this volume) as to whether global civil society (and a fortiori global citizenship) really gives an account of participation, representation and recognition, I am claiming that the elements of participation (involvement in networks, arguably democratic in an informal sense) and recognition (through the status conferred by human rights law) are already reasonably well established, though that of representation (at least in any formally democratic sense) is something that is more of a future aspiration than a current reality.

Global governance

It is generally recognized that governance is not the same as government. Government is a sub-class of governance, albeit its most common manifestation.

There are several ways in which we can think of global governance. Many writers stress the central role of rule/regulation setting in a global context, whereas others think of it more generally as the process whereby global or international relations are managed (Halliday 2000: 431) or as 'the sum of the many ways individuals and institutions, public and private, manage their common affairs' at the global level (Commission on Global Governance 1995: 2). How we conceptualize it makes a difference to how far we think global governance must or may involve global civil society, global citizenship or global democracy.

If we take the first approach, a key question is: who or what exercises 'control' (Rosenau 2000: 181) or 'command' (Council of Rome, quoted in King and Schneider 1991: 181–2) over the production or maintenance of these rules and regulations? A more traditional way of thinking about this would be to see the controllers as the formal rule setters (governments or international bodies acting as legislators), but others may say that the rule setters ought to include NGOs, economic agents, electorates, public opinion, and so on, in so far as they all substantially influence the decisions which the formal rule-setters make. Furthermore, there is a second issue: are the rules here primarily formal regulations, laws or international conventions – the province of legislators – or do they include the settled norms of behaviour which are formed and reinforced by many social influences apart from law itself?

It will be clear that if the rule-setting is thought of formally as the production of legislation (for example, international law) by formally constituted bodies, then global governance need have nothing to do with global civil society, global democracy or global citizenship. It need have nothing to do with them in two senses. First, global governance could occur (and be conduced quite legitimately) in the absence of these social phenomena or independent of their presence in a very nascent or ambiguous form: sceptics of these phenomena might not be sceptical about global governance itself. Second, even if these global phenomena are accepted as real and, indeed, as having a significant influence on the decisions taken by the rule-setters, their influence can be regarded as causal, contingent or external, rather than constitutive of governance itself. The only exceptions to this would be if some formal form of global democracy were to come into existence as something like cosmopolitan democracy (Archibugi and Held 1995), or if global citizenship were to be achieved in a fully political sense of active and formal participation in a global political order. For, in these cases, citizens would be formally participating (via authorizing their representatives to make laws) in law-making. Even here though someone might resist this conclusion, arguing that governance relates to those who do the governing and not the citizens who democratically give them the authority to govern.

On the other hand, if a broader view of governance is adopted to include in governance those who exercise a significant influence on decisions about rules, regulations and laws, or more simply contribute to how things are ordered at the public level, then there is no reason at all why those who are active in global civil society, are active global citizens or engage in global democracy (informally now or formally perhaps later), should not be seen as part of global governance.

A further qualification is needed. Whether the broader view or the narrower view is taken, there is generally assumed to be a distinctive normative aspect to governance including global governance. Governance for some involves the idea of the *art* of governing in a morally justifiable and efficient way (Halliday 2000: 431). The various influences (of NGOs, etc.), whether they are direct and constitutive or indirect and causal, are thought of as contributing to an overall goal: the management of global common affairs (Halliday 2000: 431). That is, this influence is seen as broadly appropriate. Not all influences would be regarded as part of governance on these accounts. Those of the Mafia or of international crime syndicates hardly count as part of global governance – though they may have profound influences and represent the unattractive underbelly of global civil society.

The above discussion illustrates one aspect of the largely contested character of global governance (for example, Duffield 2001; Falk 1995a). We can usefully distinguish between a basic concept of global governance and various conceptions of global governance. If the basic concept of global governance is about systems and processes of managing human relations at the global level, we can see that there are many different views about what the appropriate forms of this should be. This reflects a tension within the idea of global governance between the idea of something that already exists and something which does not already exist, except perhaps in a weak form. In the first sense, the international order in which states dominate world affairs is a form of global governance. In the second sense, what we have now simply isn't really a proper form of global governance. Global governance is a new approach with a new agenda.

In the first sense, we can say that there has been some form of global governance in the world over many hundreds of years – ever since the levels of interaction across the world led to some kind of rule-governed framework. For instance, the internationalist or Westphalian system dominated for several centuries, supplemented with colonial empires. In the twentieth century, new patterns of influence and interaction have emerged challenging the Westphalian model. For some this is a modified Westphalian model (which might be called neo-Westphalian), for others a post-Westphalian model (Linklater 1999). Which label one uses depends on the extent to which the influences of non-state actors – NGOs, economic actors, transnational movements – are seen, both descriptively and normatively, as significant, and whether this influence, if it is significant, is seen as constitutive of governance or merely as influencing, though externally, those who exercise governance.

To some extent the differences between conceptions are disputes about which conception is appropriate for a given era, as in the last case. But we also need to recognize that different forms of global governance may be appropriate to different eras. Even if the international system worked in the past, it simply is not adequate for the demands of the present. If we accept that there are degrees of global governance – both as what exists as a matter of fact and as what is desirable – then, with the identification of common global problems and with the greater degree of interdependence and transnational identities created by processes of globalization, we can say that more extensive forms of global governance are needed. Many writers who accept this necessity see the appropriate forms of global governance as indeed including non-state actors in many ways (particularly those who favour a more radical post-Westphalian view). However, as I remarked before, the acceptance of increased global governance need not involve such inclusion, especially if one refuses to link global civil society with global governance, regardless of the significance one attaches to the idea of global governance itself.

It is worth noting that one form of global governance which might emerge in the future is precisely world government. World federalists advocate this as the only form of global governance adequate to deal with our global problems (see, for example, Cohen 1954; Nielsen 1988). Whilst generally such advocates also see within world government a vital role for global civil society, a framework through which, apart from the formal status of being politically a citizen of the world, active global citizenship would be enhanced and global democracy formally instituted (World Federal Association 2002), it has to be noted that world government would guarantee none of these things. In an undemocratic world state, global civil society might at best be ignored or tolerated, at worst suppressed; global citizens might at best have most of their rights other than political rights of political participation protected, at worst have only formal membership of a tyrannous world state, and global democracy not given any expression at all.

So we can conclude from the above discussion that whilst global governance has potentially some very rich connections with the other three concepts, there is nothing in the general idea that establishes those connections. That all depends on how the particular favoured conception of each is elaborated.

Global citizenship

My underlying purpose has been to show that we can talk coherently about global citizenship having application in the modern world mainly by showing how it articulates with the other three discourses, and by showing that, although all these discourses can be so interpreted to bring out divergences, they can also be interpreted (more helpfully) so as to be seen as different routes into the same basis for descriptive and normative analyses. Is there then anything to be said for advocating global citizenship discourse in particular in preference to the other discourses? Although the correct answer is that all of them, suitably interpreted, have their role in interpreting, conceptualizing and energizing positive global change, there are three kinds of consideration worth mentioning which at least show that global citizenship discourse is an important element in such change (see also Dower 2000, 2003).

First, somewhat pragmatically, the phrase 'world citizen' or 'global citizen' is at least a 'term of art' compared with the other three phrases. Although there are many people who do not resonate to the idea of being a 'world citizen', the phrase is at least fairly straightforward.[11] Very few people, I suspect, outside circles of academics and the highly educated, would know what was being referred to in the other three phrases.

Second, the term 'global citizen' is directly addressed to individuals, whereas 'global civil society' refers to some kind of social reality, and the terms 'global democracy' and 'global governance' describe, at different levels of generality, a form of political order. The latter three are therefore more impersonal. Their normativity is more directly to do with kinds of social and political arrangements which are desirable and to be worked for, and only indirectly to do with what individuals are to do. Global citizenship addresses the individual directly: its normativity is about what individuals ought to do. If one thinks, as I do, that changes in the end stem from the normative commitment of individuals, this is precisely where the emphasis should lie. It also emphasizes the idea that individuals are *members* of a global community of some kind, in a 'global village', or, as the Commission on Global Governance called it, a global neighbourhood.

To be sure, talk of global civil society, global democracy and (in some contexts) global governance, is doubly normative: it presupposes some values and norms which *ought* to be promoted or followed in the world rather more than they are; and it advocates that these things – global civil society etc. – *ought* themselves to be strengthened. However, who is meant to do what is often left unspecified. The idea of global citizenship precisely focuses on the individual and what he or she ought to do. It highlights the thorny question of the manner and extent of exercising global *responsibility*. This is challenging and controversial, both because the idea of cosmopolitan responsibility raises the questions 'How much should we do?' and 'How do we balance such demands against the obligations normally assumed within established societies and political communities?' (see Nussbaum *et al.* in Cohen 1996a; Hutchings and Dannreuther 1999). But these questions have to be faced since the answers to them make a difference to what happens in the world – both because of what individuals do themselves and, perhaps more significantly, because of what they want and actively campaign for in respect to the policies of their governments.

Third, partly because its normativity is most obviously addressed to individuals, it is perhaps the most contested of all the concepts. Because it rests on the tripod of the ethical, the (currently) institutional and the aspirational, it allows a very large number of interpretations, depending partly on which element of the tripod is emphasized. Furthermore, the claim 'we are global citizens' can be and is defended and criticized in all of these dimensions. All the discourses raise many issues of interpretation and challenge, as we have seen, over whether they really exist and if so in what sense, and what future developments are either predicted or deemed desirable. But global citizenship, in particular, highlights the ethical dimension, and is open to much disagreement – not just over the extent of obligation, as we noted above, but also over whether we should accept a global ethic at all or rather reject it for relativist, communitarian or postmodernist reasons. Apart from outright attacks on it, there are certainly many different interpretations possible, including a wide variety of views about the appropriate 'global ethic' that should inform global citizenship.

This might seem a good reason to avoid a term that means all things to all people. On the contrary, this demonstrates its vibrancy in a changing geopolitical world in which many of the key issues about the nature and extent of the involvement of individuals in world affairs is played out through the contested claims about global citizenship. So that even if one is sceptical about what is claimed by its advocates, it is difficult to deny that the discourse of global citizenship is an immensely important one in the modern world.

My defence of global citizenship and related ideas has been in some respects a *liberal* defence. It has stressed the role of individuals, both as sources of values and bearers of human rights, and as agents with responsibility to play a part in changing the world, and it has assumed the importance of political rights, the role of democratic participation and the possibility of creating a better world by negotiation and dialogue. On the other hand, it is not a liberal view in any more precise sense of presupposing some more complex metaphysical foundation in, say, Kant or Locke. Indeed if any conception of global citizenship is to play an important role in global social change, it has to be such that it can appeal to people of many different religious and cultural backgrounds. As we grapple with global problems at the beginning of the twenty-first century, it is precisely this inclusiveness of diverse worldviews, theories or 'source stories' which has to be the hallmark of the kind of global ethic that needs to be embedded in all the discourses we have discussed.

Notes

1 This paper is part of ongoing work on the idea of global citizenship (see Dower 2000, 2003; and Dower and Williams 2002).
2 I am assuming that globalization covers a wide range of transnational phenomena, certainly not merely economic globalization. See, for example, Held and McGrew (2000) for extensive discussions of the phenomena, and Scholte (2000c) for a defence of it as a multi-faceted process of *deterritorialization*.
3 Much of this debate has centred on Peter Singer's defence of an ethic of radical sacrifice (see Aiken and LaFollette 1996, and especially Shue 1996).
4 For the former, see for example, Hutchings and Dannreuther (1999) and Heater (2002); for the latter, for example, Walzer (1995), Crocker (1998), Tomlinson (1999) and Spybey (1996). For succinct statement re global civil society, see Callahan (1999).
5 David Miller is a critic of global citizenship for this reason (Miller 1999).
6 Nussbaum (1996) relates global citizenship to the ideas of the Stoics and generally stresses the ethical aspect of cosmopolitanism. See also Heater (1998). For general accounts of global citizenship, see Cohen (1996a), Carter (2001), Heater (2002) and Linklater (2002).
7 See Linklater (1999) for the idea of the democratic deficit, though he does not endorse the argument I am considering..
8 I am grateful to Michael Kenny for drawing my attention to this.
9 For examples of 'global citizen action' in NGOs, see Edwards and Gaventa (2001).
10 See McGrew (2000) for an account of three kinds of global democracy.
11 I was reminded of this by Clare Short, UK Minister for International Development, in an exchange she had with me on this issue in February 1998.

8 Global civil society, civilians and citizens

Mervyn Frost

Things happen, the existing states of affairs change, problems arise and we have to decide what to do. This is true for all of us both at the micro level and the global level. Often what happens puts certain technical questions to us, as when a hole in the ozone layer emerged. In such cases we have to find out what caused the problem and what can be done to alleviate it. But often what happens produces problems which have not only a technical dimension but an ethical one too. For example, widespread famine poses technical questions about how to get food aid to the victims in the short term (and how to prevent it recurring in the long term). Our thinking might turn to fertilizers, new crop types and new credit lines to farmers. But it also produces a set of ethical problems about who ought to be doing what, when and how. Here questions are about whose responsibility it is to undertake the relief programmes, about what a just response would be, and so on. Beyond the technical and ethical problems what happens sometimes produces problems for us which are of a political nature, as when, in the face of famine caused by certain kinds of social arrangements we confront the question: How might we go about changing the social arrangements which produced famine in the first place?

One of the most important things which has happened in recent times is the emergence of that set of phenomena usually referred to by the catchall term 'globalization'. The term refers to a wide range of things which include the increased volume and speed of travel, communication, financial transactions, human migration, and many actions and transactions. A strong case can be made that the events of 11 September 2001 were only possible in a 'globalized' world. There is little agreement about precisely what is encompassed by globalization, but mention is often made of an emerging standardization and 'sameness' about the way things are done. Similarly it is said that a globalized world is one characterized by complex interdependence. What informs the research project guiding this book is the suggestion that globalization has brought forth a new form of society, a global civil society (hereafter referred to as GCS). A key contention of those who claim that a GCS has emerged is that this is a society within which the participants recognize one another as individuals rather than as merely members of states. In particular it is held that in GCS people recognize one another as the holders of individual human rights.

In this chapter I seek to answer the questions: Are we participants in a global civil society? If we are, what are the ethical underpinnings of this social practice? And, how does the ethicality (*sittlichkeit*) embedded in GCS contradict or reinforce the ethicality we enjoy as citizens within the society of democratic and democratizing states? And, how does it help or hinder the prospect of establishing some kind of global social arrangement within which we might enjoy global citizenship? In these questions I speak of 'we'. I take it that if GCS is truly global then this pronoun must refer to just about all of us. In order to answer these questions I shall follow the advice of Ian Clark who early on in his book *The Post Cold War Order* says that it is 'instructive to pursue the logic of our own language' (Clark 2001: 3). In what follows I shall do just this.

We all know that there are forms of ethical life embedded in the social practices in which we participate, practices like the family, academic seminars, religious practices, democratic states, the society of sovereign states and many more. Many of us are concurrently participants in several of the social forms which I have mentioned. As participants, we know, in broad outline, what the ethical underpinnings of these social forms are. For example, we could each quickly list two or three things which would constitute ethical misconduct in the context of a university seminar (plagiarism and sexual harassment spring to mind). Most of us believe ourselves to be participants in a society of states, undergirded by a certain kind of ethicality. This society is actualized in international law which includes laws specifying that it is wrong to intervene in the domestic affairs of foreign states. This law, we hold, protects the value of self-determination and is designed as a counter to the ethical wrong we refer to as 'imperialism'. That we are participants in the practices I have mentioned is self-evident to us. But are we participants in some further social practice, separate from the ones I have mentioned, a practice our participation in which is not self-evident to us? Are we participants in a practice called 'global civil society'? If we are participants in a global civil society, what form of ethical life is embedded in it and how does this square with that embedded in the society of states? Of course, we cannot answer this latter question until we have tackled the former which is about the existence of, and our participation in, a social practice called global civil society.

On the face of the matter, asking whether we are participants in GCS is a very odd question to ask, for surely if there is a GCS and we are participants in it, we would know this fact about ourselves. For in general we are aware of the practices we participate in. Thus we do not have to ask ourselves whether we are students, Christians, soccer players or citizens. It is part of the meaning of these words that they signify that we, the participants, know ourselves to be participants in the social wholes specified by these terms. The following assertions border on the nonsensical: university students who do not know of their participation in a university, Christian believers who are unaware of their participation in the Christian religion, soccer players who do not know what game they are playing, and citizens who do not know that they are members of a state. In all these cases it seems odd to imagine ourselves having to launch an inquiry as to whether the practice in question exists and whether we are indeed participants in that practice.

There are, though, some social practices which are different. Let us call them 'open practices'. There are some practices participation in which can take place without the participant(s) (in this case us) being aware of the existence of the practice or of their participation in it. Languages provide good examples of this kind of practice. For example, children can learn to speak English without being aware that what they are speaking is English and without being aware that there is a practice of speaking English which is distinct from other language practices (the practice of speaking Zulu, French, and so on). We become participants in such practices by learning how to do certain things (in this case speak English), but becoming adept at this does not require knowledge of oneself as an English speaker. The domestic legal systems within which we live provide further examples of the kind of practice I have in mind. To repeat, we learn how to participate in such practices by learning how to do certain things – in a legal system we learn how to participate by learning how to act in a law-abiding way. But doing this does not require of us that we know that we are participating in a broad social practice called a 'legal system' which is distinct from other legal systems and distinct from many other social practices. Most children are law-abiding participants in the legal system in which they find themselves, but few have a concept of the whole in which they are participating. The contrast here is with those other social practices, let us call them 'constitutional practices' which require of us, from the moment we start learning how to participate in them, that we have some notion of the constitution of the practice as a whole and some notion of what our role in it is. Games provide the easiest examples here. Consider a novice who wishes to learn how to play cricket (netball, snooker, . . .). In order to do this the novice has to learn about the game as a whole and about his or her role in it. Playing the game entails knowing what the game is. A university is a constitutional practice. Thus in order to become a student in a university one has to have some ideas about what a university is. Similarly, a state is a constitutional practice, thus to participate as a citizen in the affairs of a state – in elections, for example – one has to have some idea about what a state is.

For the purposes of the present argument, what is crucial about an 'open practice' is that those who are participating in it may not know anything in particular about the practice as a whole, may not know that what they are participating in is a social practice which is discrete from other social practices, and may not know anything about how this practice relates to other social practices. *A fortiori* they may not know anything about the ethical underpinnings of the open practices in which they are participants. It follows then that with regard to such open practices the question 'Am I a participant in a local, regional or global practice with features x, y and z?' is far from nonsensical. The preceding argument, if it is correct, opens up the possibility that many people (even most people) in the world today may be participants in many open practices without being overtly aware that they are doing so. One of these open practices may be GCS.

Following this line of thought, in this chapter I wish to argue, first, that if there is a global civil society in the contemporary world it is not a constitutional practice, but an open practice. It seems to me self-evident that there does not exist a constitutional practice called GCS such that all (or most) people everywhere know of its existence and know themselves to be participants in it. Although most people are not aware of the existence of a GCS, they do know themselves to be participants in a global constitutional practice which is the society of sovereign states. Most people are participants in this and know themselves to be such. My second argument, which is the central focus of this article, is that if there is a GCS it is best understood as an open practice – as that species of practice which may exist even though the participants in it are not at all, or not fully, aware of the parameters of the practice within which they are participating.

Whenever we confront questions about whether or not we (or others) are participants in an open social practice the *only* way to set about answering them is to examine what we (or others) say and do. An open practice consists of all those who know how to do x, (where x is the action or set of actions central to the practice in question), who understand what others are doing when they do x, and who are able to recognize in others that they have done x correctly and have not made a mistake. Those who do not know how to x, who do not understand that an x-ing has been done and who cannot recognize a mistake in the doing of x are not members of the practice in question. They are outside its borders. To put this matter another way, we can determine whether or not an open practice of x-ing exists and whether or not we are participants in it by finding out whether, with regard to x-ing, there is a company of critics to whom we feel obligated to give answers for our x-ing.

In order to make this clear, consider the easy case of the open practice of speaking English. Those who are insiders to this practice are all those who can say things in English, who can understand when something is said in English, who can criticize other people's use of the language and who understand the force of certain kinds of criticisms which might be directed at them. When I am criticized for pronunciation, grammar or vocabulary, and when I recognize the content of the criticisms directed against my use of the language, this indicates to me that I am participating in a practice and it identifies to me who my co-participants in this practice are.[1]

To summarize, some of the things we do may be done in the context of an open social practice which we have not overtly considered as such. We can explore the extent and membership of this kind of practice by identifying all those who know how to do x, who can recognize a doing of x by others, and who know how to recognize a mistake in the doing of x.

Turning now to the subject at hand, GCS, if there is a global civil society, we must be members of it. If we are not members of it then it is not global. In terms of what I have said above, evidence for its existence must be there for the finding in the language we use about what we ourselves do and the language used by others who contemplate what we have done. What do we say about ourselves and others which points to the existence of GCS? Do we use a language which suggests the existence of such a global civil society?

In a book published recently entitled *Constituting Human Rights: Global Civil Society and the Society of Democratic States*, I argued that there is indeed a global civil society.[2] It is that society within which we constitute one another as the holders of first generation individual rights. It is the society which consists of all those who claim first generation rights for themselves and recognize them in others. Let us call such people 'civilians'. We know it exists by the claims which people make and recognize and also by what they do. The defining feature of a rights claim is that it is a non-trumpable claim which only the holder may decide whether to deploy or not. The rights which define GCS are the so-called negative rights such as the rights of the person not to be killed, assaulted, tortured, the right to freedom of speech, assembly, contract, of religious belief, press freedom, academic freedom and the right to own property.[3]

There are many pieces of evidence which indicate the existence of GCS. These are to be found in what people, either as individuals or speaking as members of larger social wholes, say. Thus, for example, many states officially endorse this rights-based society. They do so in several ways: first, through including in their constitutions entrenched bills of rights; second, through their signing up to the United Nations whose charter itself entrenches a commitment to human rights; third, through the many instruments of international law which now embody a commitment to human rights; and, fourth, through regional organizations which themselves have constitutionally entrenched commitments to human rights (the African Union is one). Not only do states endorse the rights-based practice, but there are many NGOs which do so, too. Here I have in mind such organizations as Amnesty and Human Rights Watch, to mention but two. There are also many churches and associated institutions which support the rights-based practice. At the individual level many millions of people participate in this practice by claiming rights for themselves. These claims become particularly urgent when the people find themselves living in circumstances where their rights are being abused. There are very few people who assert of themselves that they have no rights.[4] The practice manifests itself in other ways too. Most importantly, the existence of this practice is made manifest through people's participation in the global market, the basic operative principle of which is that it is a practice based upon the idea of individual people making use of their rights to buy and sell what property they have, be it mobile, fixed, intellectual or property in their labour. No sense can be made of this market without a rather thick set of ideas about human rights. In participating in the market, as we all do, we make use of rights language at every point. We talk of our right to property, to make contracts, to sell things, to buy things, to form companies, and so on. From the poorest to the richest people claim for themselves, at the very least, the right to sell their labour. By doing this they signify their participation in GCS.

Crucial to this description of global civil society – this practice of claiming individual rights against one another are the following features:

First, the claims which we make in civil society are not logically tied to whether or not we are physically in, or in someway connected to, any particular sovereign state. When a person says to X: 'Don't do that, I have a right not to be killed, tortured, forcibly moved, or I have a right to speak, assemble, worship my God (and so on through the list of basic rights)', it is not the case that in order to check out the validity of such claims we first have to establish whether or not the claimant is a member of some state. If we find that there is no state in existence at the place from which the claimant is making his or her claim, this is irrelevant to the validity of the claim to have the right itself. It may, of course, be pertinent to whether the person has the capacity to enforce the right in question, but that is another matter.

Second, such claims are not dependent on whether or not the claimant is under the jurisdiction of some legal system which embodies the rights they are claiming to have. Even if the person is living in a legal system which actively opposes such rights claims (South Africa under apartheid, for example), we who are participants in this GCS would recognize the legitimacy of the claim.

Third, such claims are not dependent for their validity on whether or not the claimant has access to the necessary force required to enforce the rights claims being made. In fact, it is often in those cases where the people claiming such rights are weak and defenceless that we consider them to be most worthy of support. It seems to me to be of vital importance to distinguish very clearly between the rights claims participants in GCS make for themselves and the means which they make use of to enforce their rights. People who claim such rights for themselves make use of a whole range of devices to protect their rights. These include states (and all the machinery at the disposal of states), international organizations (such as war crimes tribunals), and private sector enforcement agencies (these are especially prevalent in Africa). But the means which they have at their disposal do not affect the validity of the claims which they make.[5]

Fourth, this society of rights holders is not confined to any geographically bounded territory. From the point of view of people who participate in it, boundaries are of no import when it comes to determining whether or not they are making a valid claim for themselves or not.

Fifth, this society of rights holders does not form a polity. It does not form a state (or any other form of polity) with its associated government. Thus it has no legislature and no policies. It has no centre. It is a dispersed practice.

In GCS, through an ongoing iterative process of making rights claims for oneself and recognizing such claims coming from others, we who do this constitute one another as actors of a certain kind.[6] It seems appropriate to call such actors *civilians*. Civilians are the participants in global civil society. For the purposes of this chapter, this is a stipulative definition which, I believe, will turn out to be useful for analytical purposes. A civilian, then, as understood in this chapter, is a participant in GCS which I have described as being a practice both open and dispersed. This practice has no defined territory, no central governmental authority, and is open to anyone who wishes to learn and use the language of individual human rights.

The actor status of civilian, a rights holder in civil society, is distinct from a different rights-holding status which is that enjoyed by a *citizen* in the practice of sovereign states. A citizen is a participant in a state (or state-like) practice which has a fixed membership, a government and a territory. The status of citizenship is not open to anyone, but is strictly controlled by the government of the polity within which it is situated. Many of us are, of course, both civilians in GCS and citizens within particular states. We need to explore the relationship between being a civilian and being a citizen, and I shall be saying more about this later in this chapter.

I have encountered two major criticisms of the view of GCS which I am putting forward here. The first is that it fails to distinguish between an ideal world and the world within which rights have acquired some form of institutional embodiment. John Charvet at the London School of Economics has raised this point. He argues that the reciprocal recognition of rights and obligations requires some form of collective coercive authority (Charvet 1996). This seems to me to be a criticism without much force. In GCS it is often the case that the making of rights claims has far-reaching and very real consequences. Let me, as I so often do, make use of a South African example. The powerless majority without the franchise claimed that they were being denied their fundamental human rights. This claim was recognized elsewhere in the GCS and it led to the formation of a worldwide political movement which came to wield substantial power. This power derived from individuals, firms, states, great powers, and superpowers. When it was at its most powerful, the Anti-Apartheid Movement influenced even the USA Congress – the legislature of a superpower.

The second major criticism which I have encountered asks with what warrant have I defined this practice in terms of first generation rights only. Why have I not included in it, not only first generation rights, but also second generation positive rights, such as rights to housing, healthcare and welfare? My answer is that claims of positive rights, such as the right to education, housing, medical care, welfare, and so on, only make sense in those circumstances where an institutional structure exists which can institute policies of taxation and redistribution. I do not deny the importance of positive rights, but I locate them amongst the rights of citizens which themselves are located in some or other institutionalized political arrangement such as a state which itself is situated in the society of states. Positive rights cannot be a component of GCS for positive rights require government and GCS has no government. It is a practice that is open and dispersed.

GCS has not always existed. For most of recorded history there was no such thing. It is a recent phenomenon. Over the last fifty years it has grown in a number of different ways. More and more people are becoming participants in it. Any particular person becomes a participant by learning how to make claims of rights for him or herself and how to recognize such claims coming from others. Once one knows how to do these things and proceeds to do so, one has become a participant – one has become a civilian. Not only are more people participating in the practice, but the discourse of human rights is being used by, and incorporated into, the practices of more and more individuals, and also institutions such as town councils, provincial governments, state constitutions and international organizations. It is being built into legal systems, both domestic and international. The discourse is being taken up in school and university curricula. Many lobby groups have emerged to promote its further institutionalization.

What is the ethical and political significance of this burgeoning GCS? I believe that it is this question which is at the heart of most scholarly interest in GCS. We cannot begin to answer this question until we have some clarity about the meaning of the terms 'ethical' and 'political'.

Ethics and politics

In both our everyday language and the language of specialists, the words 'ethics' and 'politics' are not used as synonyms. They have different uses. In everyday life we use them easily and with reasonable precision. When referring to a 'Department of Politics', we know it to be referring to something different to what would be referred to by the phrase a 'Department of Ethics'. We do not think that 'ethicist' is simply another word for 'political scientist' or 'politician'. 'She's going into politics' is not the same as 'She's going into ethics'! Most importantly, 'I am faced with an ethical problem' does not strike us as the same as 'I am faced with a political problem'. What then, in common parlance, is the distinction between ethics and politics?

In a discipline which has been exposed to constructivist insights we know that we cannot expect to find any essential difference between politics and ethics which is fixed for all time. What we can do, though, is note how the way in which we normally use these words supports a certain interpretation of a core difference between them.

We often use the term 'unethical' to indicate an act which breaches a fundamental constitutive norm of some practice within which a person is constituted as an actor of this or that kind. The breach of such fundamental norms threatens an actor's very standing as an actor in the practice in question. As examples to illustrate this, consider a soldier, government or state that indiscriminately kills civilians, a president who enriches himself at taxpayers' expense, a citizen who betrays his or her country, an academic who plagiarizes, a husband who beats his wife or sells his children. In all of these a participant in a practice breaks a fundamental constitutive rule of that practice and faces the possibility of what might broadly be termed 'excommunication' from the practice in question. To face a charge of ethical misconduct is to face a grave charge indeed. We all fear such charges because where they succeed, they threaten our very constitution, our standing, as who we understand ourselves to be. It is thus not surprising that those who face allegations of ethical misconduct will often dispute it.[7]

Ethical criticism is, one might say, always aimed at challenging an actor's behaviour or standing in terms of the values taken to underpin an existing practice at the most profound level. The formal definition of ethics then is: *Ethical conduct is conduct in accordance with the values embedded in the practices within which we are constituted as actors of this or that kind.*

On this view *all* action has an ethical dimension in that it either adheres, or fails to adhere, to the values embedded in the practice in which it takes place. Thus Robin Cook's commitment to a foreign policy with an ethical dimension was simply an articulation of what is always the case. All foreign policies (and all other policies) are open to scrutiny in terms of the ethical dimension of the practice within which they are situated. A foreign policy maker cannot opt out of this dimension. Ethical analysis then involves some or all of the following: close scrutiny of the values embedded in a given social practice, scrutiny of the fit between an individual action and the values embedded in the practice in which the act is located, and, the examination of the values embedded in one practice and those to be found in other social practices. Since we are all concurrently participants in any number of different and changing practices, it is to be expected that we would have an ongoing interest in determining whether the ethics embedded in these practices cohere or not. In international relations a major interest for all of us at present is, does the ethic embedded in GCS cohere with that to be found in the practice of sovereign states?

Politics is different. To engage in politics is to engage in a purposeful activity, an instrumental activity, of a certain kind. Not all actions are political, only some are. Most usages of 'this is politics' fit the following definition: *Political acts are words and deeds aimed at maintaining or changing the basic rules of a particular social practice.* Politics often involves concerted action. In 1968 students engaged in politics when they challenged the basic rules of association of universities. In 1999 a large body of activists at Seattle challenged the rules of association of global capitalism. Politics in states is that wide field of action which is ultimately concerned with the rules of who gets what, where, when and how. Politics is always aimed, one might say, at rearranging social practices or preventing them being rearranged.

We are now in a position to notice an interesting set of relationships between ethics and politics. It follows from the analyses produced above that although political acts are aimed at bringing about a certain result, they themselves, like all social actions, are acts which take place within given practices with their own embedded ethics. *So we may ask of any political act: Is it (or was it) ethical?* For example: Is it ethical to use campaign funds for private ends, to deploy troops for the purpose of policing, to provide international aid with conditionalities of a certain kind attached, to intervene in such cases, and so on?

Furthermore, we need to note that political actions are often prompted and motivated by ethical criticisms. The international political struggle against apartheid started with a set of ethical criticisms directed against the National Party government's policies towards Black South Africans. The government of South Africa, the international community claimed, was failing to respect the rights of a majority of South Africans to participate in democratic self-government. These ethical charges resulted in South Africa being deemed a pariah in the community of states. The *ethical* allegations, then, formed the basis for a long *political* struggle to change the constitution of the South African state.

Within any given practice an actor who is free of ethical criticism is, by definition, an actor in good standing within that practice. As such, the actor can draw authority and thus strength from the social practice as a whole. The same may be said of any collective actor which itself is constituted as an actor in a wider social practice. For example a state which is obedient to the embedded ethic of the practice of states draws strength and authority from that standing. In this connection it is instructive to contrast Norway with Libya. The insight being discussed in this paragraph is very important for those engaged in politics. A political actor (whether it be an individual political actor or a collective one such as a political party or state) who has not undermined the ethic in the practice in which he/she/it is constituted as a political actor will hold authority and legitimate power. If he/she/it is subject to successful ethical criticism he/she/it will lose that authority and power. At the limit, if the criticism sticks he/she/it ceases to be a political player. It thus follows that political actors in seeking to win their campaigns will often resort to ethical criticism of their opponents, because ethical criticism, when it works, is one of the most powerful weapons in any political arsenal. It follows that being the target of such criticism is what all actors, but especially political actors, ought to fear most. The histories of Profumo and Nixon are instructive here.

We can now return to the question: What is the ethical and political significance of GCS? The spreading and deepening of this practice does not just create ethical possibilities, it is, itself, an ethical outcome. In this practice people are recreated as that kind of actor which we know as a rights holder. People who become participants in this practice gain a lot. *They have available to them a whole menu of actions which were not open to them before.* Through their participation in GCS they become people who can claim in the context of this global practice that they have the rights to freedom of the person (not to be killed, assaulted, subject to cruel and unusual punishment, etc), freedom of speech, conscience, assembly, movement, the right to own property and the right to academic freedom. Members of GCS who make these claims cast those who abuse their rights in the role of wrongdoers. The abusers are seen as such by a global audience. Members of GCS whose rights are being abused can call on their fellow participants to at least recognize the wrong that is being done to them. Often they will call for, and be given, more than this – for example, they may be given material help of one kind or another. The ethical significance of GCS is that the rights claims of individuals are put to a global audience. The political consequences of this would be hard to exaggerate.

Although a strong case can be made to show that the founding of this rights practice owed a lot to the actions taken by states, it is, nevertheless, now the case that members of GCS can use their rights to hold states to account. The practice created by states has now taken on a life of its own. Within GCS we participants do not consider that states have a right to override the rights claims individual members of GCS make. Indeed, the language of GCS makes an even stronger claim which is that the legitimacy of states themselves now derives from the extent to which they the respect the rights civilians hold in GCS. Of course, states and individuals might not always respect the rights of participants in GCS, but this does not invalidate the point being made which is that such action will be widely condemned as unethical.

Global civil society is a dispersed practice without any central government or defined territory. As such it is itself a very specific kind of public space. In it, by granting to one another first generation rights, the participants create for themselves a space for *civilian politics.* They create for themselves a protected space within which all participants have the right to discuss the basic rules of association of all the other practices within which they are constituted as actors. What is crucial to note is that they have the liberty to discuss not only the associations to which they themselves belong, but all other social forms as well.

It is important to note that the space created for politics within GCS is only safe insofar as the participants do not undermine the basic rights-conferring rules of this association itself. This public space depends on its own constitutive rules – and the ethic that they embody – not themselves becoming subject to politics. The autonomy created for rights holders in civil society depends on the rights-conferring rules of GCS themselves being taken off the political agenda. These must not become the victim of a political attack.

To my mind, a very important aspect of global civil society is that we who participate in it (and who by so doing create a society of rights holders) provide a public space from within which civilians, making use of their rights, can discuss supplemental arrangements which might relieve the shortcomings of civil society itself.

Having extolled the virtues of the ethical standing we enjoy as civilians in GCS, it is important to note that GCS is no utopia. I do not have the space to spell out its shortcomings in detail, but the basic picture is clear enough. A society of negative rights holders is both an alienating society and one which produces huge inequalities along many dimensions. It is alienating in that in it we experience one another as rivals, competitors and strangers. It is also alienating in that the rules we encounter there appear to be external impositions on us. We did not legislate them for ourselves. It produces inequalities in that, through people making use of their property rights over time, some will become hugely wealthy and some very poor. Because there is no central authority to conduct redistributions in civil society, rights holders may quite legitimately transfer their already unequal holdings across generations, thus giving an unequal start in life to their heirs and by so doing further aggravating an already unequal set of arrangements. Happily, though, although many of us are participants in GCS, as revealed by the things we say and the claims we make, this is not the only practice in which we participate. We are indeed civilians in GCS, but we are also citizens in the society of sovereign states. Our participation in this latter practice resolves some of the problems that I have just mentioned. Our citizenship rights supplement the rights we enjoy as citizens.

The citizenship supplement

In the *Philosophy of Right* Hegel made use of a mode of social analysis which showed what, from an ethical point of view, had been achieved by the various social institutions within which he found himself. His method did not involve demonstrating human problem-solving capacities at work such that we could follow a long sequence of deliberate problem-solving that showed us changing bad states of affairs into good ones. For quite often institutions change gradually and in ways that the participants do not quite intend or plan. The institutions we live in are not always the product of some spurt of rational planning. Often they are the product of incremental changes over long periods of time. Conversely, they sometimes change in dramatic, not very well-controlled convulsions during social revolutions. Instead of looking at the detailed history of who did what to create the social institutions, Hegel made use of a holist and backward-looking method of social inquiry to show what, from an ethical point of view, had been achieved by the changes that occurred over time. Of importance for the project of this chapter is his argument that with hindsight we can see how the ethical shortcomings of civil society were solved within particular areas by the creation of modern states within which people constituted one another as citizens. As citizens *they supplemented* the ethical standing achieved in civil society and overcame the shortcomings it produced.

Since Hegel wrote early in the nineteenth century, this supplemental practice has been improved further in that civilians have constituted themselves as citizens in *democratic* states. This new form of mutual recognition is superior to that enjoyed by civilians in civil society. It is superior in that in democratic states citizens recognize one another as citizens who hold equal sets of rights to participate in the self-government of their state. The worth of citizenship rights depends not only on the mutual recognition citizens give one another within any given state but also on that accorded by the citizens of one sovereign state to those in other sovereign democratic states.

In the system of democratic and democratizing states, through our recognition of one another as holders of citizenship rights, we accord to one another that high form of value as people who are worthy of sharing in the business of self-government. Citizenship rights include the right to stand for office, the right to vote, the right to hold office holders to account, the right to form political parties, lobbies, and so on.

As the holders of citizenship rights within states, one of the important things citizens can do for one another is that they can legislate sets of positive security and welfare rights for themselves. They may decide that, without destroying the rights constituted in civil society, they can introduce taxes on civilians and redistribute the proceeds to citizens in accordance with criteria which they deem to be relevant.

As citizens who are co-constituters of a self-governing polity among other such polities, we depend on the system of mutual recognition across the system of states as a whole. The significance of this point would be hard to overstate. It is the recognition between citizens over the whole practice that constitutes us as free people.

It is fundamental to the account I have given that we remember that the superior ethical standing we gain once we are constituted as citizens depends on our not losing our prior standing as civilians. The language we now use indicates that the society of democratic states, from an ethical point of view, presupposes a global civil society. The rights we build as citizens are only of worth insofar as they are supplemental to the rights we have as civilians. It would be hard to imagine a right to stand for office (or to vote, or to form an opposition) having any value for a person who did not also enjoy the first generation rights of civil society. None of the rights of citizens would be of any worth without our having at the same time the rights of civilians.

Although the practice of civilian rights came into existence long after the system of sovereign states emerged, and although it was states that implemented and promoted human rights, this does not detract from my point that the language of individual human rights which we civilians currently use does not respect state boundaries. We who use the language of rights understand that the claims we make are not constrained by geographical boundaries.

Civilians and citizens

We who now constitute one another as civilians in Global Civil Society (GCS) are also, at the same time, people who constitute one another as citizens in a society of democratic and democratizing states. Both of these are rights-constituting practices. We have civilian rights in the one practice and citizenship rights in the other. Both practices are global. Most people in most places use language which suggests that they consider themselves to be participants in both.

Within our individual states we have no difficulty understanding how citizenship rights are supplementary to civilian rights. In the developed democracies we have long experience of how our civil society rights mesh with our rights as civilians. We understand how it would be wrong to make use of our citizenship rights to pass legislation which made inroads into our civilian rights. For example, British citizens would find something ethically repugnant in any suggestion that those British who are Welsh should be compelled to remain in Wales. There is an absurdity in supposing that it would be ethically appropriate for citizens in a democracy to pass legislation which would deprive them of their first generation rights, their civilian rights. The relationship between the two sets of rights is set up clearly in the legal constitutional arrangements which are at the foundation of the modern democratic state. These normally entrench our basic civil liberties. The constitution puts them out of bounds to intra-state politics. We can enjoy the benefits of citizenship rights only insofar as we are confident that the practice within which we do so respects our civilian rights.[8] There may be extraordinary circumstances such as those encountered during wars, when citizens might deem it appropriate to restrict civilian rights for a while. That such occasions are taken to be extraordinary supports the point that I am making.

To repeat, the citizenship rights which are established within states only overcome the shortcomings experienced by civilians insofar as it supplements their civilian rights with citizenship rights. The gains are only achieved if the civilian rights are left intact. The gains which are achieved are the overcoming of alienation, the introduction of participation in self-government, and the introduction of remedies to huge power differentials.

Because GCS has only recently come into being, because it has only recently gone global, we are still struggling with the ethical implications of this new practice for the older practice of sovereign states. If within states we would regard any attempt by our governments to deprive us of our first generation civilian rights, there is little reason to suppose that we would accept this in the international domain. We use language which suggests that we expect states and individuals everywhere to respect our individual rights. The society of democratic states, if it is to be understood as ethical, must respect the civil rights of the participants in global civil society.

What this requires in the first place is a restraint on the forms of politics which may be used in establishing and maintaining the society of democratic states. In our contemporary world, only a politics which respects civilian rights, only a civil politics, is considered justified.

What are the implications of the emergence of GCS with regard to the emergence of new forms of community and citizenship? The implications seem, to me, to be profound.

On the analysis which I have sketched, citizenship is a valued standing which builds on what is achieved in civil society and overcomes its deficiencies. In particular, by constituting ourselves as citizens within democratic political orders we overcome alienation, make possible a form of self-government, and set in place a machinery to cope with unequal power distributions. But these achievements have been most successfully realized *within* democratic states. Now that civil society has become global the problems of alienation, unequal power and lack of self-government have themselves become global. We civilians must have as a central priority the establishment of practices on a global scale to overcome these. What kind of practices might these be?

A first question must be: Does the existing system of democratic states do the trick? Does it establish a practice which can solve the ethical problems to do with alienation, unequal power and lack of self-government on a global scale? Or does the existing system of democratic and democratizing states merely reinforce these problems?

It seems to me that the answer must be that *within* well-formed democratic states these problems are addressed in some measure *for that portion of GCS covered by the state in question*. But when GCS is looked at as a whole, the problems persist both because not all states are well-formed functioning democracies, and because it is often the case that in the relationships which hold between states the three problems of GCS are maintained or even made worse. In many ways the citizens in the powerful democratic states come to dominate, alienate and govern those in weak states and in quasi states. The existing states use the apparatus at their disposal to reinforce the shortcomings of GCS rather than alleviate them. It is easy to see how this line of thought could be substantiated and developed in further detail.

Thus, it seems that we civilians in GCS ought to be dissatisfied with the existing arrangement of sovereign democratic and democratizing states. It has not set in place a global practice which enables all civilians to solve the ethical shortcomings of GCS.

What is to be done? In making use of the opportunities for civil politics opened up by the emergence of GCS, what should we civilians be aiming for? I think that some targets are clear.

Our first priority must be to extend, preserve and nurture GCS itself. This should be a priority in all we do as individuals, as members of associations, corporations, churches, lobby groups, social movements, and also as citizens within states. At every point we should pursue policies which nurture GCS. This imperative is more important than ever in the wake of the events of 11 September 2001. It seems clear to me that the reason civilians everywhere were so shocked by the events of that day was not because a superpower had been threatened or had its security put at risk. After all the events posed no serious threat to the USA *qua* state. Rather, the event was seen as a threat to GCS everywhere. The hijackers had made use of their civilian rights in a number of different parts of the world and in making use of their freedoms they had abused the civilian rights of those they had targeted. The problem they present to the world is not mainly a problem relating to the security of the system of states (they pose no threat to this), but has to do with the threat that they pose to the security of GCS as a whole. States are capable of making arrangements to prevent groups like Al Qaeda from posing any real threat to national security. But the problem is that the actions which states are likely to take in order to protect themselves from more such attacks are themselves likely to be threatening to the rights civilians enjoy in GCS. The national security agendas of states everywhere are likely to threaten the civil liberties of civilians in all places. Indeed, many states are likely to act in concert to prevent terrorist threats to national security, but in combating these they are probably going to curtail civil liberties such as free speech, free movement, free assembly, freedom of the press, and many others. The task then is to confront the threat to GCS without undermining GCS itself. The protection of GCS falls first of all to civilians themselves, but states, too, insofar as they are ethical, also have a duty to protect that portion of GCS on which they are situated. States that fail to do this adequately will themselves lose their claim to have their sovereignty respected. States derive their legitimacy from their commitment and ability to protect that portion of GCS over which they have control.

Second, we know that what we are driving at is something akin to democratic citizenship for all civilians everywhere. I am not here making a case for the utopian ideal of a global democratic state. Instead, a case can be made for saying that what we ought to be seeking is effective citizenship for all people in autonomous democratic states, where the states themselves respect the constraints imposed on them by GCS.

Third, in order to overcome the problems of GCS as a global practice it is crucial that states themselves be organized into some form of global polity which has as its aim the overcoming of the shortcomings of GCS. In order to do this the community of states would itself have to be democratic. In particular, it should have as a goal the establishment of worthwhile citizenship for all. In order to achieve this, different states will have to constitute themselves as members of a global polity – a global ethical community within which they all recognize a set of rules which imposes strict constraints on what they are entitled to do.

Fourth, the process whereby states start mutually constituting one another in an interstate polity that advances effective citizenship must be gradual so as not to threaten the gains made through the emergence of GCS. The emergence of the European Union provides a good example of the kind of arrangements which might take us forward in this respect.

Fifth, according to the argument which I am putting forward there is nothing sacrosanct about the existing set of states. We civilians might decide on different sets of states within which to constitute ourselves as citizens.

This has been a short chapter about a new global practice, GCS, within which many of us constitute one another as civilians. GCS creates a valued standing for us – that of civilian – but it also creates ethical problems to do with alienation, lack of participation in self-government and inequalities of power. These require that we create supplemental institutions within which we constitute one another as citizens who can participate in processes of self-government within autonomous polities. Citizenship, though, has to be built on the basis of respect for civilians. GCS provides us with a public platform from which we might pursue, through a process of civil politics, new forms of international community and citizenship.

Notes

1 The point here is not that all English speakers agree on all matters pertaining to the speaking of the language. There are ongoing disputes about what is to count as correct English, but the extent of the practice is identified by those who recognize what the dispute is about. Outsiders are those to whom the dispute is incomprehensible.

2 Mervyn Frost, *Constituting Human Rights: Global Civil Society and the Society of Democratic States* (Routledge: London, 2000: passim).

3 Within GCS there are ongoing disputes about what rights ought to be included on this list of basic human rights, but there is general agreement on a core set of rights.

4 There are many people who assert that *other people* of one description or another do not have rights. They typically assert that black people have not got them, or that women, like children, do not have them, and so on. But it is worth noting that such assertions are usually made about *other* people, not by the supposedly rightsless people themselves.

5 In like manner, whether or not I am able to defend my property might depend on my being suitably armed, but what armaments I have at my disposal clearly do not determine my title to the property in question.

6 On constitutive theory generally see my *Ethics in International Relations* (Cambridge University Press, 1996).

7 To test this, simply imagine a teacher's reaction when faced with a charge of ethical misconduct from one of his or her students. These might range from plagiarism, through sexual harassment, to racism. All of them, if they were shown to be true, would result in the teacher being disgraced. He or she would no longer be a teacher in good standing within the practice of teaching. See for an extended example of this happening, J.M. Coetzee's award winning novel *Disgrace*.

8 If citizens in a democracy found that their government was attempting to pass legislation depriving them of their civilian rights they would judge themselves to have been ethically harmed.

Part III

Governance and global civil society

9 Global civil society and global governmentality

Louise Amoore and Paul Langley[1]

As a group of academics interested in the conceptual and practical implications of global civil society (GCS), meeting in rural Wales in late summer 2001, we became acutely aware of the proximity (and also the disjuncture) of the relationship between our discussions and the 'real' world of global politics. The date was 11 September 2001 and questions of power, responsibility, representation, and the inclusions and exclusions of GCS came tragically to the fore. It is these questions as to the constitutive effects of the discourse of GCS that we find somewhat neglected in the debate to date. The concept of an emergent GCS, an identifiable public sphere of voluntary association distinct from the architecture of states and markets, has become voguish in some approaches to international relations (IR) and international political economy (IPE), and in the practices of global governance. It is the limitations imposed by such common-sense framings of GCS that we felt were partially responsible for our inability to find the means to begin to understand what happened on that day.

In this chapter, we refute the idea that we can isolate a clearly defined GCS sphere, and focus instead on the particular uses of the concept of GCS as it is deployed to legitimate and challenge the discourse and practice of global governance. Sensitive to what is done in the name of GCS, we are specifically interested in the specific representation that has enabled neo-liberal conceptions of global governance to flourish. Our interest should not be read as an act of closure. Rather, it is our intention to reopen areas of the GCS debate that we feel have been prematurely closed down. The policy prescriptions and commentaries of the principal international organizations have tended to treat GCS as a neutral category, populated in a pluralistic fashion by voluntary associations, thereby depoliticizing its significance in governing the global political economy. By contrast, academic discussion in IR/IPE has tended to assert the transformative potential of GCS, particularly in terms of the capacity of groups to defy neo-liberalism and democratize global governance. As the first part of this chapter shows, both positions tend to turn upon a particular representation of GCS. We characterize this by way of shorthand, thus: GCS as bounded space; GCS as voluntary associations; and GCS as agent of empowerment/resistance. In highlighting this representation, whilst we are sympathetic to the normative concerns of many of our IR/IPE colleagues, it is our view that if we are to open up meaningfully the possibilities of GCS we must recognize the politics involved in the mapping out of what a GCS might look like. Both the discourse and the practices of GCS contain contradictions – that is, they simultaneously exclude, control and discipline, even as they also hold out the potential for resistance.

In the second part of the chapter, then, we make a number of interventions that seek to disrupt common-sense understandings of GCS. First, we shift the emphasis from GCS as a bounded 'non-governmental' and non-market domain to GCS as a means of making the global political economy governable in particular ways. We see the discussion of GCS as telling us something significant about contemporary efforts to manage and transform mechanisms of government. André Drainville's observations of 'the making of a compliant citizenry' (1998: 37), coupled with the Foucauldian-inspired governmentality literature, serve to challenge the delineation of civil society from state and market on which neoliberal global governance programmes rest. Second, we question the tendency to define GCS as a bounded, coherent sphere of agency. Most accounts of GCS seem overly tempted to list institutions and actors – trade unions, church groups, women's associations, and so on – that are assumed to constitute a coherent force for 'good'. By contrast, we ask what it means for GCS to be 'representative' of particular interests. In our view, such institutional conceptions of GCS deny the unbounded, fluid and mobile character of the everyday struggles that a politicized reading of GCS would need to acknowledge. Finally, we raise questions of the image of empowerment through GCS that has accompanied the global governance debates. Following a diverse literature that warns of the 'inequality and domination' that has been 'built into the concept of "civil society" from the start' (Keane 1988a: 21), we are concerned with the exclusions and oppressions 'inscribed in civil society' (MacLean 1999: 186). In sum, our intervention does not lead us to reject the potential for a transformative GCS that some of our IR/IPE colleagues are apt to identify. Rather, we see the power relations that find expression in the governing of the global political economy, and the tensions and contradictions of an emergent GCS (not the consensus and interdependencies), as central to the politics of transformation.

Reflections on the global civil society discourse

The key contextual assumption that underpins the GCS discourse is that we are witnessing, alongside economic globalization and the end of the cold war, the construction of 'a nascent global polity' that 'is already partly extant, yet remains mostly emergent' (Falk 1998: 99). According to this view, it would appear that we have entered a process of 'becoming' in the global political economy. The international politics of sovereign states is held to be increasingly challenged in juridical and practical terms by the transnationalizing and deterritorialized character of contemporary social relations (Scholte 2000c: 132–58). Such restructuring has given rise to a range of concepts, often devised in relation to well-worn notions, that seek to characterize and bring meaning to change. Scholars in IR/IPE, for example, talk of a 'post-Westphalian' politics (Zacher 1992; Cox 1996: 153–5) or a 'new medievalism' (Bull 1977: 264–76). It is the concept of 'global governance' that has, however, become the most prominent in accounts and policy prescriptions of the decentred, multilayered and overlapping character of contemporary political authority.[2] State institutions increasingly engage in multilateral agreements (regional and international), and international organizations such as the G-7, OECD, World Bank, IMF and WTO take on an expanded importance. Meanwhile, a wide array of 'private' institutions including industrial and financial associations and professional 'experts' such as accountants, consultants and economists also come to exercise significant authority (Cutler *et al.* 1999; Hewson and Sinclair 1999). With such proclaimed global governance has come a sharp growth in the activities of so-called non-governmental organizations (NGOs) that include the likes of Oxfam, Save the Children and the Red Crescent. While forging close working relationships with international organizations to, for example, run the refugee camps and design and carry out development projects, NGOs and broader social movements have also mobilized in an attempt to shape international policies and challenge the social relations of the status quo (cf. O'Brien *et al.* 2000). It is this enormously diverse array of NGOs and social movements that tends to be the focus in a discourse of GCS that has become ubiquitous in the discussions and practices of global governance.

While we are sympathetic to the desire to map the contours of this global transformation, we are concerned to acknowledge that the ways in which we understand, frame and discuss GCS shape what it will or can become. Grounded in an awareness of the constitutive effects of the meanings ascribed to GCS, then, we are interested in the ways in which the inseparable normative and descriptive aspects of the GCS discourse impinge upon our collective capacity to understand and challenge the contemporary global political economy.

GCS as bounded space

Representatives of international organizations and academic commentators on world order tend to share the ideal-typical representation of GCS as an identifiable space, sphere, realm or 'third system' (Falk 1998: 100), bounded by and differentiated from states and governance on the one hand and economy on the other. As a consequence, GCS takes on a non-economic and, especially significant for us, a non-governmental set of characteristics.

In a statement that is representative of the discursive practices of the international organizations, the World Bank (2000: 5) describes civil society as 'the arena in which people come together to pursue the interests they hold in common – not for profit or the exercise of political power, but because they care enough about something to take collective action'. Meanwhile many in the academic community share a very similar spatial assumption. For instance, the first of Anheier, Glasius and Kaldor's three propositions for the study of GCS is that 'What we can observe in the 1990s is the emergence of a supranational sphere of social and political participation' (ibid.: 4). Not only is this sphere distinct from the practices of governance and economy, but it exists 'above and beyond national, regional, or local societies' (ibid.: 3). Falk concurs, casting GCS as a 'field of action' that provides 'an alternative ideological and political space to that currently occupied by market-orientated and statist outlooks' (Falk 1998: 100). It is this vision of GCS as a 'solidarity sphere' (Alexander 1997: 115) and its associated normative undertones of progressive transformation through collective association that, by and large, distinguishes academic commentaries from those of the international organizations. As activists in Asia, Latin America and particularly Eastern Europe recognized during the 1970s and 1980s, 'the ideal of societal space, autonomous from the state, wherein self-management and democracy could be worked out' (Baker 1999: 2) is of considerable utility to those seeking social transformation (cf. Keane 1998a: 20–2).

The representation of GCS as a bounded space filled with particular non-governmental and non-economic characteristics draws in large part on the long history of theories of civil society. Given the undoubted influence of neo-liberal economics and the ideals of liberal democracy in the contemporary global political economy, it is not surprising that liberal conceptions of civil society have also once again proved powerful (Seckinelgin 2002). International organizations such as the World Bank have been very much at the heart of propagating the neo-liberal Washington consensus. Spatial metaphors were strong in the early liberal vision of civil society associated with Smith and Hegel, a realm for the pursuit of particular interests that could be distinguished from the universality embodied by the state. Later the divorce of a liberal civil society of collective associations from the private sphere became central to development of capitalism and modernity (cf. Rosenberg 1994). Meanwhile, the Gramscian conception of civil society has proved especially influential, both explicitly and implicitly, amongst activists and academics of GCS. For Gramsci, civil society was distinct from the economic base and distinguishable from the state, characterized as 'the realm in which the existing social order is grounded' and in which resides 'the combination of forces upon which the support for a new state and a new order can be built' (Cox 1999: 4–5). That alternative theories of civil society tend to inform the different views of international organizations and the academic community has, however, done little to raise question marks over the portrayal of GCS as bounded space.

The use of spatial metaphors to discern the contours of GCS is clearly not as unproblematic as the common sense would suggest. As Hegel and those writing in the tradition of historical materialism would wish to remind us, the construction of GCS as a bounded sphere obscures the extent to which civil society, economy and state (and other institutions of governance) are necessarily intertwined and mutually constituting (cf. Chandhoke 2001; Hopgood 2000; Pasha and Blaney 1998). As Keane (2001b) is at pains to stress, GCS is in many ways 'overdetermined' by wider sets of forces. The state and other institutions of governance in particular provide the political and legal framework that institutionalizes civil society's normative prerequisites. As such it is the broadly liberal form taken by state-societies, so central to modern political economy, that by advancing and protecting basic rights has historically filled European civil society with much of its meaning. Put another way and in the terms of the great traditions of civil society, 'liberalism can not work without republicanism, the public remaking of the private' (Hopgood 2000: 2). In turn, civil associations typically focus on the state to achieve change or resist state policies that violate rights (Pasha and Blaney 1998: 421). Bracketing out contemporary GCS as a bounded sphere may obscure, then, the need to consider the practices of GCS in close relation to economic change, and the restructuring of states as part of the shifting configuration of governance. It follows that GCS cannot simply be characterized as containing a particular 'logic' of more or less transformative collective association, differentiated from the 'logic' of government and authority on the one hand and that of economy on the other. As Chandhoke (2001: 10) has it, 'we can suggest with some justification that the much-vaunted autonomy of civil society is constrained from the word go'.

GCS as voluntary associations

The second tenet of the GCS discourse upon which we would like to reflect is the tendency to equate GCS with the practices of voluntary associations. In short, GCS becomes defined as voluntary association and vice versa. Descriptions of GCS in both the documentation of the international organizations and scholarly work often read like a 'who's who' of NGOs and social movements, such that GCS becomes equivalent to what Pasha and Blaney (1998) call 'transnational associational life'. Furthermore, the associational life of GCS also becomes privileged in normative terms. Voluntary associations in the space of GCS are viewed either as *the* legitimate form of politics through which to bring improved accountability to the institutions of global governance, or as *the* principal form of a progressive politics capable of challenging and transforming the status quo. What concerns us, then, is the delimiting consequences for politics of framing GCS as voluntary associations.

The common sense that equates GCS with voluntary associations is so omnipresent in the discourse that a couple of illustrative quotations should suffice. For instance, for the Commission on Global Governance (1995: 32), the term GCS

> covers a multitude of institutions, voluntary associations and networks – women's groups, trade unions, chambers of commerce, farming or housing co-operatives, neighbourhood watch associations, religion-based organizations, and so on.

Such is the extent of the identification of GCS with voluntary organizations for the World Bank (2000) that they consistently refer to what they call 'civil society organizations'. Meanwhile, despite developing a more critical approach to GCS, leading IR/IPE scholar of GCS Jan Aart Scholte (2000: 277) engages in a not dissimilar list-making exercise that suggests that:

> we can take 'civil society' to refer to those activities by voluntary associations to shape policies, norms and/or deeper social structures. Civil society is therefore

> distinct from both official and commercial circles . . . civil society groups include academic institutes, community-based organizations, consumer protection bodies, criminal syndicates, development cooperation groups, environmental campaigns, ethnic lobbies, charitable foundations, farmers' groups, human rights advocates, labour unions, relief organizations, peace activists, professional bodies, religious institutions, women's networks, youth campaigns and more.

As is the case with the tendency to represent GCS as a bounded space, the image of GCS as voluntary associations is not simply a consequence of attempts to merely describe changes in the global political economy. Rather, it is, at least in part, a reflection of the influence of particular theories of civil society in framing contemporary conceptions. The ideas expressed in the nineteenth century by Alexis de Tocqueville on the workings of American democracy clearly loom large. For the international organizations, in particular, de Tocqueville's conclusions as to the centrality of voluntary associations to a healthy liberal democracy are by and large transposed to the present in their policy prescriptions. This is as apparent, for instance, in the World Bank's recommendations that assert the centrality of the 'social capital' supplied by civil society to economic development (cf. Seckinelgin 2002),[3] as it is in the WTO's efforts to welcome the lobbying of NGOs (Wilkinson 2002: 131–4). At the same time, the intellectual currents of thought that frame many academic accounts of GCS also encourage the representation of GCS as voluntary associations. It is far from coincidental that academic interest in GCS has overlapped with a period of constructive critical engagement with Marxism across the social sciences (e.g. Lipietz 1987; Cox 1987). The resulting neo-Marxism is apt to stress that 'the politics of civil society, articulated primarily through new social movements, has superseded the politics of class' (Lafferty 2000: 19). Civil society is no longer viewed simply as synonymous with bourgeois capitalism (cf. Rosenberg 1994; Wood 1995), but is necessary to either bring capitalism under democratic control or to find a more democratic means of economic organization (Murthy 1999). The writings of Gramsci who, contrary to Marx, was never willing to equate civil society with the bourgeoisie and instead chose to emphasize a wide range of collective associations, have once again proved especially influential in this regard.

It is important to reinforce that for both the international organizations and academic commentators, GCS as voluntary associations is regarded as a force for 'good'. While understanding the utility of a well-developed civil society to the international organizations is fairly obvious given their neo-liberal credentials and prescriptions, we have to turn to debates about the continuing relevance of Marxist thought to understand the celebration of the virtues of GCS in academic circles. Just as the proletariat is juxtaposed to the bourgeoisie under Marxism, many scholars of GCS position the 'good' of civil society against the 'bad' of state and capital (Keane 2001b: 30). Such is this trait in the discourse, also influenced by the experience of activists during the 1980s in Eastern Europe, that GCS as voluntary associations is enclosed further. For many of the leading IR/IPE scholars (e.g. Falk 1998; Cox 1999; Scholte 2000), GCS no longer refers to the bourgeoisie or even includes chambers of commerce and other associations of capital. Rather, the space of GCS is an exclusive one, occupied by the associations and movements of labour, women, environmentalists and other 'good' causes. As Cox (1999: 10) claims, 'The concept has been appropriated by those who foresee an emancipatory role for civil society'.

There is, then, a strong contested normative dimension to GCS as voluntary associations. The politics of world order is effectively 'fixed', with the associations of civil society privileged in different ways from both the 'top-down' and from the 'bottom-up' (Cox 1999). From what is described as the 'top-down', the voluntary associations of GCS form the focal point upon which turns *the* vision of a global polity painted and practised by the international organizations (Drainville 1998: 39; Baker 1999). Voluntary associations here are in many ways the signature of a 'civility' that is brought to bear in global politics, resting upon the principles of rights, plurality, legality, autonomy and freedom of association. Echoes of the liberal tradition of civil society are clear. The manner in which GCS as voluntary associations comes at once to legitimate and de-legitimate different forms of politics in the contemporary global political economy is beginning to be recognized. For instance, for Pasha and Blaney (1998: 423) the 'notions of civility that are increasingly attached to civil society, while enabling a certain form of civil life, also contribute to a narrowing of the political agenda and the exclusion of certain actors and voices'. Meanwhile, for Drainville (1998: 54), 'politics takes on the appearance of a collection of managerial problems to be solved and where the broad political attempt to settle a new order goes unexamined'. What has been less well recognized to date is that by advocating the centrality of the 'good' voluntary associations of GCS as *the* key agent for transformation, the so-called 'bottom-up' vision of a progressive global politics also has delimiting consequences. The coherence of 'good' voluntary associations is assumed and the actual and potential importance of other forms of political practice are at best obscured, and at worst devalued. For instance, social movements can be seen to have '"dual faces" which dialectically combine instrumental . . . demands with an expressive dimension orientated towards norms, values, identities, lifestyles, etc.' (Stammers 1999: 79). The privileging of GCS as a space of voluntary associations risks overvaluing instrumental political practices to the overall detriment of the progressive politics of transformation.

GCS as agent of empowerment/resistance

For both its top-down and bottom-up proponents, the medley of voluntary movements and organizations in GCS are, taken together, imagined as 'an autonomous and unambiguous agent' (Pasha and Blaney 1998: 425). The autonomy of GCS rests upon the bounding of a space of voluntary associations from states and other institutions of governance on the one hand, and economy on the other. The unambiguous qualities of GCS arise from the tendency, present in both the documents of international organizations and the writings of academic commentators, to represent the voluntary associations of GCS as a force for 'good'. Here we reflect in detail, then, on the tenet of the discourse which suggests that GCS constitutes a 'good' agent for either empowerment or resistance. We are, in particular, concerned that GCS as agent of empowerment/resistance overplays the consensual and coherent characteristics of GCS to the neglect of power relations, contradictions and tensions.

GCS constitutes an agent for empowerment in a dual sense, enabling the political participation of GCS whilst authorizing and legitimating the practices of the formal institutions of global governance. Perhaps not surprisingly, international organizations themselves are keen to invoke the assumed empowerment qualities of GCS. For example, the 1996 WTO *Guidelines for Arrangements on Relations with NGOs* clearly states that 'Members recognize the role NGOs can play to increase the awareness of the public in respect of WTO activities and agree in this regard to improve transparency and develop communication with NGOs' (Wilkinson 2002: 133). Meanwhile, the UN's actions under the so-called Global Compact have sought to encourage corporate social and environmental self-regulatory 'good practice' through a process of partnerships that includes major NGOs such as the World Wildlife Fund, Amnesty International and the International Confederation of Free Trade Unions (cf. Ruggie 2001). As the representatives of international organizations appear well aware, a nascent global polity necessarily entails not only the erosion of state sovereignty but also challenges the efficacy of liberal democracy (cf. Held and McGrew 1993). They have effectively come to confront a set of questions reminiscent of those asked by Machiavelli back in the sixteenth century – i.e. how to forge the social basis necessary for new forms of political authority.

The conclusion that the voluntary associations of GCS, and not Machiavelli's Prince, should play the key role in empowerment has, however, not only been reached by the international organizations. While often critical of the unaccountability of the institutions of global governance, many in the academic community have also asserted the centrality of GCS to the making of a democratic global polity. The international campaigns and lobbying of an NGO like Greenpeace come to be seen as the exemplar of the democratizing potential of GCS (Falk 1998: 104–5). In the first instance, the key task for the agent of GCS is 'about increasing the responsiveness of political institutions . . . the need to influence and put pressure on global institutions in order to reclaim control over local political space' (Anheier *et al.* 2001: 11). As Scholte (2000c: 278) notes

> civil society activities can contribute to a democratic legitimation of the governance of globalization. Authority is legitimate when stakeholders feel that governors have a right to govern over them and that they, as citizens, have a duty to submit to the established rules. There has been limited legitimacy in the governance of globalization to date. Most people have accepted most policies towards global relations with passivity, ignorance and resignation. Yet if civil society offers stakeholders civic education, opportunities to speak, and chances to debate options, then people can begin to feel that they 'own' global

politics and positively endorse its outputs. Such legitimacy not only renders governance more democratic; it also tends to make policies more viable.

For many academic commentators, the capacity of GCS to successfully and meaningfully empower the institutions of global governance requires that new forms of democratic participation are put in place. To return to Anheier *et al.* (2001: 11), GCS is also 'about the radicalization of democracy and the redistribution of political power'. Richard Falk (1998) talks, for instance, of the need to construct what he terms 'normative democracy'. With clear parallels to David Held's (1995) work, Falk (1998: 106–7) conceives of democracy 'as extending beyond constitutional and free, periodic elections to include an array of other assurances that governance is orientated toward human wellbeing and ecological sustainability, and that citizens have access to arenas of decision'.

It can be seen, then, that implicit in much of the academic advocacy of GCS is the belief that by acting as a progressive force for 'good', GCS provides the key to resistance in the contemporary world order. While for the likes of Falk (1998) this resistance hinges upon the establishment of more participatory and substantive democratic arrangements, others expect GCS to take the lead in a wider and perhaps ultimately more emancipatory transformation. In the Gramscian terms of many of these writers, civil society's organic intellectuals, including academics, church leaders, trade unionists, environmentalists, social activists and leaders of community organizations, are enacting a so-called counter-hegemonic war of position to establish a 'higher form of society' (Cox 1999: 16). Whilst uncertain and far from determined, the qualities of such a society seem likely to combine equitable and environmentally sustainable economic provisioning with a republican vision of democracy.

For us, however, the representation of GCS as the 'good' agent for empowerment/resistance remains highly problematic. Our concerns go beyond the observations of advocates of GCS that achievements have been 'piecemeal' and 'disparate' to date (Falk 1998: 105–6), or that in the emancipatory sense GCS remains 'something to be achieved' (Cox 1999: 11). Rather, we would seek to raise questions as to the coherent and consensual features of GCS that, as a prerequisite for empowerment/resistance, tend to be assumed. For us, civil society is constituted as much by the highly differentiated politics of power as it is by the politics of empowerment and protest. Inequalities and conflicts abound. For instance, we should recognize that the overtly neo-liberal vision of GCS propagated by the international organizations 'is established after the image of the civilized (European) male individual' and 'rests on a foundation of excluded women, who are expected to live under conditions of household despotism' (Keane 1988a: 21). At the same time, the capacity of the voluntary associations of GCS to empower the formal institutions of global governance itself requires the prior provision and protection of basic rights of association that remain far from universal or pluralist. By way of example, Anheier *et al.* (2001: 7–10) draw our attention to fault lines in GCS between those that support or wish to reform, reject or find alternatives to globalization. The liberal constitution of GCS, as currently practised by the international organizations, structurally privileges supporters of globalization and, at best, those NGOs seeking reform.

Serious doubts also remain as to the representation of GCS as a 'good' agent for resistance. As already noted, the 'good' character of GCS is initially established by banishing the associations of capital from the space of civil society, such that GCS becomes 'something like a world proletariat in civvies' (Keane 2001b: 29). This contrasts with the current situation in which the engagement between international organizations and voluntary associations is, by and large, dominated by capital (O'Brien *et al.* 2000). Even if we can accept that the associations of capital are not part of an emancipatory GCS, questions still remain as to the assumed consensus amongst labour, environmentalists, women's groups, and so on. This 'good' consensus, perceived to reflect a common opposition to neo-liberalism (Falk 1998: 102), is far from assured. As Cox (1999: 13–15) admits, a lack of consensus could leave the way clear for the dark forces of the extreme right, terrorists, organized crime and the intelligence services to enjoy further covert power. In sum, we would contend that the representation of GCS as actual and potential agent of resistance may actually divert our attention from the very power relations that we should question and challenge.

Global civil society reconsidered

In the first section of this chapter we have explored what we consider to be the dominant mode of knowledge in the contemporary framing of GCS. By positioning GCS as a non-governmental and non-market domain, constituted through voluntary association and resulting in an empowering and progressive force for good, this representation tells us 'what GCS is' and, importantly, what it is not. Given IR/IPE's predilection for identifiable and bounded agents within clearly defined structures of power, the more subtle and contradictory voices and actions of other groups have often become obscured (see Tooze and Murphy 1996; Murphy 1996). Our purpose in this section is to begin to draw together from diverse sources an alternative framing of GCS. The different strands of inquiry explored here have in common an emphasis on power and, specifically, on the intricate and intractable relationship between power and knowledge. Our knowledge of what GCS may constitute is understood to be inseparable from the power that is exercised through the framing of, for example, mechanisms of global governance. To think differently about the existence of a GCS, then, is to open up the possibility for alternative forms of politics. Drawing on a number of concrete examples of what we may call civil society practices, we intend to show that such alternative forms of politics are, indeed, already present, though obscured from view by the search for a particular kind of responsible and 'civil' global agency.

From a non-governmental space to a means of governing

The orthodox understanding of GCS, as we have suggested in this chapter, embodies a particular view of what it means 'to govern' and 'to be governed'.

Government is a function that is held to rest with formal institutions – governments, international organizations, and so on. James Rosenau and Ernst-Otto Czempiel's (1992) established argument that world affairs have shifted from a system of government to governance retains the notion that to govern is to provide the institutionalized norms and frameworks for action. A GCS, then, is necessary to provide accountability in a system of global governance. As a so-called third sphere of non-governmental politics, GCS is celebrated because it is seen as outside of government. We wish to bring our concern with power relations to front and centre by reconsidering GCS as precisely a site of government – as a place where the global political economy is shaped, regulated or deregulated, disciplined or sustained. In this alternative framing of GCS as a discursive means of governing, of making people and their actions governable, we find the potential to challenge ascribed boundaries of state–civil society and public–private, and to highlight the ambiguities of GCS. If we are to meaningfully open up the possibilities of a transformative GCS we must recognize that it simultaneously holds out the potential for resistance, while it closes down, excludes, controls and disciplines.

Michel Foucault's writing offers us a conception of government and governability that refutes conventionally held assumptions about state and civil society. Governmentality, as he termed it, is 'the ensemble formed by the institutions, procedures, analyses and reflections, the calculations and tactics, that allow the exercise of this very specific albeit complex form of power, which has as its target population' (Foucault 1979: 20). The act of government, then, is not something undertaken by institutions and individuals holding power over society. Rather, governmentality permits government from a distance, just as the global governance doctrines prescribe. Commenting on the relevance of Foucault's work to what he calls 'neoliberal subjects', Nikolas Rose depicts the kind of government that can exist through the mentalities of individuals and groups:

> An enabling state that will govern without governing 'society' – governing by acting on the choices and self-steering properties of individuals, families, communities, organizations. This entails a twin process of autonomization plus responsibilization – opening free space for the choices of individual actors whilst enwrapping these autonomized actors within new forms of control.
>
> (Rose 1999: xxiii)

The implications of the governmentality thesis for the contemporary discourse of GCS are, in our view, of great significance. For instance, in his Foucauldian study of civil society associations in the UK, John Morison uncovers a 'new breed of professionalized, well-funded, and well-organized voluntary associations' who 'use the language of risk and reward, choice, economic rationality, targeting and output as the governing concepts' (Morison 2000: 109). Focusing similar attention on transnational civil society, André Drainville points to the 'double attempt to construct global civil society and settle with it the terms of transnational civility' (1998: 46). Exploring what he terms 'transnational subjects' through the Quebec City protests of 2001, he understands the twinning of heads of states' summits and people's summits as an 'attempt to create a responsible hemispheric civil society' within which resistance becomes compliance (Drainville 2002: 27). Under orthodox neo-liberal conceptions of GCS as a bounded non-governmental public space, most personal questions of how one should live and who one should aspire to be are deemed to be private and are effectively depoliticized. The governmentality lens on GCS has the effect of re-politicizing private individual ambitions, perceptions and experiences as these are brought into networks of power. The membership of an environmental group, for example, becomes tied to the citizen as a responsible consumer and draws on numerous lifestyle habits and choices – from fair trade cappuccinos to 'anti-sweatshop' T-shirts.

The practices of global civil society, it seems to us, cannot be decisively situated in a bounded space that is 'non-governmental' and 'non-economic'. In the World Bank's framing of civil society, for example, local networks and voluntary associations become a means to mitigate the more damaging forces of the global economy. Under the heading 'what is civil society?', their website represents voluntary associations as sources of social capital that can, alongside state and market, 'contribute jointly to the provision of welfare and economic development'.[4] Offering the examples of local credit networks and rural organizations, the concept of civil society is tied to the responsibilities of individuals and groups to take 'the opportunity to participate' in development and social welfare. In the World Development Report *Attacking Poverty*, the Bank makes its use of GCS as a means of governing more explicit. In their guidelines on 'helping poor people to manage risk' they describe microfinance as a 'risk management tool' that can 'help poor households smooth consumption during an adverse shock' (World Bank 2000/01: 156). Though the report refers to NGOs such as the Self-Employed Women's Association (SEWA), HomeNet, and Women in Informal Employment: Globalizing and Organizing (WIEGO), the participation of these groups is understood to be the responsible and proactive obligation of global citizens. The critical voices that these groups bring to the inequalities of the global economy are masked by a discourse of 'harnessing global forces' and providing channels for legitimate participation that enable poor people to 'get the best' from globalization.

We are not suggesting that GCS is simply synonymous with the governing of the latest (neo-liberal, global) stage of bourgeois capitalism, far from it. Rather, spaces of GCS should be treated as ambiguous, open to contestation and often contradictory. The roles of civil society groups in relation to the governance of the global political economy are, more often than not, undecidable. Organizations may simultaneously appear to offer coping mechanisms for dealing with globalization (in effect, plugging the gaps left by the global economy), while also offering a substantive critique of the structures of global finance and production. Indeed, NGOs may themselves debate and negotiate the terms of their role in advocacy networks and partnerships, acknowledging the tensions and contradictions in their own activities to such an extent that their intra-institutional organization divorces their role in service-delivery from their advocacy work.[5] A further example can be found in local exchange trading systems (LETS). On the one hand, LETS are widely understood to be voluntary associations that have emerged as a response to the consequences of globalization (Helleiner 1998; Paccione 1997). Yet, on the other hand, their relationship to the politics of global financial exclusion is thoroughly ambiguous. In one sense, they are 'self-help' associations that also campaign for change in global finance. In another sense, the practices of LETS appeal to criteria of trust and responsibility that are not dissimilar from those applied to individuals by mainstream financial institutions. While we agree that LETS are interesting and potentially transformative sites within specific locales, we also emphasize their ambivalence – they cannot be isolated from state, market, or the existing exclusions of mainstream finance. For us, the contested and contradictory making of neo-liberal or transnational subjectivities, furthered by the global governance discourse, is part of a wider network of production, consumption and familial practices that criss-cross ascribed public and private domains.

From fixed agency to the politics of movement

'Terms like "international civil society", writes Arjun Appadurai, 'do not entirely capture the mobility and malleability of those creative forms of social life that are localized transit points for mobile global forms of civic and civil life' (2001: 7). As a concept used to explain the emergent character of contemporary global politics, GCS has done much to transcend the state-centred preoccupations of much IR and IPE. Yet, many of the habits of traditional IR/IPE inquiry remain in place: the tendency to look for identifiable and atomized agents, a focus on institutions as fixed structures of political life, and the separation of levels of analysis as though these were actually clearly delineated in everyday life. In some senses the concept of a GCS always appears in relation to a sovereign state or international organization,[6] a named list of institutions with clear membership constituencies, and a spectrum of activity from 'transnational' to 'grassroots'. For Rob Walker, 'social movements are, to the modern political imagination, most easily fixed within a sphere of social life that is distinguished from and even counterposed to the sphere of politics – within the so-called civil society' (Walker 1994: 670). Taken together with Appadurai's observations, this suggests not that we take our eyes off civil society movements or necessarily deny the potential of a transformative GCS, but that we think of them as unbounded, fluid, and mobile. In contrast to fixed and named associations, we then see a sphere of social life whose boundaries and membership are contested. Rather than an elite world of policy making that is counterposed to local and grassroots struggle, we see what Walker terms 'the transgression of these fine lines' (1994: 700). The politics of movements thus shifts from the identification of a fixed association or NGO to an acknowledgement of the ability to confound boundaries that is their very essence.

It is not unusual for an institution or organization to claim to be speaking on behalf of, or with the mandate of, GCS. To explore an example, there is increasing interest in the idea that organized labour may be, in the broadest sense, representative of the interests of civil society. Juan Somavia, Director General of the International Labour Organization (ILO), considers organized labour to be an institution of GCS, with transnational unions being 'the most organized actors and the most articulate voices in society' (Somavia 1999). It is held that the challenges posed to labour by globalization and the restructuring of production are shared by civil society more widely, and that the trade unions represent the most effective channel for communicating those interests. Put simply, effective politics is understood to reside with formalized associations that have a clear mandate. Alliances between trade unions and NGOs have been celebrated by a literature that documents the rise of a 'global social movement unionism' which transcends the narrow concerns of organized labour (O'Brien 2000; Waterman and Wills 2001). This tendency to name associations or movements as vehicles for GCS serves to fix the politics of work and labour as something that is the preserve of trade unions and NGOs. The experiences of unprotected workers, or indeed the unemployed, are exposed only via intermediary agencies that claim to speak on their behalf.

If we reconsider the agency of workers and worker groups, focusing on the mobile and contested nature of movements, we can begin to problematize the idea that formalized trade unions speak on behalf of workers as a collective body. The contemporary politics of movement within and across workplaces is as much about 'involuntary' and unplanned 'reflex' action, what Scott (1990) would call 'infrapolitics', as it is 'voluntary' and strategic action. Many of the struggles labelled 'grassroots', such as plant-level industrial action or everyday 'foot-dragging' and acts of disruption (Scott 1990), are actually central to the politics of work and confound attempts to limit this to a global social movement unionism. Soldatenko's studies of Latina garment workers in Los Angeles, for example, emphasize the intra-worker and inter-ethnic conflict within sweatshop conditions. This problematizes the treatment of workers as a collective body and exposes the difficulties of trying to 'forge an effective culture of resistance' (Soldatenko 1999: 319). To illustrate further, in *Bread and Roses*, Ken Loach's cinematic portrayal of life as an undocumented Mexican cleaner in Los Angeles, Rosa voices her contempt for the American unions that claim to represent her interests. Supporting her family through prostitution and cleaning work, she asks her white, college-educated union representative, 'what do you risk?', challenging his 'justice for janitors' campaign with an appeal for 'justice for Rosa'. In response to the union's collective 'we', Rosa replies 'don't say we, there is never we, only I' (Filmfour 2002).

When labour organizations claim to speak on behalf of a collective 'we', they avert their gaze, not only from the experiences of workers at the margins of the global political economy (cf. Anderson 2000; Chang 2000), but also from the 'silent resistances' that characterize the politics of displaced and excluded peoples (Cheru 1997). Beneath the surface of an emergent GCS lie multiple global civil societies with competing experiences of what it means to belong to a group or place, what it means to organize, and what it means to say 'we'.

Uncovering the power in empowerment

In most orthodox accounts of GCS as agent of empowerment, power is considered to be a commodity that is parcelled up, held by particular agents and groups, and wielded over the lives of others. 'The capacity to wield power as a resource over other agents', writes David Campbell, 'is an important proviso of agency' (1996: 11). The voluntary associations assumed to populate a fledgling GCS, then, can be 'empowered', literally endowed with the power resources necessary to apply pressure for global transformation. The problem, of course, is that things are rarely so straightforward in the concrete practices of organization and resistance. It is not possible to reduce power to a named group, institution or actor, as many seeking to map out a GCS would wish to do. Civil society groups or movements do not simply 'rise up' to challenge the power of global markets, they do not unambiguously resist because they are always also intricately involved in the very production of that power:

> Power is not an institution, and not a structure; neither is it a certain strength we are endowed with; it is the name one attributes to a complex strategical relationship in a particular society.
>
> (Foucault 1980: 93)

Our attention is directed to the ways in which power functions and is exercised through civil society groups, and to the inequalities and exclusions that are produced. As collective agents, global civil society networks are themselves inscribed with the power relations found in the states, markets and organizations they seek to challenge. We would agree, then, with John MacLean (1999) who reminds us that to reduce our search for transformative 'agency' to the identification of collective 'agents' leads to a misrepresentation of politics and power relations. Trade unions, universities, the media and church organizations are all historical sites of civil society uprising, but they are simultaneously spaces of representation, exclusion and control. The politics of GCS is thus running with contradictions and constantly in flux – a movement that is not always in the direction of emancipatory 'civility'.

We wish to emphasize here three aspects of GCS that become visible if we cease the search for the consolidated agent for 'good' and recognize the agitative and contradictory nature of what it means to be 'civil'. First, within a named and assumed civil society grouping there are tensions surrounding 'who' is being empowered, or 'what' is being resisted. To deny these tensions in a search for a single galvanizing manifesto or agenda is to miss the very heart of the politics of transformation. In his discussion of the popular dissent leading to the East German revolution, Roland Bleiker significantly problematizes the image of a civil society movement that empowers its members and rewards their participation:

> Despite their unusually active participation in the protest movement, East German women suffered disproportionately from the subsequent process of unification. For them the democratic dawn ushered in drastic setbacks in

> such realms as reproductive rights, access to day care or employment opportunities. A revived civil society, which identifies men with the public and women with the private sphere, further increased the masculinist character of post-Wall German politics.
>
> (Bleiker 2000: 34)

Participation in voluntary civil society activity cannot, in and of itself, be understood to empower and emancipate. 'Discursively entrenched power relations', Bleiker writes, 'cannot simply be toppled by mass demonstrations or other transversal practices of dissent' (ibid.: 170). The ability to transgress political boundaries, to organize transnationally and even to achieve democratic transformation, does not necessarily and always challenge entrenched forms of domination and exclusion. It may even deepen them. As Pasha and Blaney have it, 'transnational associational life does not so readily transcend contemporary contradiction and oppressions' (1998: 431). We are not suggesting that there is no potential for a transformative GCS sphere, but rather that the outcome can never be clear-cut, the objectives may never be fully met. As is exemplified particularly well by women's movements in former Communist Europe (cf. Pollert 1999), the achievement of apparent success in political transformation can be built on the back of gendered practices that displace risks onto women and migrant workers. The terms of reference of a civil society movement for change cannot avoid dealing with the very exclusions it seeks to oppose, and may indeed carry them into an otherwise transformed order.

Second, the assumption of GCS as a cohesive and empowered agent masks the contradictions of people's feelings of shared experience, personal wellbeing and perceptions of risk and reward. Within existing conceptions of GCS, do we have ways of thinking about the individual who is an member of Amnesty International while simultaneously holding portfolio investments in a number of large multinational corporations, the Visa cardholder who joins Reclaim the Streets, or the report from the Seattle protests that asked: 'did the protester who was filmed kicking lumps off the Nike sign while wearing Nike shoes see the irony?' (Elliott 1999). For it is in such contradictory relationships with the global political economy that we all find ourselves. Arjun Appadurai captures just such a contradiction when he asks how we can begin to understand the disjuncture of:

> Ideas about gender and modernity that circulate to create large female workforces at the same time that cross-national ideologies of 'culture', 'authenticity', and national honour put increasing pressure on various communities to morally discipline just those working women who are vital to emerging markets and manufacturing sites.
>
> (Appadurai 2001: 6)

It is these 'dark sides' of civil society activity that are so often invisible within discourses of empowerment/resistance in global governance. Just as some movements organize to challenge the boundaries that confine and restrict the movement of people, images and ideas, for example, others campaign precisely to close them down, to secure their own sense of belonging. There are currently, for example, voluntary associations springing up in the English countryside to campaign against planned asylum accommodation centres. Such groups make appeals to the threat to their own community in order to exclude migrant peoples, with one group arguing that their proximity to a prison and an army base means that they are already subject to outside threats. Indeed, even within a single protest we find some groups securing their own identity by criminalizing others – for example, consumer activist campaigners on the steps of Niketown in Seattle assisting the police in the identification and arrest of anarchists (Drainville 2002: 31). In these instances, the empowerment of civil society associations is pursued through the disempowerment of others, and the identity of a collective body is secured through the production of insecurity for others.

Finally, and a related point, we wish to emphasize again the unsettled and contested nature of an emergent GCS. As William Connolly has argued, 'a conventional pluralist celebrates diversity within settled contexts of conflict and collective action' (1995: xiii). To borrow his framing of the problem, it is our view that the conventional theorist of GCS celebrates diversity and difference within settled, defined and clearly delimited boundaries. In contrast, we ask how these boundaries come to be settled and contribute to what we would describe as GCS as a means of governing. It is the very mapping and contesting of the boundaries of GCS that we feel should receive greater attention in GCS research. To illustrate our point we will draw on Naomi Klein's 'anti-corporate' movement because it looms large in the public imagination of what it means to be resisting the forces of globalization.

Established through Klein's columns in Toronto's *Globe and Mail* and her book *No Logo* (2000), the no logo campaigns have seemed to be the epitome of an open, mobile and multi-issue movement. Indeed, Klein herself notes that, 'rather than a single movement, what is emerging is thousands of movements intricately linked to one another, much as "hotlinks" connect their websites on the Internet' (Klein 2002a: 4). Yet, Klein is also keen to settle the common context within which these movements operate, arguing that they are 'not demonstrations of one movement but convergences of many smaller ones'. The grounds for convergence are established as a common foe, an identifiable set of forces that all participants are 'against'. 'Look a little closer', she tells us, 'and it's clear that these smaller, targeted movements are indeed battling the same forces' (ibid.: 4). It seems that Klein does, after all, wish to establish a settled context for the conflicts of diverse movements. A close study of her website indicates a much more fiercely contested terrain on which the grounds for collective action are fought out.[7] As a self-proclaimed 'critic both of the Israeli occupation and of corporate-dictated globalization', Klein states that 'the globalization movement isn't anti-Semitic, it just hasn't fully confronted the implications of diving into the Middle East conflict' (Klein 2002b: 1). Again, there is an attempt to find some 'convergence', this time between the Israeli occupation and the actions of multinational companies (MNCs), and Klein finds the answer in 'self-determination: the right of people everywhere to decide how best to organize their societies and economies'. The potential diversity of GCS's political struggles is squeezed into a mould that conforms with the settled view of how things should be.

For us, Klein's desire to define the grounds for the movement's position, amidst a storm of protest in the chat room that followed, demonstrates exactly what Klein seems to deny: the contested nature of GCS as a platform for diverse political struggles. It is the perpetual struggle to define the terms of these movements that, in large part, constitutes the politics of GCS. As the anti-corporate movement again redefines its purpose with the inclusion of 'solidarity with refugees', rather than look for a convergence or a 'common threat', we point to this as the essence of GCS movements – the constant metamorphosis, fracturing and dissent. Just as Klein seeks to respond to state and corporate attempts to govern the parameters of her movement, so she herself attempts to establish the governmental grounds for the future legitimacy of that movement.

Concluding remarks

We began this chapter by commenting on the relationship between academic discussions about what GCS might be and the challenges posed by 'real' world events. It is not that 11 September 2001 represents an unprecedented watershed in IR, but rather that it is one instance among many of a provocation to our dominant modes of knowledge. Our approaches to understanding GCS will cast light on some of the dynamics of contemporary world politics, while they leave others in deep shadow. In this way the discourse of GCS constrains and delimits the possibilities for the discussion and practice of global politics. On the one hand, constraints are imposed by the specific neo-liberal representations of responsible and civil subjects, such as those furthered by the major international organizations. We would characterize such a representation of civil society as part of a neo-liberal means of governing that disciplines and excludes those who do not conform. It has been the portrayal of GCS as a bounded space of 'non-government', common to the international organizations and some academic commentaries, that has tended to obscure the very 'governing' qualities of GCS to date. On the other hand, critical academic accounts of GCS that focus their attention on the capacity of social movements to counter neo-liberal globalization neglect to recognize the consequences of their reading for global politics. Whilst the emancipatory potential of GCS is celebrated, the manner in which this assumed transformative capacity is itself open to challenge and contradiction is not explored. In our view, to continue the search for a particular kind of responsible, legitimate and civil global agency is to avert our gaze from the power relations and contestation that lie at the heart of a politicized reading of GCS.

So, what would a more politicized GCS research agenda look like? For us it would be wary of the search for a consolidated GCS, and would treat with caution claims to a fully fleshed-out map of contemporary GCS. Rather, it would attend to the modes of knowledge, dominant discourses and practices that have brought GCS into common currency. To refuse to pin down GCS definitively, and to focus instead on what is done in its name, is also to foreground the interplay between our theories and concepts and empirical research. Better understanding is needed, not only of how the GCS discourse is produced and operates concretely across and within particular institutional settings (such as international organizations and NGOs), but also of how it is translated and redefined at the level of situated experience. It is in the everyday realms of familial, associational, religious or cultural life, for example, that GCS receives its concrete context. We suggest that it is here that the sketch maps of multiple GCSs are being drawn and re-drawn, and here where the power relations, tensions and contradictions are being played out.

Notes

1 We wish to thank Marieke de Goede, Matt Smith, an anonymous development NGO official, and the editors for comments on a previous draft of this chapter.
2 For an exhaustive and provocative review of global governance debates, see Murphy (2000).
3 For detailed arguments that assert the importance of liberal civil society in supplying the collective cultural underpinnings for a successful market economy, see Fukuyama (1996) and Putnam (2000).
4 See www.worldbank.org/poverty/scapital
5 Interview with development NGO official, July 2002.
6 O'Brien *et al.* (2000), for example, assess the significance of new social movements in world politics in terms of their ability to influence the agendas of international financial institutions.
7 See www.nologo.org.

10 Managing global civil society

The WTO's engagement with NGOs[1]

Rorden Wilkinson

Introduction

Public demonstrations loom large in the folklore of global civil society. Few loom larger than the those that accompanied the third Ministerial Meeting of the World Trade Organization (WTO) in Seattle in late November–early December 1999. The Seattle demonstrations – the so-called 'Battle of Seattle' – have significance for at least three reasons: first, though they were relatively small in size (a mere 30,000 demonstrators compared to the 60,000 in Genoa in July 2001 during the Group of 8 summit, and the half a million anti-war demonstrators on the streets of Florence in November 2002), the demonstrations are generally considered to have contributed to the collapse of the WTO's Ministerial Meeting and, with it, the failure to launch a new round of trade negotiations (something that was only possible at the WTO's fourth Ministerial Meeting in Doha in November 2001). Second, for many in the anti-globalization movement Seattle stands as an example of what can be achieved by harnessing growing civil dissatisfaction with economic globalization and its system of governance (it is perhaps little coincidence that Seattle was followed in quick succession by demonstrations during the meetings of the World Economic Forum (WEF – January 2000), and the International Monetary Fund (IMF) and World Bank (April and September 2000). And third, Seattle is heralded as an important step in the development of a global civil society.

Yet, as with all remembered histories, the folklore surrounding Seattle tends to skate over certain details. For instance, the falling-out between the developed and developing members of the WTO over the shape and direction of the trade agenda was as significant in the collapse of the Seattle meeting as the demonstrations. Moreover, the Seattle demonstrations were not the result of a new, sudden and spontaneous outburst of public dissatisfaction as was suggested by elements of the news media at the time. Demonstrations, though lesser in intensity, had begun accompanying the meetings of various world and regional organizations from at least the mid-1990s and were a feature of the WTO's second Ministerial Meeting in May 1998. But more than these, the 30,000 or so protestors on the streets of Seattle did not represent a global civil society. Though the protestors drew attention to the human, ecological, developmental and political impact of WTO rules, they did not embody the richness and diversity of a global public non-state arena. Seattle was most certainly an expression of dissatisfaction with neo-liberalism and, as such, can be said to be one aspect of the wider mosaic of global civil *societies*. But it was not a reflection of a risen global civil society. Nevertheless, many of the demonstrators in Seattle considered themselves to be part of an emergent global civil society, and for that reason we must take their claims seriously. We must also take seriously the influence of other political actors in shaping the contours of a perceived global civil society. It is with one such influence – that exerted by the WTO – that this chapter is concerned.

The influence of the WTO is important in the following way. The collapse of the Seattle Ministerial Meeting, and with it the failure to launch a new round of trade negotiations, witnessed the WTO embark upon a dual strategy designed (i) to placate its developing members and, in doing so, continue to take the trade liberalization project forward; and (ii) to rehabilitate the Organization's public image in such a way that if a repeat of the Seattle demonstrations were to take place, they would be marginal in their impact.[2] This second dimension of the WTO's post-Seattle strategy drew upon and took forward a relationship that the Organization had begun to develop with NGOs – those institutions the WTO treats as synonyms for civil society (a point to which I return below). This relationship has, in turn, shaped and constrained the WTO's dealings with 'civil society' in a manner that best suits the Organization's interests. But the operationalization of this relationship, and its projection to the international policy-making community, has influenced wider perceptions of what constitutes global civil society. The development and impact of this relationship is the principal focus of this chapter.

By way of contextualization, the chapter begins by surveying the development of the post-war system of international trade regulation and the concomitant growth of popular dissatisfaction with the shape and direction of the contemporary trade agenda. The chapter then explores the development of WTO engagement with NGOs, focusing on a set of guidelines put into operation by the Organization's member states. Thereafter, the chapter traces the development of WTO–NGO relations across the Organization's first four Ministerial Meetings – those most visible events in the Organization's calendar. The chapter draws to a close by offering some concluding comments on the significance of the WTO's relationship with NGOs.

The evolution of international trade regulation and the sources of civil discontent

Contrary to popular accounts, the public scrutiny to which the WTO has been subjected did not emerge simply as a result of the Organization's establishment on 1 January 1995 or the infamous 'Battle of Seattle'. Rather, the roots of civil interest in the international mechanisms of international trade regulation are to be found in the way in which a system of international trade regulation was put into place and has developed in the post-World War II era. It is to this relatively familiar, but nevertheless important story that the chapter first turns. Crudely put, the economic malaise and political extremism that plagued inter-war Europe plunged the continent into a second full-scale conflict in a lifetime, dragging with it vast tracts of colonial and associated lands. The abhorrence with which this conflict was met ensured that early on into the war, the allied powers, and in particular the UK and US, decided that an intrinsic part of post-war reconstruction was to be the development of a world institutional framework – what was to become the United Nations Organization (UNO). Under the wider umbrella of the UNO, three institutions were to be established charged with the task of managing the global economy: the International Bank for Reconstruction and Development (IBRD or World Bank), the International Monetary Fund (IMF), and the International Trade Organization (ITO).[3] Each institution was to have jurisdiction over its own field of operations, though all were to work together as a coherent ensemble. The underwriting of private capital was to provide the wherewithal to promote reconstruction (underwritten by the World Bank), which in turn would nurture a revitalization of production. Trade arising from this revitalization was to be assisted by a process of liberalization (overseen by the ITO), and producer confidence was to be nurtured through a system of fixed exchange rates (managed by the IMF). Their collective aim, nevertheless, was to be the reconstruction of international trade. In recognition of this, the legal framework of the ITO contained a series of commitments that not only outlined its relationship with and role within the UNO, but also detailed the substance of its cooperation with its siblings, the IMF and World Bank.[4]

Reflecting the political-economic imperatives of the time, the ITO's legal framework also attributed a second-order role to the International Labour Organization (ILO)[5] – the remnant of an earlier, largely unsuccessful post-World War I attempt to construct a world institutional framework. The ILO's inclusion served two purposes: not only did it add substance to the Organization's commitment to the promotion of full employment, by committing the ITO to the maintenance of 'fair standards of labour', the ILO's insertion offered organized labour an (albeit rhetorical) degree of assurance in the face of renewed intensions to liberalize.[6] As an aside, the Havana Charter also contained a provision empowering the ITO to develop relations with NGOs.[7] The purpose of this provision was merely to enable the Organization to utilize the expertise of groups outside the ITO if and when the need arose (rather than to facilitate NGOs participation in the Organization's decision-making forums).

The intended result, then, was to be a post-war system of economic management premised around a core of three institutions – the ITO, the IMF and the World Bank – in partnership with a fourth, the ILO, with a built-in capacity to draw upon non-governmental pockets of expertise should the need arise. However, the ITO negotiations proved unable to overcome residual doubts over the content of its legal framework.[8] The Organization's fate was finally sealed when in 1950 the US announced that it would not seek ratification of the Havana Charter.

The demise of the ITO did not, however, put an end to post-war efforts to provide a focal point for the regulation of international trade. As a means of bridging the gap between the protectionism of the inter-war period and the quasi-liberal commercial order centred around the ITO, 23 states embarked upon negotiations designed to begin the process of trade liberalization. Their efforts resulted in the drafting of the General Agreement on Tariffs and Trade (GATT). Though originally intended to be provisional, the still-birth of the ITO elevated the GATT from provisional status to de facto source of international trade regulation. In doing so, however, it put into place a system of trade regulation devoid of the ITO's linkage between trade regulation, full employment and fair labour standards. Only the GATT's retention of the aim of promoting full employment in its preamble betrayed something of the relationship its more elaborate relative was intended to encompass. One consequence of the GATT's assumption of the ITO's mantle, then, was to eject organized labour from its minor stake in the governance of the global economy.

The idea of a link between trade liberalization, full employment and the maintenance of fair standards of labour was further weakened by developments in the global political economy in the late 1960s and early 1970s. The pursuit of full employment policies in the leading states began to conflict with international commitments to maintain a system of fixed exchange rates. The inflationary impact of demand management policies in acting as a stimulus to growth in times of economic recession sat uncomfortably with the need to keep inflation at bay and maintain the price of the national currency under the shadow of industrial stagnation. What resulted was an awkward system of 'stop–go' management wherein national economies proceeded through a series of expansions and retractions in an effort to maintain congruity with the rhythms of the global economy. By the early 1970s it became impossible to maintain a system of fixed exchange rates. The result was a decision to end the Bretton Woods system and move towards a system of free convertibility (de facto from 1973, but formalized by the 1976 Jamaica Meeting of the IMF), signalling the end of the post-war settlement.

The move away from the Bretton Woods system of fixed exchange rates had a significant impact on the evolution of international trade regulation. Whereas the failure of the ITO and the subsequent rise of the GATT had unhinged the linkage between trade and labour regulation, the demise of the welfare state and the end of the Bretton Woods system sealed the fate of such notions. This movement was consolidated by the concomitant ideological sea change from Keynesianism to monetarism and then neo-liberalism as the preferred form of economic management in the lead industrial states, and the absorption of that ideology by the multilateral institutions of world economic management.

This ideological sea change had a profound effect on the world of work, accelerating the shift from Fordism to more flexible methods of production. In this movement, the partnership between worker and employer was reconfigured. In the industrial core, efforts to reduce costs were manifest in a movement away from longer-term employment towards short-, temporary and fixed-term contracts;

non-monetary remuneration, such as health care and pension provision, was whittled away; and labour markets were increasing deregulated to promote flexibility.[9] Beyond this, production began to move away from large centres employing sizeable workforces located in core cities and states, towards the sub-contraction of production to smaller sites in the national and international periphery producing goods and services on demand. Central to this reconfiguration was the implementation of systems of legislation designed to facilitate and embed more flexible approaches to production.

For organized labour, key to the restructuring of production has been the liberalization of trade and finance. Greater capital mobility, in part the result of liberalization and in part a consequence of the conditionality attached to structural adjustment programmes,[10] ushered in an internationalization of production wherein the sub-contracting model began to be utilized across previously unconnected places. One consequence of this internationalization was the heightening of competition among firms. This, in turn, led to growing pressure to reduce production costs in an effort to bolster competition. The search for ever-lower production costs brought with it downward pressure on existing labour standards. These pressures focused attention on the GATT, along with its Bretton Woods siblings, as legitimate points of engagement in abating the growth of worker insecurity. It is perhaps unsurprising, then, that the first discussions within the GATT over labour issues should have occurred at the same time as those seeking to extend the General Agreement's body of rules to further facilitate the internationalization of production. The Tokyo Round (1973–9) witnessed tentative discussions on both labour standards[11] and intellectual property. Neither, however, was successful. US and EEC efforts to introduce a code on intellectual property ownership failed, as did efforts to establish a foundation from which future discussion of trade liberalization and labour standards could ensue. A similar fate befell a second attempt to initiate some discussion within the GATT. A US-sponsored initiative on the question of 'worker rights' raised during a Preparatory Committee meeting in the run-up to the Uruguay Round proved unsuccessful, resulting in labour issues being omitted from the Ministerial Declaration;[12] and a re-raising of the issue during the closing stages of the Uruguay Round was sidelined in favour of a decision to discuss 'additional items' under the auspices of the WTO once it had been established.[13]

Civil dissatisfaction and the WTO

For certain sections of the international labour movement, the creation of the WTO proved disappointing, for others it was what had been expected. The absence of a clear linkage between trade and worker rights in the WTO's legal framework ran contrary to aspirations that the WTO would parody the ITO's labour provisions. It was left to the WTO's first Ministerial Meeting (Singapore) to discuss the issue of a link between trade liberalization and labour standards. But organized labour's hopes of securing a commitment to certain basic worker rights – so-called core labour standards – within the WTO's legal framework suffered a significant setback during the meeting. The outcome of the meeting – the Singapore Ministerial Declaration – attempted to settle the issue by declaring the Membership's commitment to core labour standards, but in doing so identifying the ILO as the appropriate body to set and deal with those standards.[14] What resulted was, for some among the international labour movement at least, an awkward compromise. The Declaration committed Members of the WTO to the observance of core labour standards without suggesting how this commitment could be operationalized; it attempted to put an end to suggestions that the WTO should have any responsibility in this area beyond a commitment to further trade liberalization in the belief that this would naturally bring about improvements in working conditions; it rejected the use of labour standards as veils behind which more protectionist motives could be hidden, thus safeguarding the comparative wage advantage of developing countries; and it pointed to the continuation of existing collaboration between the WTO and ILO secretariats.[15]

Organized labour was not, however, the only group to bemoan absences in the WTO's legal framework. Environmental NGOs pointed to the lack of environmental sensitivity in WTO agreements, noting that while the preamble to the WTO's Establishing Agreement committed member states to the 'objective' of sustainable development supported by a light scattering of references to the language of environmental protection,[16] few legally binding measures existed.[17] The relative absence of environmental sensitivity was compounded by the failure of the WTO's Committee on Trade and Environment (CTE) to make any substantive headway in its deliberations on the relationship between trade and the environment.[18]

The WTO's dispute settlement mechanism has also been the focus of civil criticism for the content of several rulings deemed to have significant environmental consequences, the most notorious of these being the shrimp–turtle case.[19] Criticism has also been drawn from an insistence on the part of the WTO to take 'scientific' knowledge – knowledge which is itself often essentially contested – as the ultimate source of arbitration in settling disputes involving the environment. This was particularly the case during a dispute between the EU and US over imports of hormonally modified beef.[20] Relatedly, the WTO has come in for considerable criticism over the tension between the Agreement on Trade Related Intellectual Property Rights (TRIPs) and the environment. The move to patent so-called 'innovations' in biotechnology, and the codification of these patents in international law has led many to suggest that the WTO is too quick to offer legal protection to scientific 'advancements' that have potentially damaging effects on human and animal life, as well as on the biosphere.[21]

The inequalities between North and South have also been the source of much criticism levelled at the GATT/WTO. Among the many points of grievance are: the lack of adequate political representation during the original negotiation of the GATT; the continuation of asymmetries in negotiating power between North and South; the failure of previous initiatives to alter the adverse trading fortunes of the developing countries; the crowding out of development issues by so-called new issues (intellectual property, services, investment, e-commerce); the political fall-out from the election of the second WTO Director General; and a relative disadvantage in technical and legal expertise.

Labour, the environment and development have not been the only areas in which the WTO is deemed to be deficient. The WTO has been much criticized for a lack of transparency and accountability in its decision-making processes – characteristics that prompted EU Trade Commissioner Pascal Lamy to liken the WTO to a mediaeval institution.[22] There are four distinct charges here: first, that WTO working practices are shrouded in secrecy and closed from public view; second, that the interests of various governments, particularly the leading industrial powers, are over-represented in WTO decision-making forums; third, that multinational corporations are perceived to have a disproportionate degree of access, and thus influence, in WTO decision-making; and fourth, that the broad representation of interests in the WTO does not include those who suffer most from increased trade liberalization and accompanying changes in production processes. As Tony McGrew puts it, these charges

> sit uneasily alongside the official view of the WTO as an institution in which the principles of one state, one vote, of consensus decision-making, and of accountability though governments are considered the hallmark of its democratic credentials.[23]

Although the sources of dissatisfaction are many and varied, much cross-issue sympathy can be found among those critical of the WTO. That said, the strategies and final objectives pursued by the broad array of public groups engaged in this issue are varied, as are the ideological dispositions from which they derive influence. Crudely, and somewhat artificially, three broad types of groups can be identified.[24] First, there are those that, though critical of aspects of the WTO, are broadly supportive of the notion of a world body regulating trade on liberal lines. Among others, this group includes business associations such as the International Chamber of Commerce (ICC) and particular quasi-autonomous think tanks, such as the UK-based Royal Institute of International Affairs (RIIA).[25] Second, there are those that are critical of the activities of the WTO, but seek to engage with the Organization in an effort to bring about change. Among these we can count a number of trade union bodies such as the ICFTU and NGOs such as Oxfam, Christian Aid and the World Wide Fund for Nature (WWF). Third, there are those groups that are fundamentally opposed to the WTO and seek its abolition. This group includes those that are ideologically opposed to economic liberalism as well as those that perceive the WTO as one feature of a world government; all, however, are united in their opposition to the Organization. The groups encompassed here are People's Global Action (PGA), Globalize Resistance, GATT/WTO Watch and the Third World Network.

That said, the array of groups critical of the WTO is such that these categories are largely artificial. Some groups inhabit the hinterland between, say, those that favour some kind of engagement and those that seek the WTO's abolition; others oppose some aspects of the Organization's remit, but are broadly supportive of others. What is instructive, however, is that the WTO has sought to quell some of the criticisms from those loosely inhabiting categories 1 and 2, and, in the process, marginalize the views of those comprising the third by pursuing a particular kind of relationship with civil society. It is to this relationship that we now turn.

Managing civil society

In July 1996 the WTO released an outline of the terrain upon which it was prepared to engage with civil society organizations. This terrain came in the form of a set of six broad guidelines (see below) directed at codifying the WTO's position but which at the same time revealed much about the Organization's perception of civil society and the legitimacy of particular NGOs. It is important to explore briefly each guideline in turn as each puts into place a key dimension of the WTO's strategy for dealing with NGOs.

Guideline I is significant as it reiterates at the outset that the development of relations with NGOs is an activity embarked upon at the *discretion* of the WTO's General Council, and that such activity is to be directed towards developing relations with *only* those NGOs that can demonstrate a concern with matters related to those of the WTO. Here the WTO clearly specifies that the balance of the relationship lies with itself rather than with those NGOs it chooses to develop a relationship with. Furthermore, in specifying the parameters within which the WTO is prepared to operationalize the provisions of Article 5, Paragraph 2 (the provision that empowers the WTO to develop relations with non-governmental actors), the Organization chose to equate civil society with NGOs, rather than pursuing a broader, more inclusive and representative spectrum of public opinion. The WTO has yet to determine exactly what it deems an 'NGO' to be, but recent practice points to a preference for non-profit-making bodies with interest 'directly related to those of the WTO', though a distinction is not made between groups representing business and civil interests.[26]

Guideline II emphasizes the role that NGOs can play in increasing public awareness of WTO activities and uses this as the justification for improving transparency and communication procedures.[27] Yet, while the inclusion of this guideline was clearly included to unlock some of the inertia within a WTO membership hesitant at any movement in this direction (in that it provides justification for a move towards greater transparency and communication), it also has another function: to outline that it is principally what NGOs can do for the WTO, rather than the converse, that broadly defines the relationship between the two.

Guideline III complements the second by adding a modicum of flesh to the Organization's commitment to increasing transparency. Here we see this commitment to transparency interpreted simply as a need for greater derestriction of WTO documents and access to these documents through the WTO's website, rather than for a more wholesale laying open of WTO working procedures.[28]

1996 WTO guidelines for the development of relations with NGOs

I. Under Article V: 2 of the Marrakesh Agreement establishing the WTO 'the General Council may make appropriate arrangements for consultation and cooperation with non-governmental organizations concerned with matters related to those of the WTO'.

II. In deciding on these guidelines for arrangements on relations with non-governmental organizations, Members recognize the role NGOs can play to increase the awareness of the public in respect of WTO activities and agree in this regard to improve transparency and develop communication with NGOs.

III. To contribute to achieve greater transparency Members will ensure more information about WTO activities in particular by making available documents which would be derestricted more promptly than in the past. To enhance this process the Secretariat will make available on on-line computer network the material which is accessible to the public, including derestricted documents.

IV. The Secretariat should play a more active role in its direct contacts with NGOs who, as a valuable resource, can contribute to the accuracy and richness of the public debate. This interaction with NGOs should be developed through various means such as inter alia the organization on an ad hoc basis of symposia on specific WTO-related issues, informal arrangements to receive the information NGOs may wish to make available for consultation by interested delegations and the continuation of past practice of responding to requests for general information and briefings about the WTO.

V. If chairpersons of WTO councils and committees participate in discussions or meetings with NGOs it shall be in their personal capacity unless that particular council or committee decides otherwise.

VI. Members have pointed to the special character of the WTO, which is both a legally binding intergovernmental treaty of rights and obligations among its Members and a forum for negotiations. As a result of extensive discussions, there is currently a broadly held view that it would not be possible for NGOs to be directly involved in the work of the WTO or its meetings. Closer consultation and cooperation with NGOs can also be met constructively through appropriate processes at the national level where lies primary responsibility for taking into account the different elements of public interest which are brought to bear on trade policy-making.

Source: WTO, 'Guidelines for arrangements on relations with NGOs', Document WT/L/162, 18 July 1996.

The WTO's desire to have managerial control over all the content of its relations with civil society continues in Guideline IV. Here, though also reiterating its perception that NGOs are 'a valuable resource' particularly in contributing to the 'accuracy and richness' of public debate, the WTO outlines something of how a relationship between the WTO and NGOs is to be developed. Relations are to be developed through a variety of means ranging from the organization of issue-specific symposia, to the development of provisions to enable NGOs to submit information for the contemplation of 'interested delegations'.[29] However, as Marceau and Pedersen note, even the mention of 'symposia' in the guidelines is a fairly safe exercise. Its inclusion, they argue, is

> largely due to the success of the first symposium [on trade and environment, held in June 1994 in the run up to the formal establishment of the WTO] and the fact that Members found it to be a useful, if arms-length, exercise in NGO–WTO relations, with the Secretariat serving as 'buffer' between Members and NGOs.[30]

Guidelines V and VI constitute the most managerial and constraining dimensions of WTO–NGO relations. Guideline V states that when engaged in 'discussions' or 'meetings' with NGOs, WTO officials do so in a personal capacity, unless a previous decision has been taken to contrary.[31] This is complemented by Guideline VI which states that under no circumstances is the development of relations with NGOs to result in the dilution of the 'intergovernmental character of the WTO', nor are NGOs to be involved in either the work of the WTO or its meetings. Furthermore, the guidelines state that the largest share of the responsibility for nurturing relations with NGOs lies with member governments, where a diversity of opinion can be reflected in national trade policy, rather than with the WTO.[32]

What arises from the WTO's operationalization of the provisions of Article 5, Paragraph 2, then, is a framework which, though appearing broad, tightly constrains civil society interaction and ensures that the balance of power in the relationship remains firmly with the WTO. The emphasis is on the development of relations with NGOs, rather than with more informal, less well-organized tracts of public opinion. By committing itself to court only those willing to engage with the WTO, large sections of more critical public opinion are marginalized. The resulting effect is a legitimization of certain NGOs (and, in extension, their constituencies) and a delegitimization of others. Even then, however, the guidelines locate responsibility for dealing with civil society concerns firmly at the door of member states, rather than with the Organization. Indeed, it is the Organization's reluctance to accept any substantive responsibility for dealing with civil society concerns that has frustrated many within the NGO community.

Ministerial Meetings: the evolution of WTO–NGO relations

The constraints imposed by the WTO's guidelines are not, however, the only factors shaping the Organization's relations with NGOs. As important in shaping the contours of WTO–NGO relations have been the WTO's first four Ministerial Meetings: Singapore (December 1996), Geneva (May 1998), Seattle (November/ December 1999) and Doha (November 2001).

Singapore

The run up to the Singapore Ministerial Meeting was characterized by a degree of nervousness on both sides. Many within the WTO were uneasy about the development of any kind of relationship with civil society; whereas, among those NGOs that had successfully applied for official recognition at the Ministerial Meeting, few knew what to expect. For its part, the WTO, in conjunction with the Singaporean Government, provided what were generally deemed to be good facilities for the NGO representatives, and various proceedings were broadcast to the NGO centre. However, a number of factors served to cloud the NGO experience. In line with WTO guidelines, NGO delegations were only permitted from those organizations that could demonstrate that their interests were directly related to those of the WTO. Those deemed not to have a legitimate interest within the WTO's remit as defined by the Organization's secretariat were excluded from the meeting.[33]

For the WTO, the invitation to attend the Singapore Ministerial Meeting was not intended to set a precedent, nor was it to lead to a formalization of WTO–NGO relations.[34] Nevertheless, the experience of Singapore bred a perception among the more critical Members of the WTO that this first engagement with civil society had been relatively unthreatening, particularly as it had taken place against the backdrop of some limited discussion of the thorny issue of trade and labour standards. As a consequence, no objections were raised to the further accommodation of NGOs at the Organization's second Ministerial Meeting.[35]

Geneva

However, the WTO's Geneva Ministerial Meeting proved quite different from Singapore. The relative political freedom of Switzerland enabled a series of demonstrations, organized by a loose coalition of NGOs and grassroots movements, to take place illustrating a level of dissatisfaction with the WTO that had been absent in Singapore. Though it would be a mistake to suggest that a direct causal relationship existed between the protests and what took place inside the Meeting, the amount of time given over to civil society issues in the statements of key people did not go unnoticed. In a candid opening address to the Ministerial Meeting, Renato Ruggiero, the then Director-General of the WTO, suggested that among the main challenges facing the WTO was the need to tackle issues of public concern. He cited financial instability, development, marginalization, the environment, employment, health and cultural diversity as among the most pressing, and suggested that, by way of moving forward, the WTO divert some energy towards strengthening its relationship with civil society.[36] Although Ruggiero's comments did not suggest that the WTO was about to reverse its decision to exclude NGOs from the workings of the Organization, they were followed by comparably supportive declarations from the US and EU.[37] While to some these intentions appeared largely symbolic, they were raised in conjunction with calls for a new trade round to follow the Organization's third Ministerial Meeting in Seattle, raising hopes that that the proposed 'Millennium Round' would take issues of public concern more seriously. Geneva, then, appeared to be a significant moment in the development of WTO–NGO relations, a point from which a deeper relationship could emerge. Such hopes were, however, short-lived.

Table 10.1 NGO attendance at WTO Ministerial Meetings

Ministerial Meeting	*Number of NGOs registered*	*Number of NGOs attending*
Singapore	159	108
Geneva	152	128
Seattle	738	not available
Doha	647	not available

Source: Drawn from data available on the WTO website www.wto.org.

Seattle 1: the meeting

The run up to the WTO's third Ministerial Meeting in Seattle witnessed a series of events that enflamed public tempers and alienated many among the Organization's Membership. The election of Mike Moore to the post of Director General proved particularly messy. The Member states could not agree upon a successor to Ruggiero until four months after the end of his tenure (at the end of April 1999). The political turbulence that followed witnessed the South's preferred candidate, Supachai Panitchpakdi, lose out to the US-backed, and initially much unfancied, compromise candidate, Moore. In an effort to abate some of the ill-feeling generated among the South, Moore's tenure was limited to three years, whereupon he would be replaced with Supachai, who would serve a similar term. Combined with an historically poor record on development and the spectre of a Millennium Round designed to discuss new issues rather than to address old ones, many from the South arrived in Seattle in a combative mood.[38]

However, this was not the only alienation that was to have a profound impact on the Meeting. The spectre of a new round of trade negotiations resulting from the Seattle Meeting, set against the backdrop to the US presidential elections, provided fertile ground for anti-WTO protests. Fearing that those gathered in Seattle would attempt to disrupt the Ministerial Meeting, Moore gave two speeches which contributed to the anti-WTO feeling. First, two days prior to the start of the Ministerial Meeting, in an address to the International Confederation of Free Trade Unions (ICFTU), Moore announced that he believed the issue of worker rights and their relationship with the WTO to be in many ways a 'false debate'. Rather, he argued, it is poverty not trade that is the principal cause of poor working conditions.[39] Though acknowledging that work insecurity is a common feature of the contemporary global economy, he argued that more, rather than less, trade liberalization was the answer. Second, and a day later, Moore told a gathering of NGOs that the WTO is not a world government, nor does it have any intention of becoming one; it does not override national law, dictate to countries, 'kill turtles or lower wages or employ children in factories'.[40] In both instances, Moore appeared to misunderstand many of the arguments surfacing from the labour and NGO communities. Moreover, his views were interpreted, at best, as insensitive, and, at worst, patronizing. Moore's comments, unsurprisingly, proved ineffectual in dissipating the growing hostility towards the WTO in and around Seattle. In the following days a series of co-ordinated and ad hoc demonstrations, coupled with an over-zealous reaction from the US National Guard, caused serious disruption to the meeting.

Seattle 2: the aftermath

The events in Seattle caused much embarrassment and were the source of much soul-searching within the Organization, none more so than by Mike Moore. Seattle was in many ways a critical juncture for the WTO, particularly with regard to the Organization's relationship with civil society. Rather than persist with its prior policy of tolerating, but nevertheless keeping at arm's length public scrutiny of the Organization, a distinct change in WTO policy towards NGOs occurred, albeit still constrained by the Organization's six guidelines. The first and most obvious dimension of this change of tack was the active engagement by the WTO in a public confidence-building exercise, and a concomitant effort to improve and increase the Organization's general profile.[41] One part of this strategy saw a response to accusations that the Organization lacked an appropriate degree of transparency manifest in an increase in the usage of the WTO's website: first, through a decision to speed-up the derestriction of WTO documents and for these to be made available electronically; and second, shortly thereafter, relaunching the website in conjunction with the release of a series of public relations documents designed to promote the work of the Organization as well as to quell popular misconceptions.[42] As a complement to the increased availability of documents on its website, the WTO also sought to increase the level of public involvement through the development of various electronic forums, including, among other things, on-line forums on trade issues, as well as the creation of virtual chat rooms and notice boards.

A second dimension of the WTO's post-Seattle public relations strategy has seen the Organization commit itself to engaging in a number of 'dialogues and briefings' designed, at one and the same time, to improve the Organization's public image as well as to disseminate knowledge about the work of the WTO. These range from 'lunchtime dialogues' wherein NGO representatives have the opportunity (at the WTO's discretion) to attend an informal discussion of their work with interested delegations and secretariat officials, through 'open dialogue' discussions on specific issues to NGO briefing sessions after key WTO meetings. Moreover, the WTO has committed itself to exploring 'opportunities' to allow NGO representatives to attend technical seminars on particular issues or aspects of the WTO's remit. Provisions have also been put into place for the convening of 'stand alone' workshops organized around issues of specific interest to NGOs. And, the WTO has developed an NGO outreach section on its website comprising, among other things, NGO position papers, an NGO bulletin, and a dedicated NGO website during Ministerial Meetings.

Nevertheless, these provisions have not meaningfully expanded access to the Organization. In the first instance, the vast majority of forums take place in Geneva. Only the 'stand alone' workshops have the potential to take place beyond the immediate hinterland of the Centre William Rappard (the WTO's Geneva headquarters). Moreover, as is the case in attending Ministerial Meetings, participants are chosen by the WTO from those deemed to have a legitimate interest in trade issues. The majority of meetings in the WTO are set to remain behind closed doors. The result is that the WTO's post-Seattle regime for dealing with NGOs continues to favour those well-organized, northern-based NGOs that can demonstrate a legitimate interest in WTO affairs, who pursue a largely unthreatening agenda, and who have access to the internet – precisely those NGOs that already have access to the WTO.

A third dimension to the WTO's post-Seattle strategy has seen the Organization take a more active interest in the internal workings of those NGOs expressing a desire to attend its Ministerial Meetings. As well as demonstrating that an NGO's activities are concerned with matters that relate directly to those of the WTO, it was decided (effective May 2001) that NGOs should provide general information on the institutional structure of their organization, including details of national, regional, and international representation, the number of staff, size of membership, financial statements, as well as a statement of whether they have previously attended WTO Ministerial Meetings.[43] Moreover, as had been the initial intention of including a provision enabling the Organization to develop relations with NGOs in the Establishing Agreement, the WTO has begun to put greater emphasis on what NGOs can do in nurturing trade capacity in developing countries, rather than simply as scrutineers of good practice.

Doha (November 2001)

The WTO's fourth Ministerial Meeting in Doha in November 2001 proved to be a markedly different affair from Seattle. Not only were the demonstrations that had accompanied the Seattle Meeting absent, a changed global political climate and the WTO's post-Seattle energies ensured that the Meeting finally resulted in the launch of the much delayed Millennium Round (albeit renamed the 'Development Round' to reflect an apparent change of focus in the negotiations). Nevertheless, Doha had a significant impact on the evolving relationship between the WTO and civil society. First, the General Council's January 2001 acceptance of Qatar's invitation to host the fourth Ministerial Meeting in Doha provided the WTO with a near perfect climate in which to manage WTO–NGO relations, both in terms of the Gulf state's relative isolation and its intolerance of public demonstration. The WTO secretariat was thus able to carefully select those non-governmental representatives able to attend the meeting. Of those NGOs that applied to attend the meeting, 647 were granted permission, albeit only one representative from each was permitted.[44]

Second, the Doha meeting was profoundly affected by the terrorist attacks on Washington and New York of September 11, 2001. Occurring only two months prior to the meeting, the attacks initially raised questions over whether the Ministerial gathering would take place. But it is the changed political climate that the attacks generated that had the most significant impact on the meeting. Although the WTO secretariat had done much in the run-up to the meeting to ensure agreement among the delegates over the launch of a new round, the climate of cooperation and defiance generated by the terrorist attacks further ensured their success. This climate also spilled over into WTO–NGO relations. Many of the NGO delegates at the meeting were at pains to play down any opposition to the Organization, emphasizing instead their broad commitment to a rules-based trading system in conjunction with a need for some moderate reforms. The events of 11 September also had a marked impact on public demonstration. Whereas the WTO's third Ministerial Meeting had been greeted with demonstrations, not only in Seattle but in major cities across North America and Western Europe, no such sideshow accompanied Doha. One consequence of the September 11 attacks for the WTO, then, was to quell popular criticism of the Organization and, in doing so, enable it to divert attention towards addressing the tensions within the membership that had contributed to the breakdown of the Seattle meeting. Doha, it seems, was a panacea for the WTO.

Concluding remarks

What, then, can we conclude about the shape of WTO–NGO relations? We see that the 1996 guidelines have locked the WTO into a particular kind of relationship with civil society that is, for both sides, deeply constraining. For civil society, the guidelines enable only those bodies that can demonstrate an interest in the WTO's remit to engage with the Organization. This invariably means that those groups representing business interests and some more acceptable NGOs are included. Even then, however, the substance of this relationship is particularly shallow.

There is another, more worrying, consequence. These 'acceptable' groups are among those more likely to gain access to global decision-making anyway.[45] It is those least likely to be able to exercise their voice that will again find themselves debarred. Here, we are not only thinking of those bodies that do not want to engage with the WTO, such as the PGA, but also those that are unable to make representations on the international stage, particularly from the South. The sum of this legitimizing/delegitimizing dichotomy is that the views of those already able to be heard can quickly become reduced to a representative picture of public opinion. Without doubt, such an outcome will reinforce the Western bias already existent in the WTO particularly, and global governance more generally. Those not represented will suffer further and more acute alienation.

For the WTO, its insistence on a set of guidelines that ensure its preponderance in any relationship simply confirms its unwillingness to take account of public opinion. An increasing elaboration of its Internet provisions, or the organization of symposia which in themselves do not influence policy making, will not alter this perception in the slightest. The task ahead for the WTO is to develop procedures that take account of the broadest range of public opinion at the core of the Organization, rather than to continue in the dogmatic pursuit of unhindered trade liberalization. The WTO also needs to think more critically about the intrinsic value of expanding the boundaries of its accountability. For instance, in defending the content of the WTO's courtship of NGOs, Marceau and Pedersen suggest that 'some would argue that interest groups should not have "two bites at the same apple" – one domestically and one internationally'.[46] But it is precisely because of a perceived lack of representation at the national level, coupled with a widely held belief that states are losing something of their agency, that civil society organizations have arisen and are lobbying international organizations. Furthermore, business groups are over-represented at national and international levels; it is in recognition of this that NGOs have sought to engage and redress some of the balance.

More broadly, there are as many problems with NGOs as there are with the world economic organizations they seek to confront. First, many NGOs do not want to be seen to be getting into bed with the IMF, World Bank and WTO. But, by not doing so, they run the risk of further marginalizing their views from the arena of public debate. Second, while a good number of world and regional organizations resemble autocratic, oligopolistic or monarchical regimes, the same can also be said for certain NGOs.[47] When thinking about whether or not the inclusion of NGOs in the decision-making structures of a world organization has the capacity to counter greater concentrations of power,[48] we need also to think about the democratic credentials of NGOs themselves.

Beyond this, the significance of the WTO to civil society folklore ensures that the impact of the Organization's management of its relationship with NGOs in part shapes the wider realm of what is popularly conceived of as global civil society. It is less important, then, to suggest that a truly global civil society is in ascendancy; rather, the global civil society that is imagined in public discourse is a civil society of particular NGOs deemed legitimate by the kinds of relationships entered into by the WTO. It is to these relationships, then, that scholarly attention must also be directed when assessing the analytical utility of global civil society.

Notes

1 This chapter draws upon, updates and revises earlier work on the WTO's relationship with NGOs. I am grateful to Randall Germain and Mike Kenny for their comments on this chapter.
2 See Rorden Wilkinson (2002) 'The World Trade Organisation', *New Political Economy* 7(1) (March): 129–41.
3 For a more extensive account see Rorden Wilkinson (2000) *Multilateralism and the World Trade Organisation*, London: Routledge, chapter 1.
4 See Article 3 (paragraph 2), Article 11, Article 24 (paragraphs 1–8), and *Ad* Article 24 of the Final Act and Related Documents, UN Conference on Trade and Employment, 21 November 1947 to 24 March 1948, Havana, Cuba.
5 Article 2 (paragraph 2), Article 7 (paragraphs 2–3) and the Resolution to the Economic and Social Council Relating to Employment of the Final Act and Related Documents, UN Conference on Trade and Employment, 21 November 1947 to 24 March 1948, Havana, Cuba.
6 For a more detailed discussion of the ILO's role within the post-Second World War system of economic governance see Rorden Wilkinson, 'Peripheralising Labour: The ILO, WTO and the completion of the Bretton Woods project', in Jeffery Harrod and Robert O'Brien (eds) (2002) *Globalized Unions? Theory and Strategies of Organized Labour in the Global Political Economy*, London: Routledge.
7 Article 87 of the Final Act and Related Documents, UN Conference on Trade and Employment, 21 November 1947 to 24 March 1948, Havana, Cuba.
8 See William Diebold Jr. (1952) 'The End of the ITO', *Essays in International Finance*, No. 16, International Finance Section, Department of Economics, Princeton University; J.E.S. Fawcett (1951) 'The Havana Charter', *The Yearbook of World Affairs* 5; Herbert Feis (1948) 'The Geneva Proposal for an International Trade Charter', *International Organization* 2: 1; Richard N. Gardner (1956) *Sterling–Dollar Diplomacy: Anglo-American Collaboration in the Reconstruction of Multilateral Trade*, Oxford: Clarendon Press; Jacob Viner (1947) 'Conflicts of Principle in Drafting a Trade Charter', *Foreign Affairs* 25: 4; and Clair Wilcox (1949) *A Charter for World Trade*, London: Macmillan.
9 See Guy Standing (1999) *Global Labour Flexibility*, Basingstoke: Macmillan, pp. 49–82.
10 Eddy Lee (1997) 'Globalization and Labour Standards: A Review of Issues', *International Labour Review*, 136(2) (Summer): 175.
11 Nigel Haworth and Steve Hughes (1997) 'Trade and International Labour Standards: Issues and Debates over a Social Clause', *Journal of Industrial Relations*, 39(2):184.
12 Steve Charnovitz (1987) 'The influence of international labour standards on the world trading regime: a historical overview', *International Labour Review*, 126(5): 565, 574–5.
13 Decision on the Establishment of the Preparatory Committee for the World Trade Organisation, Paragraph 8(c)(iii).
14 *WTO Singapore Ministerial Declaration*, Paragraph 4, 13 December 1996.
15 Steve Hughes and Rorden Wilkinson (1987) 'International Labour Standards and World Trade: No Role for the World Trade Organisation?', *New Political Economy*, 3(3) (November): 378.

16 See, for example, the Decision on Trade in Services and the Environment and the Decision on Trade and Environment, the preamble to the Agreement on the Application of Sanitary and Phytosanitary Measures, and the preamble to the Agreement on Agriculture.
17 The only legally binding provisions safeguarding the environment relate to the already existing 'general exceptions' clause of the GATT (Article XX) and a comparable clause incorporated into the GATS (Article XIV).
18 Marc Williams and Lucy Ford (1999) 'The World Trade Organisation, Social Movements and Global Environmental Management', *Environmental Politics*, 8(1) (Spring): 278–9.
19 An October 1998 ruling by the WTO's Appellate Body found the US to be discriminating against imports of shrimp from India, Malaysia, Pakistan and Thailand. The discrimination was deemed to have resulted from prohibitions on imports of shrimp harvested without the employment of measures designed to reduce the number of associated sea turtle deaths (by using turtle excluder devices or so-called 'tow-time' restrictions).
20 See WTO Appellate Body Report, 'EC Measures Concerning Meat and Meat Products (Hormones)', WT/DS26/AB/R, WT/DS48/AB/R, (16 January 1998).
21 See Ian Neale, 'The WTO and issues associated with TRIPs and agrobiotechnology', in Annie Taylor and Caroline Thomas (eds) (1999) *Global Trade and Global Social Issues*, London: Routledge, pp. 114–32.
22 Lamy is reported to have made this comment during the Seattle Ministerial Meeting, though he has since tried to distance himself from it. See Pascal Lamy, Speech to the Confederation of British Industry, 6 July 2000.
23 Tony McGrew (1999) 'The World Trade Organisation: technocracy or banana republic?', in Taylor and Thomas (eds) *Global Trade and Global Social Issues*, p. 202.
24 See also Williams and Ford (1999) 'The World Trade Organisation, Social Movements and Global Environmental Management', pp. 269, 276–8, 282–6.
25 See, for example, written and oral evidence presented by Duncan Brack, Head of the Energy and Environmental Programme, Royal Institute of International Affairs (Chatham House), presented to the House of Lords Select Committee on the European Union, 'The World Trade Organisation: The EU Mandate After Seattle', (10th Report), 13 June 2000.
26 Gabrielle Marceau and Peter N. Pedersen (1999) 'Is the WTO Open and Transparent? A discussion of the relationship of the WTO with non-governmental organisations and civil society's claims for more transparency and public participation', *Journal of World Trade*, 33(1): 14.
27 WTO, 'Guidelines for arrangements on relations with NGOs', paragraph 2.
28 WTO, 'Guidelines for arrangements on relations with NGOs', paragraph 3.
29 WTO, 'Guidelines for arrangements on relations with NGOs', paragraph 4.
30 Marceau and Pedersen (1999) 'Is the WTO Open and Transparent?', p. 11.
31 WTO, 'Guidelines for arrangements on relations with NGOs', paragraph 5.
32 WTO, 'Guidelines for arrangements on relations with NGOs', paragraph 6.
33 For an account of the Singapore experience see Robert O'Brien, Anne Marie Goetz, Jan Aart Scholte and Marc Williams (2000) *Contesting Global Governance: Multilateral Economic Institutions and Global Social Movements*, Cambridge: Cambridge University Press.
34 Marceau and Pedersen (1999) 'Is the WTO Open and Transparent?', p. 13.
35 Marceau and Pedersen (1999), 'Is the WTO Open and Transparent?', p. 17.
36 Renato Ruggiero, WTO Director General, Opening Address to the Second Ministerial Meeting, (Geneva, 18 May 1998).
37 See statements to the WTO Geneva Ministerial Meeting by Leon Brittan, Vice President of the European Commission (18 May 1998), Charlene Barshefsky, US Trade Representative (18 May 1998), and Bill Clinton, US President (18 May 1998).

38 See Rorden Wilkinson (2001) 'The WTO in Crisis: exploring the dimensions of institutional inertia', *Journal of World Trade*, 35(3) (June).

39 Mike Moore 'Labour issue is a 'False Debate' . . . ', WTO Press Release, No. 152 (28 November 1999).

40 Mike Moore, 'The WTO is not a World Government. . .', WTO Press Release, No. 155 (29 November 1999).

41 See, for instance, former special advisor to the Director-General of the WTO, Philippe Legrain's defence of the Organisation in *The Guardian*, 12 July 2001.

42 Principal among these were '10 benefits of the WTO trading system' and '10 common misunderstandings about the WTO' (see *www.wto.org*).

43 WTO document WT/MIN(01)/INF/3.

44 WTO Press Release, '647 non-governmental organisations to attend the Doha Ministerial', No. 240, 13 August 2001.

45 Scholte, in a study of the IMF's interaction with civil society, makes just this point. See Jan Aart Scholte (1998) 'The IMF meets Civil Society', *Finance and Development*, 35(3) (September).

46 Marceau and Pedersen (1999) 'Is the WTO Open and Transparent?', p. 43.

47 For a discussion of the potentials and pitfalls of a civil society contribution to the promotion of democracy in global governance see Jan Aart Scholte (2002) 'Civil Society and Democracy in Global Governance', *Global Governance*, 8(3) (July–September).

48 Warkentin and Mingst argue that, given the right conditions, global civil society does have such a capacity. See Craig Warkentin and Karen Mingst (2000) 'International Institutions, the State, and Global Civil Society in the Age of the World Wide Web', *Global Governance*, 6(2) (Apr–June): 254.

11 Global modalities of financial governance

The public sphere and civil society

Randall Germain[1]

Global finance and the puzzle of governance

The problem of governance in a rapidly globalizing financial system presents a puzzle to students of monetary and financial affairs. Historically, the governance of finance – to the extent that it has occurred at a global or international level – has taken one of two forms: either it has been imposed on financial institutions by a single undisputed financial hegemon, or it has been the product of highly centralized and complex market-based interactions that incline financial institutions to act in certain ways. Today neither condition prevails, yet financial governance at a global level exists and is (arguably) improving. In this chapter, I argue that we can only understand this peculiar state of affairs with reference to the formation of a clearly functioning and increasingly globalized public sphere. At the same time, in order to understand how a public sphere has itself emerged, we need to take account of and analyse the growing role of what many in this volume call 'global civil society' – that is, the interconnected set of non-commercial and non-government organizations (or, following Nancy Fraser's (1996: 133) definition: non-economic and non-administrative) involved in influencing and shaping the incentive matrix within which we act collectively and individually.

For governance to occur under the contemporary condition of a privately organized and decentralized global financial system, a public sphere must exist in which norms and principles can be formulated, codified and used as barometers against which best practice can be developed and measured. A globalized public sphere, however, does not simply develop of its own accord. It is the result of a complex interaction of a range of agents whose activities *together* constitute a public space that also has rule-making attributes – what Nancy Fraser (1996: 136) calls a 'strong public'. Crucial among these agents are those identified here as part of civil society. Their key role in the emerging modality of financial governance is twofold: to elevate the *publicness* of different perspectives concerning the issues and stakes represented by voices of authority, and to help impose on public and private (commercial) agents a limited sense of accountability. Although the actions of a globalizing civil society do not by themselves determine the effectiveness of the public sphere, they have played a crucial role in its emergence and will continue to do so.

The argument of this chapter is pursued in two parts. First, the idea and role of the public sphere is developed within the context of financial governance, highlighting the way in which the consensual development of the norms and principles of governance now take place within what I describe as the newly anchored global financial public sphere. To make the argument for the novelty of this development, I briefly indicate the contours of what many now call the 'new global finance', precisely in order to distinguish the governance problematic today. The second part then explores the role of a globalizing civil society in this new framework of governance that includes a public sphere. In particular, I highlight the contradictory struggles which occur between competing facets of civil society, and indicate how the countervailing impulses located within civil society help both to maintain the publicness of debate and extend the rather limited lines of accountability that exist within the elites which hitherto have governed finance. Finally, I stand back and assess how firmly anchored the global financial public sphere has become and reflect on the relationship of civil society to the broader contours of the capitalist global economy.

Governance and the public sphere

The changing governance problematic

To speak of the history of 'global' financial governance is, by and large, to invoke a fiction. The growth of both our knowledge about how to govern or regulate financial institutions and the actual record of such governance is overwhelmingly dominated by national authorities. The early modern roots of financial governance lie in the long drawn-out struggles of competing national authorities to subject financial actors to their needs and demands (Braudel 1982). Over the course of centuries, national authorities triumphed, and the majority of financial institutions became indelibly associated with national economies and national currencies (Gilbert and Helleiner 1999). Yet a determined international sphere of financial activity remained during this time, associated with what Karl Polanyi (1944) called 'haute finance' and the operation of the international gold standard. It is within this context that we can identify the earliest trends towards a 'global' level of financial governance.

Here, two conditions were historically crucial in determining the scope and scale of financial governance at the global level: the degree of centralization of the financial system, and the existence of a financial hegemon or leading power. In the nineteenth-century governance of the global financial system was made possible by the high degree of systemic centralization, while in the Bretton Woods period it was the aspirations and resources of the American government that provided what governance the global financial system experienced. Today, however, neither condition applies. Instead we have entered what many consider to be a condition of 'new global finance'.[2]

Three principal structural features dominate the 'new global finance'. First, it is characterized by decentralized globalization, in which there is no single financial centre that provides guidance and direction to the entire global financial system (Germain 1997; Langley 2002). There are multiple centres which serve as nodal points for the operations of globally-oriented financial institutions. Credit markets have also taken on a life of their own; that is, they are no longer closely connected to the actual trade in goods and services that constitutes the so-called 'real' global economy (Drucker 1986; Strange 1998). Second, the multiple forms which financial institutions take are without historical precedent – the decentralized yet globalized organization of credit markets has produced a staggering operational differentiation among financial institutions. At the heart of this operational differentiation is the repackaging of risk, which has in turn made the collection, analysis and distribution of information one of the core activities of financial institutions (Sinclair 2000). Creating value through the use of information is therefore one of the defining hallmarks of the 'new global finance'. And third, the 'new global finance' is not dominated by a single financial power as the Bretton Woods era was dominated by the US. Although the US remains the single most influential public authority within the global financial order, it can no longer impose its preferences and demands unilaterally on a pliant world (Germain 2001).

Governing the 'new global finance' in the absence of a financial hegemon requires the adaptation of decision-making mechanisms. During the Bretton Woods era these mechanisms were associated with the overwhelming power and influence of the US, while during the era of the international gold standard these mechanisms were associated primarily with the centralized credit networks at the heart of the City of London (including the privately owned Bank of England). Today, however, the 'new global finance' ensures that these mechanisms can no longer operate effectively or efficiently.

Governance, 'publicness' and consensus

Nevertheless, financial governance both exists and is arguably improving. It exists because the modalities of governance are everywhere in evidence. All states with functioning financial systems have of course the full panoply of governance agencies, usually a combination of treasury ministry, central bank and financial regulator(s). But beyond this there has been an explosion of recent initiatives at the global level to coordinate governance better and address regulatory gaps, including most importantly the formation of the Financial Stability Forum (FSF) and the G-20. Regional level initiatives also have their place – for example, the Executives' Meeting of East Asia–Pacific Central Banks (EMEAP) in Asia. Alongside established mechanisms of financial governance such as the IMF and G-7, these new bodies have been developing standards, codes and benchmarks that offer guidance and direction to the exercise of public authority at the national level. Financial governance, in other words, has become more genuinely global and interlinked over the past half decade. Figure 11.1 represents schematically what might be called the emerging inter-state financial architecture (cf. Germain 2001).

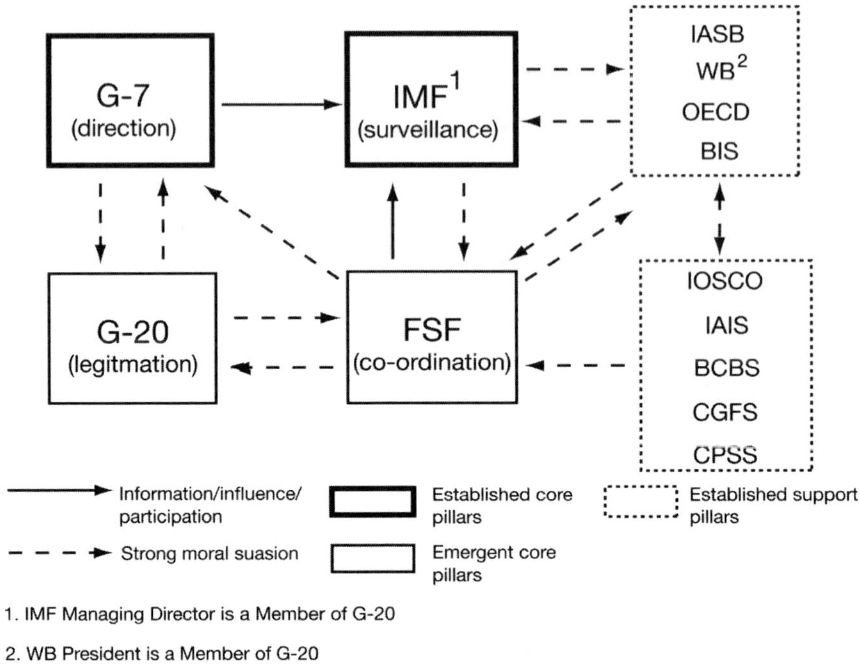

Figure 11.1 Inter-state financial architecture

Source: Originally published in *Global Governance: A Review of Multilateralism and International Organizations* 7(4) (Oct.–Dec. 2001): 417. © Lynne Rienner Publishers. Reprinted with permission.

By broadening-out the decision-making process, the structure of financial governance has become both more global and more legitimate. Two noteworthy aspects of this new governance structure are worthy of discussion. The first noteworthy aspect is its increased 'publicness'. Previously, financial governance at the global level was confined primarily to elite-level deliberations among a select set of relatively opaque institutions, such as the G-10, the OECD's Working Party 3 (where codes of liberalization were first discussed), and the Bank for International Settlements (BIS). Today, however, even though the actual meetings of the FSF and the G-20 (and indeed many of the more specialized agencies such as the Basle Committee on Banking Supervision, or BCBS) are closed to immediate public scrutiny, the results of these meetings are published and an extensive system of outreach has been put in place to ensure a dialogue occurs among as wide a cross-section of the public as possible. For example, the FSF conducts regular meetings with non-members to ensure communication and foster dialogue about the regulatory issues with which it is concerned. The BIS makes similar outreach efforts, and has recently opened an office in Hong Kong to consolidate its Asian presence. Taken together, these efforts are an indication of the extent to which official debate and dialogue on matters of financial governance have become increasingly 'public' over the past several years.[3]

The second noteworthy aspect to the new structure of financial governance is its consensual nature. The turn towards a more consensual decision-making structure has been prompted by the emergence of a specialized division of labour within the international financial architecture between the G-7, IMF, FSF and G-20. At one level, we might observe that the G-7 provides signals for the general direction of financial governance; the IMF provides surveillance on behalf of the international community; the FSF provides coordination among regulatory agencies; and the G-20 provides political legitimacy for the broader process through its inclusion of emerging market economies.[4] At another level, however, this structure of governance brings together in different ways the overlapping parts of public authority that together constitute financial governance. Central banks, who are in the main responsible for the stability and soundness of domestic financial systems, work primarily through the FSF and G-20, where central banks from the most systemically-significant financial markets are represented. Treasury ministries work in part through the G-20 and FSF, but the larger share of their efforts are directed through the IMF and, where they are members, the G-7. National regulatory authorities for financial institutions and associated services (accounting, insurance, stock exchanges) work through the FSF and other specialized institutions such as the International Organization of Securities Commissions (IOSCO), which feed into discussions and debates at the BIS and IMF as well.

The very complexity of this division of labour undercuts the possibility of direct coercion being exercised between the various elements of the financial governance structure. Not only are finance ministries, central banks and regulators driven by different sets of dynamics, in many instances they are statutorily independent from both each other and central government. As central bank independence has become more widespread, for example, the ability of treasury ministries to bend central banks to their needs has declined. This has had knock-on effects at the global level, where the fragmentation of authority is even more pronounced. Regulatory agencies are subject to a similar dynamic insofar as they are increasingly acquiring a statutory independence from central government. This is further complicated by the multiplicity of regulators at work; in many countries there are separate regulators for banks, insurance companies and securities firms (as in the US). The trend toward unified financial supervision, as occurs in the UK, is not yet far advanced.

This complex division of labour actively discourages coercion and encourages consensus as a key hallmark of international decision-making. An example of this is the recent overtures by the IMF (and US Treasury) to further investigate the problem of sovereign debt rescheduling (Krueger 2002). Although in the past this has been fiercely resisted by successive American administrations (as well as the American financial community and the IMF), concerted and persistent international pressure from German, British and other governments has finally succeeded in opening up an official multilateral dialogue. The formulation of many of the standards and codes by the FSF and BCBS has followed a similar consensual pattern in terms of being the products of widespread international consultation.[5] In terms of the operation of the new global architecture of financial governance, then, consensus appears to be one of its most important cornerstones.

We should not, of course, be blind to some of the more problematic aspects of consensual decision-making, such as the acceptance of a widely diffused ideational framework (in this case, a refined version of free-market neoliberalism), the continued centrality of the US and its financial community for all decisions, the constrained nature of emerging market participation, and the continued exclusion of important participants and issues from the dialogue that consensus promotes (some of which will be taken up in the final section of the chapter). We should also be alert to the possibility that one government's consensus is another's coercion. At the same time, we should acknowledge the significant progress in terms of developing the effectiveness and legitimacy of financial governance which this development represents. Consensual decision-making demands and requires a certain kind of discourse for its very existence, one that looks to evidence, argument and reason as the guiding precepts of dialogue. And even though consensual decision-making cannot ignore the material constraints that shape the flow of dialogue and act as barriers to the realization of whatever goals are mutually agreed, looking to the use of a very public form of reasoning for verification, authentication and legitimation is a tremendous progressive step in the history of the structure of financial governance. Taken together, the elevation of consensus and the heightened sense of 'publicness' within the international decision-making mechanisms of global financial governance indicate that something new is at work here. I identify this new development as the emergence of a genuine public sphere within the global financial system.

Mapping the public sphere

James Bohman has defined the 'public sphere' as an institutionalized arena of discourse and dialogue where issues of public concern are considered and addressed within a context of specific audiences able to engage in social, cultural and political criticism, and in which a certain form of public reasoning holds sway (Bohman 1998; 1999).[6] This definition adapts the understanding of the public sphere made prominent by Jürgen Habermas (1989) and critically extended by others (Calhoun 1996).[7] Its chief utility for our purpose lies in helping to explain how governance is actually achieved in a global financial system marked by decentralized globalization and the absence of a single financial hegemon. The signal advantage of the idea of a 'public sphere' is that it illuminates some of the key mechanisms through which decision-making is pursued under conditions of decentralized consensus formation, which I have argued is precisely the contemporary condition of the global financial system.

Beyond this, the idea of a 'public sphere' directs our attention to one of the most important contemporary arenas for forging the incentives that guide financial behaviour. Typically, scholars of monetary and financial relations assume that institutional preferences are constructed privately, on the basis of material interests, and then mediated to the broader global financial system either through the power of such institutions or through the disciplining power of markets (Strange 1998; Gill 1999; Hardt and Negri 2000). In different ways, these scholars consider the incentive structure of financial governance to be coercively imposed upon all actors. However, under conditions of decentralized globalization, such direct or indirect coercive imposition is difficult to achieve. Instead, a discursive construction or evolution of the incentive structure is underway. This discursive dialogue of course reflects prevailing material interests, but more than this it also takes place in and through a particular kind of debate undertaken in a public and political space. This arena is the 'global financial public sphere'.

We may identify the global financial public sphere as an enabling environment anchored by the interaction of four key globally institutionalized configurations of power. These are a government-led institutional framework at the global level, the global operation of financial markets, a global media, and civil society (Scholte 2000c). It is within this environment that the principal operational features of a global financial public sphere have become instantiated – namely, clear modes of public reasoning, a plurality of participants and a growing critical reciprocity between participants. Figure 11.2 represents schematically the global financial public sphere as an interactive set of institutionalized configurations of power. I will take each element of the public sphere in turn.

The global financial public sphere is anchored in the first instance around a complex institutional framework that enables dialogue and communication to occur within the context of policy development. This institutional framework has been identified in Figure 11.1, and comprises the key institutions that transform what might otherwise remain simply as a public 'space' – a space purely for dialogue or, in Nancy Fraser's terminology, a *weak public* (Fraser 1996: 136) – into an operational sphere where actual decisions are made. The complex division of labour at the heart of the global architecture of financial governance – which encompasses the key public authorities in their individual and collective formulations (i.e. as the US *and* the G-7, for example) – both debates and makes policies. It is a 'strong public' insofar as this is where the major discussions about the future shape and operational imperatives of global finance develop.

This 'strong public' is further anchored in the second instance around the operation of global financial markets. Why should we think of financial markets as part of the public sphere? The first part of our answer is that markets are important channels of information with regard to issues that are central to financial governance. They are often also 'public' channels of information, so that in effect they provide information which can be used to help evaluate competing

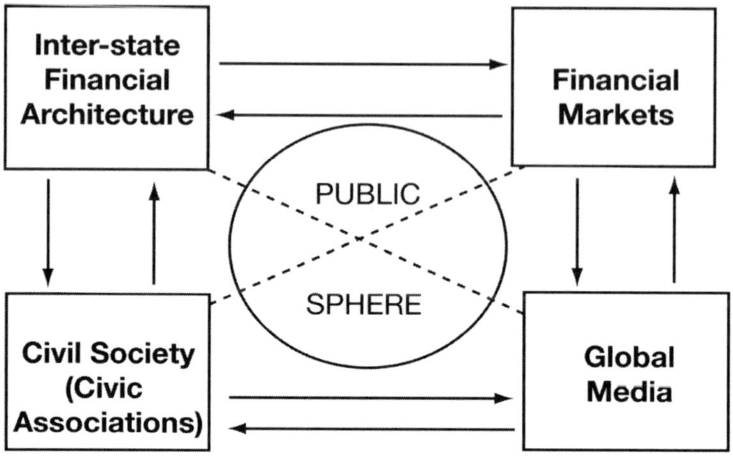

Figure 11.2 Global financial public sphere

claims about the scope and impact of actually existing financial governance. Markets provide important clues to the effective achievement of financial governance. The second part of our answer is that markets help to produce and shape the organizations which are the objects of governance. They produce the actors that governments are in fact trying to govern. As such, markets have a crucial role to play in the evolution of the financial institutions that form, in effect, the terrain of governance. These institutions, in turn, attempt to shape and direct the exercise of financial governance, and in many ways are active participants in the government-led institutional framework outlined in Figure 11.1.

The third anchor point for the global financial public sphere is the global media. The media (principally television, radio and print, but increasingly also Internet-based outlets) is one of the key mechanisms promoting communication and exchange within the public sphere. Significant here is the growth in the interest in and reporting of financial issues, both among the financial press and the more broadly focused popular press. The widespread impact of financial crises and the sheer number of near meltdowns since the 1992 ERM debacle have brought home to the general public the stake they have in the general health of the financial system. It is important to note, however, that the media on its own does not necessarily promote a public sphere (Bohman 1999; Stevenson, in this volume). Rather, it both makes possible a wider audience and helps to educate that audience – that is, to make it more literate. In this sense the media is crucial in the dissemination of a mode of public reasoning which subjects established views to critical engagement. And while we must be alert to the place of the media within the contours of the material interests of the global economy (it is often owned by transnational corporate interests such as the stable of media outlets controlled by Rupert Murdoch), the sheer diversity of media outlets does enable contestation and struggle to inform a broader public debate. In other words, the media in all its forms is a key channel through which debate about financial governance proceeds.

The final configuration of power around which the global financial public sphere is anchored might be termed civil society – or, more exactly, the organizations which many have identified as belonging to civil society (Scholte and Schnabel 2002). These are organizations that neither fall formally under the rubric of government nor are fully active in markets. Rather they are non-state and non-commercial actors that, starting from a variety of motivational purposes, attempt to influence the arrangements of financial governance in directions that are consistent with their core principals. They range from religiously inspired organizations, to organizations of conscience, to broad-based social movements, to oppositional organizations that exist in contest with either government agencies or market-based institutions (Scholte 2002). These organizations engage in the debate over financial governance primarily by either seeking to influence governments and inter-governmental institutions directly or through mass protest, and sometimes both. They contribute to the anchoring of a public sphere precisely because they have become part of the intended audience of the world's financial discourse.

Within each of these anchor points an institutionalized configuration of power exists. Within the institutional framework, for example, the configuration of power privileges representatives of mature financial systems over representatives of emerging market financial systems and, in particular, representatives of capital market-based financial systems rather than bank-based financial systems. One way of thinking about this configuration of power is in terms of the G-7 versus G-20, or the FSF versus the IMF. Within financial markets, to take another example, transnationally oriented financial institutions are privileged over nationally oriented financial institutions, and ideas sympathetic to capital mobility tend to hold greater sway than ideas sympathetic to greater degrees of domestic control over capital mobility. This configuration of power can take the form of contests between large integrated universal banks based in G-7 economies versus many banks based in emerging market economies who primarily lend to domestic businesses in their home economy. Transnationally oriented financial institutions are well organized and represented through groups like the G-30 and the Institute of International Finance, while domestically oriented financial institutions are poorly organized and represented.

It is within the global media and civil society, however, that the configuration of power has become institutionalized in a particularly open and fluid manner. For example, although many global outlets such as *The Economist*, the *Wall Street Journal* and *The Banker* publicize and support a classically liberal outlook on economic organization (privileging market fundamentalism, competition and limited government intervention), there are others which promote the desire to embed markets into broader social purposes such as a reformed national welfare state (*New York Times*, *The Guardian*, *Le Monde*). For every libertarian think-tank, such as the Cato Institute or the Institute for Economic Affairs, there is a much more social democratic or liberal internationalist outfit, such as the Institute of International Economics or the Fabian Society. Civil society organizations and the global media have also been used as outlets for experts who disagree with prevailing policy, serving in effect as a platform for the dissemination of positions highly critical of government initiatives. The contested configuration of power within these two anchors has enabled the actualization of the public sphere over the last ten years. We can see this actualization in the three principal features of the public sphere's operation.

First, there are clear modes of public reasoning that inform the dialogue concerning governance issues within the public sphere. Michel Camdessus (1999), for example, has spoken about the global financial system as a 'global public good' – that is, a good which is undiminished through consumption, non-excludable and for the benefit of all (cf. Kaul *et al.* 1999, ch.1; Wyplosz 1999). Such a claim can only be invoked within the context of a specific mode of public reasoning. In this case, legitimating the claim of a 'public good' invites the use of evidence over assertion; it acknowledges the different starting points of participants (for example, developed vs. emerging markets); and it values historical practice as a counterweight to ideological claim. In other words, one of the central operating features of the public sphere enables different understandings of the issues concerning global finance to be aired in public forums following acceptable rules of critical engagement. In a public sphere, dialogue follows established rules for engagement that determine how it can proceed.

We can see the way that modes of public reasoning operate to confirm the existence of a global financial public sphere in the example of the Highly Indebted Poor Countries Initiative (HIPC), initially launched by the IMF and World Bank in 1996. HIPC itself was initially resisted by the Fund and the Bank (and its main shareholders), but concerted pressure from a wide range of non-state actors (chiefly organizations we might characterize as belonging to civil society) and more sympathetic governments eventually prevailed in extracting a coordinated multilateral response to debt relief. When the initial take-up from highly indebted countries themselves proved lacklustre due to the dubious advantages of participating in the programme, however, a further movement under the banner of 'Jubilee 2000' formed to argue for the enhancement of the HIPC initiative. Many of Jubilee 2000's arguments were acknowledged and addressed in1999, when the HIPC initiative was refined to make it more attractive as a multilateral option for sustained debt reduction (Dawson and Bhatt 2002; Gariyo 2002; Durbin and Welch 2002). On this reading, the primary significance of Jubilee 2000 was in terms of its capacity to engage critically with multilateral dialogue and – by force of argument, reason and evidence – make an impact. It is unlikely that this train of events would have occurred without the benefit of a public sphere.

The second key operational feature of the global financial public sphere is a plurality of participants. One of the most striking departures of the contemporary period lies in the extension of the literate 'audience' for financial governance beyond the self-interested parties of government (chiefly central bankers and regulators) and the financial community. Despite the formidable levels of expertise usually demanded as the price of entry into financial discussions, there has been an explosion of participants in debates concerning financial governance. On the official governmental side, we have witnessed since 1999 a significant extension of participation into emerging markets in the form of the formation of the G-20 and Financial Stability Forum (Germain 2001). Both of these new forums include representation from emerging market economies on a scale without historical precedent with respect to the actual governance of finance.[8] When contrasted to the limited scale of representation that occurred during the last great exercise in recasting global financial governance between 1973 and 1977, which was technically limited to the Committee of Twenty (and, practically, to the G-10), the scale of representation today is substantially broader and deeper in scope.[9]

But it is the extension of the 'audience' of financial discourse into what many would identify as the organs of civil society (Scholte 2002) that is possibly the more significant development in terms of widening participation in the public sphere. This extension of the audience first became apparent in the industrialized economies from about 1995 on, when a number of critical organizations such as the Bretton Woods Project were formed. These were essentially loose, elite-level organizations that inserted into debates about the international financial architecture critical alternative points of view that in some ways picked up on a history of elite opposition to the financial arrangements preferred by what some have identified as the transnational capitalist class (van der Pijl 1984; 1998). These academically led organizations were eventually joined after 1997 by a set of southern-based NGOs and think-tanks responding to the devastation of the 1997/8 Asian financial crisis, such as 'Focus on the Global South' in the Philippines, 'Third World Network' in Malaysia and the 'Public Interest Research Center' in India. To the academic arguments invoked by northern-based organizations, these southern NGOs added an activist urgency born of dealing with the catastrophic post-Asian crisis decline in living standards. Finally, civil society organizations began to insert themselves dramatically into the consciousness of developed countries with the 'Battle of Seattle' and other pitched encounters at G-7 and IMF meetings (RIPE 2000; Millennium 2000). From a polite discussion among educated gentlemen, the debate over global financial governance had by the end of the twentieth century metamorphosed into a much more bruising, contested and public exercise.

Widening participation links to the third key operational feature of the public sphere –namely, a growing critical reciprocity within the context of the debate over financial governance. While pitched battles in Seattle, Gothenburg and Genoa may grab headlines, it is the ongoing debate over issues such as capital controls, benchmarks and codes, and prudential standards where the new critical reciprocity is most in evidence. Two examples will illustrate this new feature: the debate over capital account liberalization, and the debate over prudential standards.

Prior to the outbreak of the financial crisis in Thailand in 1997, the IMF was intent on refashioning its articles of agreement to include the pursuit of capital account liberalization as one of its core missions. With the collapse of fixed exchange rates across Asia, the reintroduction of capital controls in Malaysia and eventually defaults (and devaluations) in Russia and Argentina, the issue of capital account liberalization became neutralized. But crucially it was not that the IMF gave up pushing liberalization (e.g. Fischer 1997; cf. Eichengreen 1999; Stiglitz 2002). Rather, it was because the economic and political arguments against capital account liberalization persevered. Liberalization without the basic building blocks of adequate financial regulation was *argued* to be simply wrong, both analytically and practically (as the experience of Indonesia, among other countries, demonstrated). It may be correct to observe that long-standing arguments against the wisdom of pursuing capital account liberalization (and ultimately in favour of adopting staged and targeted capital controls) could not have triumphed on their own without the actual experience of the catastrophic post-1997 consequences so plainly in evidence. But at the same time, the actual existence of these consequences does not explain the about-face either, as the experiences of the early 1930s so amply demonstrates. It was the existence of a public sphere in which critical reciprocity of argument could occur that was a necessary element in the explanation.

Similarly, with respect to the debate over prudential supervisory standards, many have noted how this debate is occurring within a more inclusive decision-making framework and under better knowledge of the trade-offs between developed and emerging market economies (Germain 2001; Eichengreen 2002; Stiglitz 2002). The point here to note is that unlike previous debates over prudential standards – which were conducted under strict conditions and with limited participants – the current debate both extends the circle of practitioner-participants beyond the old elite and involves a wider cross-section of arguments, including those concerned with what might be termed cosmopolitan democracy (Porter 2001).[10] In fact, the very turn towards developing a global regulatory framework based on wide-spread participation and ownership of the resulting standards requires a public sphere for their development. Neither the debate over capital account liberalization or prudential regulatory standards (or sovereign debt rescheduling, or debt relief, etc.) could have been sustained without the existence and operation of a public sphere.

Governance and civil society

I have argued that under the conditions of the 'new global finance', financial governance is organized around a complex division of labour that requires a public sphere for its effective operation. Although the actual exercise of governance continues to depend upon the active direction of public authorities – the legacy of the public organization of authority consolidated during the Bretton Woods era remains formidable – this direction is now circumscribed by the need for consensus to be reached among those charged with exercising it (principally governments of developed economies and key emerging market economies) and the recipients of governance (financial institutions in all of their diversity).[11] The public sphere operates by enabling debate based upon accepted arguments and established evidence to occur, and by providing a degree of surveillance to occur which enforces the broad outlines of agreement. In the absence of a financial hegemon, and when the global financial system is marked by 'decentralized globalization', what Nancy Fraser (1996) has called a 'strong public' is indispensable for governance.

Civil society organizations, whether formal NGOs, broader civic organizations or more dispersed social movements (Walker 1994; O'Brien *et al.* 2000), have a significant role to play within the operation of the public sphere. Partly because of the increased 'publicness' of the new structure of financial governance, civil society organizations have access to debates that twenty years ago were closed to them. Part of this access comes through media coverage of organized protests, but part also comes through engaged debate between contending views which depend upon the weighing up of evidence for their resolution. Such forms of participation are examples of how the involvement of civil society in the public sphere (a) operates through existing the institutional framework (e.g. media), (b) helps to cement the connections within the public sphere (e.g. between the media and governmental institutions), and (c) challenges prevailing relationships (e.g. within the market). Furthermore, the impact of this kind of participation is replicated at each anchor point, where configurations of power spill into the public sphere and interact with each other.

This conception of the role of civil society organizations, although it accepts to a certain extent the representation of civil society as standing somewhere between the state (i.e. government) and market (cf. Kaviraj and Khilnani 2001; chapters by Sassoon and Gamble and Kenny in this volume), also refuses to see civil society (and civil society organizations) as independent actors in their own right, or as necessarily positive in their impact (cf. Amoore and Langley in this volume; Cox 1999; Scholte 2002). Rather it sees civil society as part of the interconnected milieu of governance, which has been enabled, in terms of agency, precisely because of the rise of the public sphere and its participation within it. It also stresses the republican insight that even though agents (public, private and civic) bring to the public sphere expectations, beliefs and preferences, it is their actual participation within the public sphere that helps to mould those expectations, beliefs and preferences in particular directions (Onuf 1999, ch. 10; Cochrane 2001).

This last insight provides a suitable departure point for evaluating the contribution of civil society to financial governance. For if preferences, beliefs and expectations can be influenced by participation in a public sphere, then the contribution of the civil society organizations to governance is threefold. First, in instrumental terms the public sphere makes possible a wider and deeper debate about particular policy directions, informed by a wider audience than in the past. This extension of the audience, insofar as it includes civil society organizations, helps to support the premium which the public sphere places on argument and evidence, even if ideological predispositions continue to be a robust part of the debate. In this way, civil society can be considered as an active force of deliberative agency within the context of financial governance, and one which helps to maintain its new level of *publicness*.

Second, in a broader vein, civil society's involvement with the structures of governance help to round out the terrain over which power is contested within the financial system. The particular way in which agency is organized within civil society provides at least some avenues of engagement with the key institutional frameworks of financial governance: civil society organizations engage with the IMF and/or WTO (O'Brien *et al.* 2000, ch. 5; Wilkinson, in this volume); grassroots activists confront the G7; and mass protesters challenge corrupt governments like Soeharto. All of these avenues of engagement are routed through the public sphere, and from there feed into other constituent parts of the governance structure. In this sense, the contribution of civil society to global financial governance is to further broaden the decision-making structure along the lines that reinforce the broadening out of the financial architecture as outlined in Figure 11.1.

Finally, civil society's deeper engagement with the emerging global architecture of finance suggests that the limited degree of accountability afforded by the architecture to both public and private authority can be enhanced. To be precise, by remaining engaged with those involved in formulating the structure of incentives associated with guiding global finance, civil society organizations force public authorities to justify their actions and reasoning in a language which is not just technocratic but also political. Public authorities must either make a technocratic language – such as that used to discuss prudential standards – understandable to the broader public, or they must introduce into technocratic discussions clear political priorities that speak to basic political needs. For example, they must be able to explain the link between certain kinds of prudential standards, financial stability and general economic welfare. Civil society engagement, in other words, increases the political accountability of public authorities to their ultimate constituents – citizens, in the collective sense.

It is therefore accurate to label civil society participation in global financial governance as a sufficient condition for the continued operation of the current framework, but not a necessary condition of its continued viability. It is rather the combined ensemble of interactions which together provides the basis for the global financial public sphere to exist. In this sense, civil society rests alongside the organization of public authority, the operation of the market and the global reach of the media to provide a mechanism of decision-making suitable for an era of decentralized globalization. Governance under the 'new global finance' has itself assumed a more decentralized format.

Conclusion: global capitalism, the public sphere and civil society

It would be too much to claim that civil society now plays a determining role in global financial governance, or that civil society organizations on their own make the actual processes of governance more effective and legitimate. What is acceptable to claim, however, is that a public sphere has emerged with respect to global finance, and that civic organizations and indeed various agents within civil society have played a not insignificant role in this achievement. It is also worthwhile acknowledging that this achievement is itself a novel development, and to ask whether it will persist. In other words, how firmly anchored is the global financial public sphere, and what is its likely future relationship to financial governance?

Two developments could indeed derail the consolidation of the public sphere. First, global financial markets could themselves once again become highly centralized, thus enabling governance to emanate in large part from the accumulation of multiple decisions made by financial institutions. Financial governance, in this sense, would become in effect the by-product of market decisions, as occurred under the nineteenth-century gold standard. Private authority would substitute for public authority.

Is this likely to happen? On present trends this is most unlikely to occur. With the continued development of global financial markets (in bonds, equities, foreign exchange, derivatives, futures, etc.) anchored in different financial centres, the centralization of the financial system under the direction of one set of financial institutions is remote. Yet this is exactly what would be required for an effective form of governance to emerge from private authorities. Decentralized globalization is going to be the key structural feature of the 'new global finance' for some time to come, with the concomitant requirement for a public sphere.

Second, if the US were to regain its post-1945 position as a genuine financial hegemon, de facto financial governance could once again proceed without recourse to a public sphere. Such governance would not require as wide a consensus on rules, standards and benchmarks as is now demanded, simply because the overweening power of the US to set the rules, produce the standards and enforce the benchmarks would be re-established. This however is unlikely to occur, simply because the material basis upon which American hegemony was constructed after 1945 is unlikely ever to be refashioned again. One caveat to this is provided by those scholars who argue that a reconstructed transnational neo-liberal hegemony can be seen to be emerging (Overbeek 1993; van der Pijl 1998; Gill 2003). Such a refashioned hegemony, however, will still require a public sphere for its realization, principally because of the way that neo-liberalism as a discourse works to instantiate a particular understanding of identity and citizenship. In short, where new forms of hegemony are dependent upon a reconfigured sense of the individual and collective self, the public sphere becomes one of the crucial ideational battlegrounds over which these identities are contested (Villa 1992). The global financial public sphere is most likely to remain firmly anchored to the broader structure of governance into the indefinite future.

The debates surrounding the idea of the public sphere, however, are themselves premised on the continued vitality of global capitalism as the background canvas over which the thematic concerns of governance are played out. As much as proponents of the public sphere might contend, the public sphere in effect relies on the dispersion of formal power that capitalism promotes in its liberal and competitive phase. Where capitalism operates to create and distribute wealth according to comparative (and even competitive) advantage, enabling development to spread and inhibiting highly unequal concentrations of wealth to form, governance will rely on broad participation and a relatively egalitarian process of consensus formation. In other words, we cannot completely separate the exercise and provision of governance from the broader social processes which underpin the creation and allocation of wealth within the global economy. The question this poses then is one of the transformative capacity of the public sphere.

And here the jury is out. On one hand, the public sphere makes possible the participation of a new range of agents in a variety of ways and through mechanisms which many did not have access to previously (civil society via the media, for example). At the same time, participation in the public sphere disciplines agents in a way which may well blunt their more radical (and transformative) motivations (Hardt and Negri 2000). The public sphere is a mediated space, after all, which is shot through with the configurations of power that originate in the constituent institutional arrangements of the global political economy such as governments, markets, media, etc. (cf. Amoore and Langley in this volume). It is not a transformative space in and of itself; rather, it should be viewed as an enabling environment that can be used in particular ways by agents motivated to protect, preserve or unseat established privileges. Mapping the global financial public sphere and the engagement within it of civil society actors and others only provides us with a first cut at some of the mechanisms of governance in the twenty-first century. But at least it directs attention to the actual way in which the ensemble of governance operates today, thereby establishing the limits of the possible in terms of financial governance.

Notes

1 I would like to thank Mike Kenny and Geoffrey Underhill for helpful comments on an earlier draft. The arguments of this chapter have also been improved by comments received at previous presentations to the University of Amsterdam Department of Political Science, the 'Approaches to Global Finance' workshop at the University of Warwick, and the 2002 annual conference of the British International Studies Association. Any remaining errors are mine. Finally, I would like to acknowledge the support of the Nuffield Foundation, the British Academy, the University of Wales (Aberystwyth) and the ESRC for funding the larger research project upon which this chapter draws.

2 See Cohen (1996), Andrews and Willetts (1997), Dombrowski (1998), Cerny (1998), Lukuaskas (1999) and Kirshner (2000) for overviews of recent literature on this subject.

3 I take up later the issue of non-official participation in these debates by civil society organizations.

4 I provide a fuller account of these different functions in Germain (2001).

5 One might argue that the formation of the FSF itself, and possibly the G-20, were also the products of such a consensual approach, although they also met different national interests as well.

6 There are many other foundational elements central to the consolidation and operation of a 'public sphere', such as equality among participants, non-use of force, indefinite audiences, etc. For purposes of space I will touch on these only as required for the argument (for extended discussions, see Bohman 1999; Fraser 1996; Cochrane 2001).

7 I am for the moment ignoring the republican and pragmatic formulations of the public sphere provided by Hannah Arendt and John Dewey (see Cochrane 2001; Hohendahl 1996; Benhabib 1996a).

8 There have been precedents for widespread representation of less-developed countries in conferences whose remit included financial governance (principally the 1944 Bretton Woods Conference and the 1922 Genoa Conference), but what is novel today is that such representation extends to the fashioning of the day-to-day rule-making which is the hallmark of governance activities.

9 Crockett (1977) provides an overview of the reform efforts of the mid-1970s, while Mayobre (1999) details the contribution of developing countries to the governance of the global financial system since 1972.

10 It must be stressed that as Porter (2001) argues, transnational interests and the arguments they use in favour of developed country standards (for example as with the Basle II process of capital adequacy ratios) remain extremely powerful. Nevertheless, the very fact that other arguments are in play and indeed being actively considered should reinforce the broader claim that a public sphere in which critical reciprocity among participants exists helps to explain the development of recent prudential supervisory standards, and the acceptance of their necessarily uneven application across emerging markets and developed economies.

11 But see the countervailing arguments provided by those who argue that the role of 'private authority' in the global economy is growing (e.g, Strange 1996; Gill 1995; Cutler, Haufler and Porter 1999; Hall and Biersteker 2001).

12 Understanding global civil society

Contestation, citizenship, governance

Randall Germain and Michael Kenny

Global civil society and world order

The preceding chapters suggest the conceptual and practical significance of thinking about an emergent global civil society as part of our understanding of world order in the contemporary period. In this concluding chapter, rather than retrace the contribution of each author, we draw together some of the arguments contained within their chapters and, on this basis, delineate an agenda for further inquiry into the character and implications of the idea of global civil society.

Two distinctive thematic concerns arise out of the contributions to this volume. The first is how to configure the relationship between the multiple meanings of a 'global' civil society with previously established moral and political arguments about a civil society bounded by the territorial state. This theme directs our attention to the problematic ways in which global civil society relates to the territorial state, and especially to the tension in play between actually existing political authority and the new transnational or global terrain of social relations. This tension demands that we adjust some of the more traditional ethical claims arising out of civil society to a new milieu.

Here we must acknowledge that, although the concept of civil society has emerged as a broadly liberal ideal within Western modernity, it also possesses classical roots (as Hutchings and Onuf in this volume remind us). This has allowed different theoretical traditions to lay claim to the mantle of civil society since its inception, and has enabled theorists to harness it to a variety of political and ethical projects. Several of the authors in this volume, for example, stress the ideological complexities surrounding contemporary invocations of a globalized version of civil society (e.g. Gamble and Kenny, and Sassoon), while others stress the different historical traditions out of which claims on behalf of civil society have emerged (e.g. Onuf, Frost, Dower, and Hutchings).

One important shared emphasis which arises out of these discussions is therefore that a 'progressive' political agenda needs to be actively constructed in relation to a globalizing civil society, rather than being seen as immanent within its unfolding. This idea is present too in philosophical debates about the necessary and sufficient conditions of an emergent form of global citizenship, and in the idea that transnational public spheres are expanding and altering the character of civic participation. By thinking about the possibilities represented by an emergent and globalizing form of civil society, we may be able to fashion arguments and practices that advance citizenship beyond the narrow confines of national boundaries (Murphy 1994; Held 1995; Linklater 1998).

But the ethical potential of global civil society resonates beyond arguments for a reconfigured form of citizenship or a globally constituted public sphere. If Gamble and Kenny are right, the narratives that underpin different visions of global civil society represent a new phase in the ideological struggle that has taken an unforeseen turn in the wake of the terrorist attacks of 11 September 2001. One of the central contests in contemporary geopolitical life therefore stems from tensions between the civic, ideological and cultural goals that individuals and groups pursue on a transnational basis, and the many attempts by states to deal with and control the identities and aspirations that these express.

A second thematic concern linking the contributions to this volume involves the claim that the relationships and networks which comprise global civil society must themselves be understood as instantiated within broader relations of power. All of the essays in this volume support a pronounced scepticism towards the characterization of global civil society as an autonomous domain free of the usual constraints associated with political and economic life. As Stevenson notes, the way in which civil society is represented through the media immediately privileges certain social actors by lending to them an opinion-forming capacity and rendering as 'others' cultures and agents upon whom the gaze of the metropolitan West falls. Or, as Amoore and Langley suggest, the broader governmentality of civil society itself is a 'project' for those elites supportive of a global economy organized along neo-liberal lines. The idea of 'governmentality' invites us to consider more critically who are the winners and losers in the systems of globalized governance currently under construction – a point illustrated by the case studies examined by Germain and Wilkinson. These arguments chime with claims central to a recent literature that explores how the capacity to govern rests not only on the formal institutional ability to exercise direct power over outcomes, but also on how the different ways in which the underlying terrain of discussion and debate is itself shaped (Cutler, Haufler and Porter 1999; Hall and Biersteker 2002).

At the same time, several of the contributors to this volume suggest that a focus upon the dynamics and processes through which power is produced and reproduced within global civil society must also include an integral role for the ideational, normative and visionary aspects of social agency. Thinking about a transnational social order encourages an appreciation of the motivational dynamics that drive individual and collective actors to identify with and promote specific kinds of social arrangements and identity. Such a concern provides a useful corrective to the tendency in contemporary International Relations (IR) and International Political Economy (IPE) scholarship to elevate material over ideational and cultural dynamics. By examining the diverse normative and cultural impulses that give rise to specific civil society formations in the contemporary period, we are better positioned to understand how claims to power can either establish or reinforce the privileges of existing social relations, or undermine and transform them. Rather than following the established models used by scholars in the fields of IR and IPE, the contributors to this volume all share a commitment to delineating and interpreting the ideational and normative contours of social and political struggle. They highlight the importance of conflicting conceptions of civil society to contending visions of world order, as well as rival accounts of the moral and political relationship between individual citizen, nation-state and global institution. Social order, our contributors remind us, is not simply determined according to the calculus of material resources or formal entitlements. Within both national and international politics, it is crucially forged through the formation of ideas and mentalities and their instantiation in particular social and institutional relations.

Interpreting global civil society: three avenues of inquiry

Through their focus on the normative potential of civil society and its associated relations of power, the contributors to this volume suggest some distinctive lines of inquiry for the increasingly salient task of mapping and understanding global civil society. Below, we highlight three particularly important interpretative suggestions to arise from their contributions, all of which pertain to the general theme of how we might interlink our understanding of global civil society with interpretations of world order. These consist of: (1) an examination of the character of the balance between consent and coercion that arises from the social relations of a globalizing civil society; (2) a consideration of the implications for transnational social mobilization made possible by a new language of citizenship; and (3) an exploration of the interrelations between global society and the networks of globalized governance. Underlying each of these suggestions is the notion that the ethical potential of global civil society is contingent upon an open-ended set of political struggles. Within the latter, the character and constitution of authority in global political life are especially important. These lines of inquiry all lead to an enhanced sensitivity to the fluidity associated with transnational and/or globalized forms of social relations – an idea invoked, for instance, through Frost's discussion of 'open practices', or the 'politics of movement' identified by Amoore and Langley. These three lines of inquiry are sketched below.

Coercion and consent

In the wake of the destruction of the World Trade Center in New York on 11 September 2001 and the subsequent US-led interventions in Afghanistan and Iraq, the hopes enunciated by Western international political analysts for a liberal order founded upon the legitimacy of international law and the United Nations, have receded. Instead, the patchy, uneven and conflictual terrain of international society that has emerged at the beginning of the twenty-first century is threatened by an unstable amalgam of fundamentalist movements, 'rogue' states, terrorist groups and a chasm in power and voice between the powerful and powerless. Until recently, Western states were arguably connected to each other through common strategic interests, shared enemies, and a unified civilizational heritage. Today, in the aftermath of the determination of the US to effect regime change in Afghanistan and Iraq, the stable patterns these linkages once provided have been weakened. The main counter-trend to this centripetal reconfiguration of international affairs arises from the power of American-led globalization. Yet even in relation to the global economy, national and regional trajectories are still apparent, not least due to the uncertainties generated for multilateral rule-based systems (such as trade and finance) by unilateral, American-led initiatives (see Wilkinson in this volume).

The analysis of 'world order' in this geopolitical situation necessitates looking beyond the intellectual matrices that have guided much scholarly enquiry into international politics. It means attending to the contested visions advanced by various socio-political forces and delineating the mechanisms through which consent for emergent transnational governance networks and social relations is secured. Understanding the legitimization of these arrangements necessitates a consideration not just of transnational forms of authority, but also of the continuing significance of publicly constituted authorities, norms and institutions – be these national, regional or transnational in kind. As Hutchings points out in her chapter in this volume, it is important to perceive how the coercion exercised by the state makes possible, and supports, the consensual attributes of civil society.

In order to unpack the social and moral dynamics shaping contestation, coercion and consent within global civil society, analysts need to look beyond an immediate assessment of states' interests and the usual indicators of power (typically calibrated in either 'hard' or 'soft' modalities). This implies attention to the role of particular visions of world order, and their political articulation and institutional embodiment. We need to consider not only *what* states do to fashion an order amenable to their interests, but *how* their actions reflect and perpetuate particular conceptions of order and justice. Equally, we should examine the various cultural and political obstacles standing in the way of contending visions of world order.

In this volume, Dower, Hutchings, Onuf and Frost argue in different ways for a more rigorous ethical conceptualization of the individual as citizen, civilian, or rights-bearer in the global political community. It may be worthwhile supplementing this lexicon with other forms of collective subjectivity defined by, for instance, relations of clan, culture and class. By redeploying the insights of various political traditions into the organization of consent within civil society, we can understand more deeply the moral deficiencies of current political and social arrangements and develop a sense of the various possible trajectories that social developments might pursue.

Mobilization and citizenship

However coercion and consent are organized in a social formation, they are achieved in relation to the contingencies and complexities of the exercise of individual human agency. As several of the contributors to this volume acknowledge, in the Western political tradition this capacity is crucially shaped by the vernacular of citizenship. This language helps define the political identities that embolden individual actors in democratic states to exercise agency in a meaningful way. It also helps to frame the character of their political and ethical relations with their fellows.

While citizenship constitutes a central problematic in Western political thought, it sits awkwardly with the normative preferences and assumptions of scholars in the fields of IR and IPE. The latter tend to regard the foregrounding of politico-ethical discourse as a mistaken privileging of morality and individual agency on a terrain where states, social interests or socio-economic processes can be assumed to prevail. One of the main contributions of the arguments presented in this volume, we suggest, is to challenge the exclusion of individual agency and ethical norms from conventional understandings of the modalities of world order.

An assessment of the shifting loci of citizenship – both as a meaningful identity and as a set of formal entitlements – ought to be central to the project of understanding how world order is maintained and challenged in the current period. The increasingly pervasive language of human rights and the dissemination of an ethical discourse about transnational citizenship are, as Onuf and Frost suggest, intricately linked with the generation of new kinds of socio-political subjectivity in global politics. And within an emergent institutional environment that is organized, in part, in response to such normative claims, this point is even more applicable. Far from being on the periphery of structurally determined patterns of agency and activity, the notion of 'citizenship' and 'the citizen' are in important ways key driving forces in global political society. Interrogating the civic potentiality and ethical underpinnings of a globalizing civil society represents an important step towards this wider understanding. It enables us to consider the interrelation between the spread of ethical claims in international life about rights and citizenship, and various forms of collective struggle over resources and values. Although social mobilization is often still orientated towards the state, it is increasingly likely to aim beyond any single national space or public authority.

The diffusion of these kinds of mobilization should not be understood as entirely spontaneous or organic in character, as some of the dominant 'liberal' interpretations of civil society suggest (Kenny 2003). They are affected and mediated by several factors: the prior existence of legal rights and obligations within particular nation-states (such as the freedom to associate); the technological capacities that enable broad-based mobilization to occur, and which are in turn related to the flows of wealth and power in the global economy; and the spillage of social tensions, cultural conflicts and religious differences beyond the domain of the nation-state (Keane 2001b). Democratic theorists of global civil society should regard such inequities and disparities of opportunity as integral, not incidental, to its character. Otherwise, a highly romantic and misleading picture emerges, where global civil society as the source of a heroic alternative to the new global empire, as for example in the form of *biopower* (Hardt and Negri 2000)), takes hold – a stance that different contributors to this volume question. The effective operation of the global *capitalist* economy necessarily privileges powerful, elite groups with disproportionate access to fungible resources such as capital, and these groups are active in powerful ways within the social relations that comprise civil society.

By imagining the growth of the idea of a transnational citizenship as a wellspring for transnational forms of social mobilization, some commentators are able to invest in the achievement of a global civil society the hope of a new kind of progressive alternative to neo-liberal globalization (Dunn 2002). Some intellectual voices cast this potentiality in terms of a widely shared 'subaltern' humanism, and see in it a rebellion against the legalistic projects favoured by Western liberals (Falk 1995b; Baker 2002). Various contributions to this volume, however, point towards a rather different kind of politico-ethical understanding. At the heart of this perspective is the notion of establishing a more egalitarian conception of social responsibilities and a commitment to the dissemination and protection of a more substantive set of human rights than Western cosmopolitanism tends to stress. Grappling with the implications of an emergent global civil society, we suggest, may therefore help those committed to the pursuit of such values as justice and emancipation. Interestingly, this focus allows for the normative critique of familiar liberal conceptions of citizenship and social justice, as much as it enables their spread (as both Frost and Dower indicate in this volume). While the contributors to this book tend to stress the contingent moral character of global civil society, all remain committed to the possibility of a progressive harvesting of its ethical and political potential.

Governance, power and discipline

Understanding the contours of world order today involves looking beyond the 'objective', material power of states and the disciplinary injunctions of the global economy. It requires, in both analytical and normative terms, a simultaneous appreciation of the 'pull' of values and normative claims as well as the 'push' of material interests and resources. It necessitates, too, a sensitivity to path-dependency as well as the possibility of newly evolving socio-political trajectories. And, we maintain, it needs analyses that permit an appreciation of the role of individual agency within broader social and institutional contexts. These different commitments suggest that the problematic of world order needs to be approached with a sensitivity to the fluid and changing social topography on which it rests.

Several contributions to this volume remind us that states and inter-state organizations have at times consciously sought to enable the formation of a particular form of transnational civil society. These processes are important and unduly neglected in scholarly research. There are of course many possible advantages for public authorities in generating a broadly compliant, de-politicized and supportive civil society, the legitimacy of which spans particular national contexts (Chandhoke 2002). Exactly this kind of development is invoked and legitimated by some of the projects that promote forms of global governance.

The chapters by Wilkinson and Amoore and Langley, for example, observe the opportunity to enhance international political legitimacy by tieing 'respectable' parts of civil society into transnational networks shaped in the first instance by the prevailing interests of international institutions in the existing political order. For these authors it is this which explains the enthusiasm of states and global institutions for these networks. The latter are thus able to represent themselves as responsive and accountable, all the while limiting external access to, and influence upon, their policies and programmes. The extent to which this form of civil society inclusion can filter out alternative political voices, and thereby legitimate the social and political purpose of these institutions, should be central questions for researchers, for they bear directly on the broader question of the emerging character and possibilities of a globalizing form of civil society.

This governance-led 'making' of civil society also demands that we look beyond the state to understand how social discipline and authority are instantiated within the institutions that fashion world order. When we turn to consider the deployment and meanings of such values as democracy, security and liberty in a globalizing context, how much room is there to advance alternatives to the prevalent liberal and conservative understandings of these norms as propagated by the central organs of global order? The groups and organizations that have moved into the interstices between national and transnational civil society, particularly those based in the geopolitical orbit of the Northern hemisphere, play an important role as carriers of these values. These groups might be viewed as sources of legitimation in zones where, for instance, American power is regarded suspiciously (Macdonald 1997). Far from always being a progressive and emancipatory force, civil society can also be viewed as an integral component in the overall global power structure.

A realistic appraisal of these processes is vital, we suggest, to a rounded interpretation of the moral and social character of the emerging transnational social order. Yet the ethical significance of global civil society is not exhausted by the imprint that relations of power and domination leave upon it. Among the different promises and sources of hope encoded in its development is the possibility of a variegated and robust set of public spheres. Various social forces – from above and below – have combined to bring into being incipient forums and spaces that do not belong in any straightforward way to national authorities or corporate elites. If these developments are accorded constitutional and political protection from the overbearing powers of commerce, the possibility of establishing a domain wherein contending visions of world order and different moral standpoints are allowed to sustain a broad, on-going international dialogue, becomes an important and realistic prospect (Bellamy 1995; Castiglione 1995).

Summary

This collection represents an attempt to respond to the moral, political and social concerns which a focus on the idea of global civil society presents. The emphasis here on relatively novel social and cultural phenomena should not be taken to lend weight to the idea that a new 'stage' in the unfolding of the historical process has been reached, or that we need to junk the intellectual and political baggage of the past. Rather, we and the contributors to this volume maintain that various political traditions have much to offer to our understanding of these developments, and that the intellectual anchorage they provide may help us avoid the hype, gloom and exaggerated hopes that have tended to inform recent Western analyses of global civil society.

Such is the fluidity and open-ended political character of some of the developments considered in this volume that it is vital that analysts of international and global politics retain a wide-angled interpretative approach. This should involve a commitment to delineating both the material *and* ideational processes through which political and economic elites are struggling to bring about world order, as well as the many ways in which resistance to these attempts are being formulated. For such an interpretative sensibility to take hold, a less defensive and exclusive self-understanding is overdue for practitioners in the fields of International Relations, International Political Economy and normative Political Theory. One overriding intellectual implication of engaging with the idea and ideal of global civil society is to reveal the narrowness and artificiality of the separation of distinctive lines of inquiry in these respective but related sub-fields. Some will object to the lack of parsimony such a move heralds in terms of possible explanations of global political phenomena. Yet such a response betrays an approach to international politics that fails to grasp that social fluidity, political uncertainty and ideological contestation are constitutive of the character of world order, rather than extraneous factors to it. The different essays in this volume offer fertile indications, we believe, of how analyses of global civil society might proceed, and point to some of the moral possibilities which this domain and the social relations it harbours may herald.

References

Adam, Barbara (1997) 'Re-vision: the centrality of time for an ecological social science perspective', in Scott Lash, Bronislaw Szersynski and Brian Wynne (eds) *Risk, Environment and Modernity*, London: Sage.

Ades, Dawn, Benton, Tim, Elliott, David and Whyte, Iain Boyd (1995) *Art and Power, Europe under the Dictators (1930–1945)*, London: Hayward Gallery.

Aiken, William and LaFollette, Hugh (eds) (1996) *World Hunger and Morality*, Englewood Cliffs: Prentice Hall.

Albright, Madeleine K. (2000) *Focus on the Issues, Strengthening Civil Society and the Rule of Law, Excerpts of Testimony, Speeches and Remarks by US Secretary of State Madeleine K. Albright*, Washington, DC.

Albrow, Martin (1996) *The Global Age: State and Society Beyond Modernity*, Cambridge: Polity Press.

Alexander, Jeffrey C. (1997) 'The Paradoxes of Civil Society', *International Sociology* 12(2): 115–33.

Alexander, Jeffrey C. and Jacobs, Ronald N. (1998) 'Mass communication, ritual and civil society', in Tamar Liebes and James Curran (eds) *Media, Ritual and Identity*, London: Routledge.

Alexandrowicz, Charles H. (1958) 'The Theory of Recognition *in Fieri*', *British Year Book of International Law* 34: 176–98.

Anderson, Benedict (1983) *Imagined Communities: Reflections on the Origin and Spread of Nationalism*, London: Verso.

Anderson, Bridget (2000) *Doing the Dirty Work: The Global Politics of Domestic Labour*, London: Zed Books.

Anderson, Perry (2002a) 'Internationalism: A Breviary', *New Left Review* 14: 5–25.

—— (2002b) 'Internationalism: Metamorphoses of a Meaning', Stanford S. Elberg Lecture in International Studies: Institute of International Studies, University of California, Berkeley at http://globetrotter.berkeley.edu/Elberg/Anderson/anderson-elb1.html.

Andrews, David and Willett, Thomas (1997) 'Financial interdependence and the state: international monetary relations at century's end', *International Organization* 51(3): 479–511.

Anheier, Helmut, Glasius, Marlies and Kaldor, Mary (2001) 'Introducing global civil society', in Helmut Anheier, Marlies Glasius and Mary Kaldor (eds) *Global Civil Society 2001*, Oxford: Oxford University Press.

Appadurai, Arjun (2001) 'Grassroots globalization and the research imagination', in Arjun Appadurai (ed.) *Globalization*, Durham, NC: Duke University Press.

Archibugi, Danielle (1995) 'From the UN to cosmopolitan democracy', in Danielle Archibugi and David Held (eds) *Cosmopolitan Democracy: An Agenda for a New World Order*, Cambridge: Polity Press.

Archibugi, Danielle and Held, David (eds) (1995) *Cosmopolitan Democracy: An Agenda for a New World Order*, Cambridge: Polity Press.

Axtmann, Roland (2002) 'What's wrong with cosmopolitan democracy?', in Nigel Dower and John Williams (eds) *Global Citizenship: A Critical Reader*, Edinburgh: Edinburgh University Press.

Baker, Gideon (1999) 'The taming of the idea of civil society', *Democratization*, 6(3): 1–29.

—— (2002) 'Problems in the theorisation of global civil society', *Political Studies* 50(5): 928–43.

Barber, Benjamin R. (1996) *Jihad vs. McWorld: How Globalism and Tribalism Are Reshaping the World*, New York: Ballantine.

—— (1998) *A Place for US: How to Make Civil Society and Democracy Strong*, New York: Hill and Wang.

Baudrillard, Jean (1994) *The Illusion of the End*, Cambridge: Polity Press.

Beitz, Charles R. (1979) *Political Theory and International Relations*, Princeton, NJ: Princeton University Press.

Bell, Daniel A. (2000) *East Meets West: Human Rights and Democracy in Asia*, Princeton, NJ: Princeton University Press.

Bellah, R. (1996) *Habits of the Heart: Individualism and Commitment in American Life*, Berkeley, CA: University of California Press.

Bellamy, Richard (1995) 'The political form of the constitution: the separation of powers, rights, and representative democracy', *Political Studies* 44(3): 436–56.

Benhabib, Seyla (1996a) 'Models of public space: Hannah Arendt, the liberal tradition, and Jürgen Habermas', in Craig Calhoun (ed.) *Habermas and the Public Sphere*, Cambridge: MIT Press.

—— (ed.) (1996b) *Democracy and Difference: Contesting the Boundaries of the Political*, Princeton, NJ: Princeton University Press.

Bevir, Mark (2000) *The Logic of the History of Ideas*, Cambridge: Cambridge University Press.

Bhabha, Homi K. (1992) *The Location of Culture*, London: Routledge.

Bleiker, Roland (2000) *Popular Dissent, Human Agency and Global Politics*, Cambridge: Cambridge University Press.

Bobbio, Norberto (1979) 'Gramsci and the conception of civil society', in Chantal Mouffe (ed.) *Gramsci and Marxist Theory*, London: Routledge.

Bohman, James (1998) 'The globalization of the public sphere', *Philosophy and Social Criticism* 24(2/3): 199–216.

—— (1999) 'Citizenship and norms of publicity: wide public reasoning in cosmopolitan societies', *Political Theory* 27(2): 176–202.

—— (2001) 'Cosmopolitan republicanism: citizenship, freedom and global political authority', *The Monist* 84(1): 3–21.

Bourdieu, Pierre (1996) *On Television*, New York: New Press.

Braudel, Fernand (1979/1982) *Civilization and Capitalism, 15th to 18th Centuries, Volume2: The Wheels of Commerce*, trans. Sian Reynolds, London: Collins/Fontana.

Brouwer, Gordon de (2002) 'The IMF and East Asia: a changing regional financial architecture', unpublished paper.

Brown, Chris (1992) *International Relations Theory: New Normative Approaches*, New York: Harvester and Wheatsheaf.

—— (2001) 'Border and Identity in International Political Theory', in Albert Mathias, David Jacobson and Yosef Lapid (eds) *Identities, Borders, Orders: Rethinking International Relations Theory*, Minneapolis: University of Minnesota Press.

Bull, Hedley (1977) *The Anarchical Society: A Study of Order in World Politics*, New York: Columbia University Press.

Calhoun, Craig (ed.) (1996) *Habermas and the Public Sphere*, Cambridge, MA: MIT Press.

Callahan, David (1999) 'What is "global civil society"?', *Civnet* (3)1.

Camdessus, Michel (1999) 'International financial and monetary stability: a global public good?' remarks to the IMF conference 'Key Issues in Reform of the International Monetary and Financial System', Washington, 28 May 1999: http://www.imf.org/external/np/speeches/(1999)/(0528)99.html.

Camilleri, Joseph A. and Falk, Jim (1992) *The End of Sovereignty? The politics of a Shrinking and Fragmenting World*, Aldershot: Edward Elgar.

Campbell, David (1996) 'Political prosaics, transversal politics, and the anarchical world', in Michael J. Shapiro and H.R. Alker (eds) *Challenging Boundaries: Global Flows, Territorial Identities*, Minneapolis: University of Minnesota Press.

Caney, Simon (2001) 'International distributive justice', *Political Studies* 49(5): 974–97.

Carter, April (2001) *The Political Theory of Global Citizenship*, London: Routledge.

—— (2002) 'Associative democracy', in April Carter and Geoffrey Stokes (eds) *Democratic Theory Today*, Cambridge: Polity.

Carter, April and Stokes, Geoffrey (2002) *Democratic Theory Today*, Cambridge: Polity.

Castells, Manuel (1997) *The Power of Identity; The Information Age: Economy, Society and Culture*, Vol. 2, Oxford: Blackwell.

Castiglione, D. (1995) 'The political theory of the constitution', *Political Studies* 44 (3): 417–35.

Cerny, Philip (1998) 'Politicising international finance', *Millennium*, 27(2): 353–61.

—— (2000) 'Restructuring the political arena; globalization and the paradoxes of the competition state', in Randall D. Germain (ed.) *Globalization and Its Critics: Perspectives From Political Economy*, Basingstoke: Palgrave.

Chandhoke, Neera (2001) 'The "civil"and the "political", in civil society', *Democratization* 8(2): 1–24.

—— (2002) 'The limits of global civil society', in Marlies Glasius, Mary Kaldor and Helmut Anheir (eds) *Global Civil Society 2002*, Oxford: Oxford University Press

Chang, Grace (2000) *Disposable Domestics: Immigrant Women Workers in the Global Economy*, Cambridge, MA: South End Press.

Charvet, John (1996) 'What is nationality, and is there a moral right to national self-determination', in Simon Caney, David George and Peter Jones (eds) *National Rights, International Obligations*, Boulder: Westview Press.

Cheru, Fantu (1997) 'The silent revolution and the weapons of the weak: transformation and innovation from below', in Stephen Gill and J. Mittelman (eds) *Innovation and Transformation in International Studies*, Cambridge: Cambridge University Press.

Clark, Ian (2001) *The Post Cold War Order*, Oxford: Oxford University Press.

Cochran, Molly (2001) 'Conceptualizing international public spheres', paper delivered to annual conference of International Studies Association, Chicago (USA).

Cohen, Benjamin (1996) 'Phoenix risen: the resurrection of global finance', *World Politics* 48(1): 268–96.

Cohen, Jean L. (1997) 'A bid for hegemony: the contemporary American discourse', paper presented to 'Gramsci and the Twentieth Century' conference, 15–18 April, Cagliari.

Cohen, Jean L. and Arato, Anthony (1992) *Civil Society and Political Theory*, Cambridge, MA: MIT Press.

Cohen, Joshua (ed.) (1996a) *For Love of Country: Debating the Limits of Patriotism*, Boston: Beacon Books.

—— (1996b) 'Procedure and substance in deliberative democracy', in Benhabib, S. (ed.) *Democracy and Difference: Contesting the Boundaries of the Political*, Princeton, NJ: Princeton University Press.

Cohen, Joshua and Rogers, Joel *et al.* (1995) *Associations and Democracy*, London: Verso.

Cohen, L. Jonathan (1954) *The Principles of World Citizenship*, Oxford: Blackwell.

Cohen, Stanley (2001) *States of Denial: Knowing about Atrocities and Suffering*, Cambridge: Polity Press.

Colás, Alejandro (2001) 'The promises of international civil society: global governance, cosmopolitan democracy and the end of sovereignty?' at www.theglobalsite.ac.uk.

Commission on Global Governance (1995) *Our Global Neighbourhood*, New York: Oxford University Press.

Connolly, William (1995) *The Ethos of Pluralization*, Minneapolis: University of Minnesota Press.

Cox, Robert W. (1987) *Production, Power and World Order: Social Forces and the Making of History*, New York: Columbia University Press.

—— (2002) *The Political Economy of a Plural World*, London: Routledge.

Cox, Robert W. with Sinclair, Timothy J. (1996) *Approaches to World Order*, Cambridge: Cambridge University Press.

—— (1999) 'Civil society at the turn of the millennium: prospects for an alternative world order', *Review of International Studies* 25(1): 3–28.

Crocker, D.A. (1998) *Transitional Justice and International Civil Society*, Working Paper No. 13, University Park, MD: National Commission on Civic Renewal.

Crockett, Andrew (1977) *International Money: Issues and Analysis*, New York: Academic Press.

Curran, James and Park, Myung-Jin (2000) 'Beyond globalisation theory', in James Curran and Myung-Jin Park (eds) *De-Westernising Media Studies*, London: Routledge.

Cutler, Claire, Haufler, Virginia and Porter, Tony (eds) (1999) *Private Authority and International Affairs*, Albany: SUNY Press.

Dahlgren, Peter (1998) 'Enhancing the Civic Ideal in Television Journalism', in Kees Brants, Joke Hermes and Liesbet van Zoonen (eds) *The Media in Question: Popular Cultures and Public Interests*, London: Sage.

Dawson, Thomas and Bhatt, Gita (2002) 'The IMF and civil society: striking a balance', in Jan Art Scholte and Albrecht Schnabel (eds) *Civil Society and Global Finance*, London: Routledge.

De Grazia, Victoria (1992) *How Fascism Ruled Women: Italy (1922–1945)*, Berkeley: University of California Press.

De Oliveira, M.D. (1995) 'The case for global civil society', *National Civic Review*, Spring 1995, pp. 130–2.

Devereux, E. (1996) 'Good causes, God's poor and telethon television', *Media, Culture and Society* 18: 47–68.

Dillon, Michael (1995) 'Sovereignty and governmentality: from the problematics of the "New World Order" to the ethical problematic of the world order', *Alternatives* 20: 325–68.

Dombrowski, Peter (1998) 'Haute finance and high theory: recent scholarship on global financial relations', *Mershon International Studies Review* 42(1): 1–28.

Dower, Nigel (1998) *World Ethics: The New Agenda*, Edinburgh: Edinburgh University Press.

—— (2000) 'The idea of global citizenship: a sympathetic assessment', *Global Society* 14(4).

—— (2003) *An Introduction to Global Citizenship*, Edinburgh: Edinburgh University Press.

Dower, Nigel and Williams, John (eds) (2002) *Global Citizenship: A Critical Reader*, Edinburgh: Edinburgh University Press.

Drainville, André C. (1994) 'International political economy in the age of open Marxism', *Review of International Political Economy* 1(1): 105–32.

—— (1998) 'The fetishism of global civil society: global governance, transnational urbanism and sustainable capitalism in the world economy', in Michael P. Smith and Luis E. Guarnizo (eds) *Transnationalism from Below*, London: Transaction Publishers.

—— (2002) 'Quebec City (2001) and the making of transnational subjects', *Socialist Register* (2002): 15–42.

Drucker, Peter (1986) 'The changed world economy', *Foreign Affairs* 64(4): 768–91.

Duffield, Mark R. (2001) *Global Governance and the New Wars*, London: Zed Books.

Dunn, J. (2002) 'Indiscreet as war on terror' *The Times Higher Education Supplement* 22(3): 27.

Dunne, Tim and Wheeler, Nicholas (eds) (1999) *Human Rights in Global Politics*, Cambridge: Cambridge University Press.

Durbin, Andrea and Welch, Carol (2002) 'The environmental movement and global finance', in Jan Aart Scholte and Albrecht Schnabel (eds) *Civil Society and Global Finance*, London: Routledge.

Earth Charter (2002) http://earthcharter.org/.

Edwards, Michael (1999) *Future Positive*, London: Earthscan.

Edwards, Michael and Gaventa, John (2001) *Global Citizen Action*, London: Earthscan.

Ehrenberg, John (1999) *Civil Society: The Critical History of an Idea*, New York: New York University Press.

Eichengreen, Barry (1999) *Toward a New International Financial Architecture: A Practical Post-Asia Agenda*, Washington: Institute for International Economics.

—— (2002) *Financial Crises and What to do about Them*, Oxford: Oxford University Press.

Elliott, L. (1999) 'Unless WTO cleans up its act there will be more issues for the protesters to trade on' *The Guardian*, 6 December.

Elster, Jon (ed.) (1998) *Deliberative Democracy*, Cambridge: Cambridge University Press.

Ethical Consumer (2002) http://www.ethicalconsumer.org/.

Falk, Richard (1995a) *On Humane Governance: Toward a New Global Politics*, Cambridge: Polity Press.

—— (1995b) 'The world order between inter-state law and the law of humanity: the role of civil society institutions', in Danielle Archibugi and David Held (eds) *Cosmopolitan Democracy*, Cambridge: Polity Press.

—— (1998) 'Global civil society: perspectives, initiatives, movements', *Oxford Development Studies* 26(1): 99–110.

—— (1999) *Predatory Globalization: A Critique*, Cambridge: Polity Press.

—— (2002) 'An emergent matrix of citizenship: complex, uneven, and fluid', in Nigel Dower and John Williams (eds) *Global Citizenship: A Critical Reader*, Edinburgh: Edinburgh University Press.

Featherstone, M. (1999) 'Technologies of post-human development and the potential for global citizenship', in Jan N. Pieterse (ed.) *Global Futures: Shaping Globalisation*, London: Zed Books.

Filmfour (2002) *Bread and Roses*, Ken Loach.

Fine, Robert (1997) 'Civil society theory, enlightenment and critique', *Democratization* 4(1): 7–28.

Fischer, Stanley (1997) 'IMF: the right stuff. Bailouts in Asia are designed to restore confidence and bolster the financial system', *Financial Times*, 16 December.

Foucault, Michel (1979) 'On governmentality', *Ideology and Consciousness* 6: 5–22.
—— (1980) *The History of Sexuality Volume I: An Introduction*, New York: Vintage.
Fraser, Nancy (1993) 'Rethinking the public sphere', in Bruce Robbins (ed.) *The Phantom Public Sphere*, Minneapolis: University of Minnesota Press.
—— (1996) 'Rethinking the public sphere: a contribution to the critique of actually existing democracy', in Craig Calhoun (ed.) *Habermas and the Public Sphere*, Cambridge, MA: MIT Press.
Freeden, Michael (1978) *The New Liberalism: an Ideology of Social Reform*, Oxford: Clarendon.
—— (1996) *Ideologies and Political Theory: A Conceptual Approach*, Oxford: Clarendon.
Frost, Mervyn (1996) *Ethics in International Relations*, Cambridge: Cambridge University Press.
—— (2002) *Constituting Human Rights: Global Civil Society and the Society of Democratic States*, Routledge: London.
Fukuyama, Francis (1992) *The End of History and the Last Man*, Harmondsworth: Penguin.
—— (1996) *Trust: The Social Virtues and the Creation of Prosperity*, New York: Free Press.
Galston, William A. (1991) *Liberal Purposes: Goods, Virtues and Diversity in the Liberal State*, Cambridge: Cambridge University Press.
Gariyo, Zie (2002) 'Civil society and global finance in Africa: the PRSP process in Uganda', in Jan Aart Scholte and Albrecht Schnabel (eds) *Civil Society and Global Finance*, London: Routledge.
Garnham, Nicholas (1992) 'The media and the public sphere', in Craig Calhoun (ed.) *Habermas and the Public Sphere*, Cambridge, MA: Massachusetts Institute of Technology.
Germain, Randall D. (1997) *The International Organization of Credit*, Cambridge: Cambridge University Press.
—— (2000) (ed.) *Globalization and Its Discontents: Perspectives From Political Economy*, Basingstoke: Palgrave.
—— (2001) 'Global financial governance and the problem of inclusion', *Global Governance* 7(1): 411–26.
—— (2004) 'Globalizing accountability within the international organization of credit: financial governance and the public sphere', *Global Society* 18(3): 217–42.
Giddens, Anthony (1979) *Central Problems in Social Theory: Action, Structure and Contradiction in Social Analysis*, Berkeley and Los Angeles: University of California Press.
—— (1984) *The Constitution of Society: Outline of the Theory of Structuration*, Berkeley and Los Angeles: University of California Press.
—— (1990) *The Consequences of Modernity*, Stanford, CA: Stanford University Press
—— (1994) *Beyond Left and Right: The Future of Radical Politics*, Stanford, CA: Stanford University Press.
Gilbert, Emily and Helleiner, Eric (eds) (1999) *Nation-States and Money*, London: Routledge.
Gill, Stephen (1995) 'Globalisation, market civilisation and disciplinary neoliberalism', *Millennium* 24(3): 399–423.
—— (1999) 'The geopolitics of the Asian crisis', *Monthly Review* 50(10): 1–10.
—— (2003) *Power and Resistance in the New World Order*, London: Palgrave.
Gillespie, Marie (2000) 'Transnational communications and diaspora communities', in Simon Cottle (ed.) *Ethnic Minorities and the Media*, Buckingham: Open University Press.
Gills, Barry (ed.) (2000) *Globalization and the Politics of Resistance*, Basingstoke: Palgrave.
Giroux, H. (1999) *The Mouse that Roared: Disney and the End of Innocence*, Oxford: Rowman and Littlefield.
Gramsci, Antonio (1971) *Selections from the Prison Notebooks*, London: Lawrence and Wishart.
—— (1975) *Quaderni del carcere*, vols. I–IV, Turin: Einaudi.

Gray, John (1998) *False Dawn: The Delusions of Global Capitalism*, London: Granta.
—— (2002) 'Review of W. Hutton, "The World We're In"', *New Statesman*, 10 May.
Habermas, Jürgen (1989) *The Structural Transformation of the Public Sphere*, Cambridge: Polity.
—— (1990a) *Moral Consciousness and Communicative Action*, Cambridge: Polity.
—— (1990b) 'Discourse ethics: notes on a program of philosophical justification', in Seyla Benhabib and Fred Dallmyr (eds) *The Communicative Ethics Controversy*, Cambridge MA: MIT Press.
—— (1996) *Between Facts and Norms*, Cambridge: Polity.
—— (2001) *The Post-National Constellation: Political Essays*, Cambridge: MIT Press.
Hall, Rodney and Biersteker, Thomas (eds) (2002) *The Emergence of Private Authority*, Cambridge: Cambridge University Press.
Halliday, Fred (2000) 'Global governance: prospects and problems', in David Held and Anthony McGrew (eds) *The Global Transformations Reader*, Cambridge: Polity Press.
—— (2002) *Two Hours that Shook the World. September 11, 2001: Causes and Consequences*, London: Saqi Books.
Hallin, Daniel C. (1994) *We Keep America on Top of the World*, London: Routledge.
Hamelink, Cees J. (1994) *The Politics of World Communication; A Human Rights Perspective*, London: Sage.
—— (1995) *World Communication; Disempowerment and Self-Empowerment*, Zed Books: London.
Hamilton, Alexander (1961 [1787]) 'The Federalist No. 9', in Jacob Cooke (ed.) *The Federalist*, Middletown CT: Wesleyan University Press.
Hannerz, Ulf (1992) *Cultural Complexity; Studies in the Social Organisation of Meaning*, New York: Columbia University Press.
Hardt, Michael and Negri, Antonio (2000) *Empire*, Cambridge, MA: Harvard University Press.
Haug, Wolfgang Fritz (1999) 'Rethinking Gramsci's philosophy of praxis from one century to the next', *Boundary 2* 26(2): 101–17.
Heater, Derek B. (1996) *World Citizenship and Government: Cosmopolitan Ideas in the History of Western Political Thought*, Basingstoke: Macmillan.
—— (2000) 'Does cosmopolitan thinking have a future?', *Review of International Studies* 26 (Special Issue): 179–97.
—— (2002) *World Citizenship: Cosmopolitan Thinking and its Opponents*, London: Continuum.
Hegel, G.W.F. (1991 [1821]) *Elements of the Philosophy of Right*, H.B. Nisbet (trans), Cambridge: Cambridge University Press.
Heiman, G. (1971) 'The sources and significance of Hegel's corporate doctrine', in Zbigniew A. Pelczynski (ed.) *Hegel's Political Philosophy: Problems and Perspectives*, Cambridge: Cambridge University Press.
Held, David (1995) *Democracy and the Global Order: From the Modern State to Cosmopolitan Governance*, Cambridge: Polity Press.
—— (2002) 'The transformation of political community: rethinking democracy in the context of globalisation', in Nigel Dower and John Williams (eds) *Global Citizenship: A Critical Reader*, Edinburgh: Edinburgh University Press.
—— (2003) 'Cosmopolitanism: globalisation tamed?', *Review of International Studies* 29(4): 465–80.
Held, David and McGrew, Anthony (1993) 'Globalization and the Liberal Democratic State', *Government and Opposition* 28: 261–85.
—— (eds) (2000) *The Global Transformations Reader*, Cambridge: Polity Press.

Held, David, Anthony McGrew, David Goldblatt and Jonathan Perraton (1999) *Global Transformations*, Cambridge: Polity.

Helleiner, E (1998) 'Think globally, transact locally: Green political economy and the local currency movement', paper presented to 39th Annual Convention of the International Studies Association, February, Washington DC.

Herman, Ed S. and McChesney, R.W. (1997) *The Global Media: The New Missionaries of Global Capitalism*, London: Cassell.

Hewson, Martin and Sinclair, Timothy J. (1999) 'The emergence of global governance theory', in Martin Hewson and Timothy J. Sinclair (eds) *Approaches to Global Governance Theory*, New York: SUNY, pp. 1–25.

Hirst, Paul (1994) *Associative Democracy*, Cambridge: Polity.

—— (2002) *War and Power in the Twenty-First Century: The State, Military Conflict and the International System*, Cambridge: Polity.

Hobbes, Thomas (1991 [1651]) *Leviathan*, Richard Tuck (ed.) Cambridge: Cambridge University Press.

—— (1998 [1642]) *On the Citizen*, Richard Tuck and Michael Silverthorne (ed. and trans) Cambridge: Cambridge University Press.

Hobsbawm, Eric (1994) *Age of Extremes: The Short Twentieth Century: 1914–1991*, London: Michael Joseph.

Hoggart, Richard (1995) *The Way We Live Now*, London: Pimlico.

Hohendahl, Peter Uwe (1996) 'The public sphere: models and boundaries', in Craig Calhoun (ed.) *Habermas and the Public Sphere*, Cambridge MA: MIT Press.

Honneth, Axel (1995) *The Struggle for Recognition: The Moral Grammar of Social Conflicts*, Joel Anderson (trans) Cambridge: Polity Press.

Hoopes, Stephanie (1999) 'A political science response to a global politics agenda', in Martin Shaw (ed.) *Politics and Globalization: Knowledge, Ethics and Agency*, London: Routledge.

Hopgood, Stephen (2000) 'Reading the small print in global civil society: the inexorable hegemony of the liberal self', *Millennium: Journal of International Studies* 29(1): 1–25.

Huntington, Samuel (1998) *The Clash of Civilizations and the Remaking of World Order*, New York: Touchstone Books.

Hutchings, Kimberley (1999) 'Political theory and cosmopolitan citizenship', in Kimberley Hutchings and Roland Dannreuther (eds) *Cosmopolitan Citizenship*, New York: St Martin's Press.

Hutchings, Kimberley and Dannreuther, Roland (eds) (1999) *Cosmopolitan Citizenship*, New York: St Martin's Press.

Ignatieff, Michael (2004) *The Lesser Evil: Political Ethics in an Age of Terror*, Princeton, NJ: Princeton University Press.

Isin, Engin F. and Wood, Patricia K. (1999) *Citizenship and Identity*, London: Sage.

Johnston, Josee and Laxer, Gordon (2003) 'Solidarity in the age of globalization: lessons from the anti-MAI and Zapatista struggles', *Theory and Society* 32(1): 39–91.

Kaldor, Mary (1999a) 'Transnational civil society', in Tim Dunne and Nicholas J. Wheeler (eds) *Human Rights in Global Politics*, Cambridge: Cambridge University Press, pp. 195–213.

—— (1999b) *New and Old Wars: Organized Violence in a Global Era*, Cambridge: Polity.

—— (2000) '"Civilising", globalisation? The implications of the "Battle in Seattle"', *Millennium*, 29(1): 105–14.

—— (2004) *Global Civil Society: an Answer to War*, Cambridge: Polity.

Kant, Immanuel (1991 [1797]) *The Metaphysics of Morals*, excerpted in Hans Reiss (ed.) and H.B. Nisbet (trans) *Kant: Political Writings*, 2nd edn, Cambridge: Cambridge University Press.

Kaul, Inge, Grunberg, Isabelle and Stern, Marc (eds) (1999) *Global Public Goods*, Oxford: Oxford University Press for UNDP.

Kaviraj, Sudipta and Khilnani, Sunil (eds) (2001) *Civil Society: History and Possibilities*, Cambridge: Cambridge University Press.

Keane, John (1988a) (ed.) *Civil Society and the State: New European Perspectives*, London: University of Westminster Press.

—— (1988b) 'Introduction', in John Keane (ed.) *Civil Society and the State: New European Perspectives*, London: University of Westminster Press.

—— (1998) *Civil Society: Old Images, New Visions*, Cambridge: Polity Press.

—— (2001a) 'Who's in charge here?', *The Times Literary Supplement* 18(5): 15–18.

—— (2001b) 'Global civil society?', in Helmut Anheier, Marlies Glasius and Mary Kaldor (eds) *Global Civil Society 2001*, Oxford: Oxford University Press, pp. 23–50.

—— (2003) *Global Civil Society?*, Cambridge University Press: Cambridge.

Kellner, D (1995) 'Intellectuals and new technologies', *Media, Culture and Society* 17(3): 427–48.

Kelsen, Hans (1961) *General Theory of Law and the State*, Anders Wedberg (trans) New York: Russell and Russell.

Kenny, Michael (2001) 'Interpreting "global civil society"', paper presented to 'Global Civil Society: Critical Engagements and Ethical Encounters' conference, 10–12 September 2001, Gregynog, Wales.

—— (2003) 'Global civil society: a Liberal-Republican argument', *Review of International Studies* 29 (Dec. 2003): 119–44.

Keohane, Robert and Milner, Helen (eds) (1996) *Internationalization and Domestic Politics*, Cambridge: Cambridge University Press.

King, Alexander and Schneider, Bertrand (1991) *The First Global Revolution: A Report of the Council of Rome*, New York: Pantheon.

Kirshner, Jonathan (2000) 'The study of money', *World Politics* 52(3): 407–36.

Kissinger, Henry A. (1994) *Diplomacy*, New York: Simon & Schuster.

Klein, Naomi (2000) *No Logo*, London: Flamingo.

—— (2002a) 'Farewell to the "end of history": Organization and vision in anti-corporate movements', *Socialist Register* 2002: 1–14.

—— (2002b) 'Sharon, Le Pen and anti-Semitism', www.nologo.org/article.pl?sid=02/04/24/(1319)201.

Kohlberg, Lawrence (1984) *Essays on Moral Development*, Vol. 1, San Francisco: Harper and Row.

Krueger, Anne (2002) 'New approaches to sovereign debt rescheduling: an update on our thinking', address given to conference on 'Sovereign Debt Workouts', Institute for International Economics, 1 April (www.iie.com/papers/krueger(0402).htm).

Kumar, Krishan (1993) 'Civil society: an inquiry into the usefulness of an historical term', *British Journal of Sociology* 44(3): 375–95.

Küng, Hans and Kuschel, Karl-Josef (1993) *A Global Ethic: The Declaration of the Parliament of the World's Religions*, London: SCM Press.

Kymlicka, Will (1995) *Multicultural Citizenship*, Oxford: Oxford University Press.

Kymlicka, Will and Norman, Wayne (2000) 'Citizenship in culturally diverse societies: issues, contexts, concepts', in Will Kymlicka and Wayne Norman (eds) *Citizenship in Diverse Societies*, Oxford: Oxford University Press.

Lafferty, George (2000) 'The Dynamics of Change: Class, Politics and Civil Society – From Marx to post-Marxism', *Democracy and Nature*, 6(1): 19–26.

Langley, Paul. (2002) *World Financial Orders*, London: Routledge.

Larmore, Charles E. (1997) *Patterns of Moral Complexity*, Cambridge: Cambridge University Press.

Lash, Scott (2001) 'Technological forms of life', *Theory, Culture and Society*, 18 (1): 105–20.

Linklater, Andrew (1982) *Men and Citizens*, London: Macmillan.

—— (1998) *The Transformation of Political Community: Ethical Foundations of the Post-Westphalian Era*, Cambridge: Polity Press.

—— (1999) 'Cosmopolitan citizenship', in Kimberley Hutchings and Roland Dannreuther (eds) *Cosmopolitan Citizenship*, New York: St Martin's Press.

—— (2002) 'Cosmopolitan citizenship', in Bryan S. Turner and Engin F. Isin (eds) *Citizenship Studies: A Handbook*, London: Sage.

Lipietz, Alain (1987) *Mirages and Miracles: The Crisis of Global Fordism*, London: Verso.

Lively, Jack and Reeve, Andrew (1997) 'The emergence of the idea of civil society: the artificial political order and natural social orders', *Democratization* 4(1): 68–80.

Lukauskas, Arvid (1999) 'Managing mobile capital: recent scholarship on the political economy of international finance', *Review of International Political Economy* 6(2): 262–87.

Lynch, Marc (2000) 'The dialogue of civilisations and international public spheres', *Millennium* 29(2): 307–30.

Macdonald, L. (1994) 'Globalising civil society: interpreting international NGOs in Central America', *Millennium* 23(2): 267–85.

—— (1997) *Supporting Civil Society: the political role of non-governmental organizations in Central America*, Basingstoke: Macmillan.

Maclean, John (1999) 'Towards a political economy of agency in contemporary international relations', in Martin Shaw (ed.) *Politics and Globalisation: Knowledge, Ethics and Agency*, London: Routledge.

MacLean, Sandra, Quadir, Fahimul and Shaw, Timothy (2000) 'Structural adjustment and the response of civil society in Bangladesh and Zimbabwe: a comparative analysis', in Barry Gills (ed.) *Globalization and the Politics of Resistance*, Basingstoke: Palgrave.

McGrew, Anthony (ed.) (1997) *The Transformation of Democracy*, Milton Keynes: Polity and Open University Press.

—— (2000) 'Democracy beyond borders?', in David Held and Anthony McGrew (eds) *The Global Transformations Reader*, Cambridge: Polity Press.

Maffesoli, Michel (1996) *The Time of Tribes: The Decline of Individualism in Mass Society*, London: Sage.

Maine, Henry Sumner (1970) *Ancient Law: Its Connection with the Early History of Society and its Relation to Modern Ideas*, 10th edn, Gloucester, MA: Peter Smith.

Marden, P. (1997) 'Geographies of dissent: globalization, identity and the nation', *Political Geography* 16(1): 37–64.

Marquand, D. (2002) 'The liberal nation', *Prospect*, March: 22–5.

Marshall, Thomas H. (1973) *Class, Citizenship and Social Development*, Westport CN: Greenwood Press.

Martell, Luke and Anker, Christien van den (2001) *Social Democracy: Global and National Perspectives*, Basingstoke: Palgrave.

Martin-Barbero, Jesus (1993) *Communication, Culture and Hegemony: From the Media to Mediations*, E. Fox and R.A. White (trans.), London: Sage.

Mattleart, A. (2001) 'Against global inevitability', http://www.wacc.org.uk/media/mattelart.htm.

Mayobre, Eduardo (ed.) (1999) *G-24: the developing countries in the international financial system*, Boulder: Lynne Rienner.

Millennium (2000) 'Seattle: December 1999?', 29(1): 103–40.

Miller, David (1995) *On Nationality*, Oxford: Clarendon Press.

—— (1999) 'Bounded citizenship', in Kimberley Hutchings and Roland Dannreuther (eds) *Cosmopolitan Citizenship*, New York: St Martin's Press.

—— (2001) *Citizenship and National Identity*, Oxford: Blackwell.

Miller, P. and Rose, N. (1990) 'Governing economic life', *Economy and Society* 19(1): 1–31.

Morison, John (2000) 'The government–voluntary sector compacts: governance, governmentality, and civil society', *Journal of Law and Society* 27(1): 98–132.

Morley, David (2000) *Home Territories: Media, Mobility and Identity*, London: Routledge.

Morley, David and Robins, Kevin (1999) *Spaces of Identity: global media, electronic landscapes and cultural boundaries*, London: Routledge.

Morton, Adam (2003) 'Historicizing Grasmci: situating ideas in and beyond their context', *Review of International Political Economy* 10 (1): 118–46.

Mosco, Vincent (1996) *The Political Economy of Communication*, London: Sage.

Mouffe, Chantal (ed.) (1979) *Gramsci and Marxist Theory*, London: Routledge.

—— (1992) *Dimensions of Radical Democracy*, London: Verso.

—— (1993) *The Return of the Political*, London: Verso.

Mulgan, Geoff (1997) *Connexity; How to Live in a Connected World*, London: Chatto and Windus.

Murdock, Graham (1992) 'Citizens, consumers, and the public culture', in Michael Skovmand and Kim Schroder (eds) *Media Cultures*, London: Routledge.

—— (1994) 'Money talks: broadcasting, finance and public culture', in Stuart Hood (ed.) *Behind the Screens: The Structure of British Television in the Nineties*, London: Lawrence and Wishart.

—— (1999) 'Rights and representations: public discourse and cultural citizenship', in Jostein Gripsrud (ed.) *Television and Common Knowledge*, London: Routledge.

Murphy, Craig (1994) *International Organization and Industrial Change*, Cambridge: Polity Press.

—— (1996) 'Seeing women, recognising gender, recasting international relations', *International Organization* 50(3): 513–38.

—— (2000) 'Global governance: poorly done and poorly understood', *International Affairs* 76(4): 789–803.

Murthy, Viren (1999) 'Leftist mourning: civil society and political practice in Hegel and Marx', *Rethinking Marxism* 11(3): 36–55.

Narlikar, Amrita and Wilkinson, Rorden (2004) 'Collapse at the WTO: a Cancun post-mortem', *Third World Quarterly* (25) 3.

Neilsen, Kai (1988) 'World government, security and social justice', in Stephen Luper-Foy (ed.) *Problems of International Justice*, Boulder: Westview Press.

—— (1995) 'Reconceptualizing civil society for now: some somewhat Gramscian turnings', in Michael Walzer (ed.) *Toward A Global Civil Society*, Oxford: Berghahn.

Nerfin, M. (1987) 'Neither prince nor merchant: citizen', *Development Dialogue* No. 1.

Nussbaum, Martha C. (1996) 'Cosmopolitanism and patriotism', in Joshua Cohen (ed.) *For Love of Country: Debating the Limits of Patriotism*, Boston: Beacon Press.

Nussbaum, Martha C. and Sen, Amartya (eds) (1993) *The Quality of Life*, Oxford: Clarendon.

O'Brien, Robert (2000) 'Workers and world order: the tentative transformation of the International Union Movement', *Review of International Studies* 26(4): 533–56.

O'Brien, Robert, Goetz, Anne Marie, Scholte, Jan Aart and Williams, Marc (2000) *Contesting Global Governance: Multilateral Economic Institutions and Global Social Movements*, Cambridge: Cambridge University Press.

Onuf, Nicholas G. (1998) *The Republican Legacy in International Thought*, Cambridge: Cambridge University Press.

—— (2001) 'Speaking of policy', in Vendulka Kubálková (ed.) *Foreign Policy in a Constructed World*, Armonk NY: M.E. Sharpe.

—— (2002) 'Institutions, intentions and international relations', *Review of International Studies* 28: 211–28.

Onuf, Peter and Onuf, Nicholas (1993) *Federal Union, Modern World: The Law of Nations in an Age of Revolution, 1776–1814*, Madison WI: Madison House.

Otto, D. (1996) 'Nongovernmental Organizations in the United Nations System: the emerging role of international civil society', *Human Rights Quarterly* 18: 107–41.

Overbeek, Henk (ed.) (1993) *The Global Political Economy: The Rise of Transnational Neoliberalism in the 1980s*, London: Routledge.

Pacione, M. (1997) 'Local exchange trading systems as a response to the globalisation of capitalism', *Urban Studies* 34(8): 1179–99.

Parekh, Bhikhu (2000) *Rethinking Multiculturalism: Cultural Diversity and Political Theory*, Macmillan: Basingstoke.

Pasha, Mustapha K. and Blaney, David L. (1998) 'Elusive paradise: the promise and peril of global civil society', *Alternatives* 23(3): 417–50.

Pateman, Carole (1970) *Participation and Democratic Theory*, Cambridge: Cambridge University Press.

Peters, John D. (1999) *Speaking into the Air*, Chicago and London: University of Chicago Press.

Pieterse, Jan N. and Parekh, Bhikhu (1995) *The Decolonisation of the Western Imagination*, London: Zed Books.

Pijl, Kees van der (1984) *The Making of an Atlantic Ruling Class*, London: Verso.

—— (1998) *Transnational Classes and International Relations*, London: Routledge.

Pilger, John (2002) *The New Rulers of the World*, London: Verso.

Pitkin, Hanna (1967) *The Concept of Representation*, Berkeley and Los Angeles: University of California Press.

Plant, Raymond (1980) 'Economic and social integration in Hegel's political philosophy', in Donald P. Verene (ed.) *Hegel's Social and Political Thought: The Philosophy of Objective Spirit*, New Jersey: Humanities Press.

Polanyi, Karl (1944) *The Great Transformation*, Boston: Beacon Press.

Pollert, Anna (1999) *Transformation at Work: The New Market Economies of Central Eastern Europe*, London: Sage.

Porter, Tony (2001) 'The democratic deficit in the institutional arrangements for regulating global finance', *Global Governance* 7(4): 427–39.

Putnam, Robert (1993) *Making Democracy Work*, Princeton: Princeton University Press.

—— (2000) *Bowling Alone*, New York: Simon and Schuster.

Rawls, John (1971) *A Theory of Justice*, Cambridge MA.: Belknap Press of Harvard University Press.

—— (1999) *The Law of Peoples*, Cambridge, MA: Harvard University Press.

Review of International Political Economy (RIPE) (2000) Special themed section: 'The Battle of Seattle' 7(3): 465–504.

Riedel, Manfred (1984) *Between Tradition and Revolution: The Hegelian Transformation of Political Philosophy*, Cambridge: Cambridge University Press.

Risse, Thomas (2000) 'Transnational civil society and human rights', in Anna Florini (ed.) *The Third Force: The Rise of Transnational Civil Society*, Tokyo/Washington DC: Japan Centre for International Exchange and Carnegie Endowment for International Peace.

Robins, Kevin (1997) 'Cyberspace and the world we live in', in Mike Featherstone and Roger Burrows (eds) *Cyberspace/Cyberbodies/Cyberpunk; Cultures of Technological Embodiment*, London: Sage.
Robins, Kevin and Webster, Frank (1999) *Times of the Technoculture; From the information society to the virtual life*, London: Routledge.
Robinson, W. and Harris, J. (2000) 'Towards a global ruling class? Globalization and the transnational capitalist class', *Science and Society* 64(1): 11–54.
Rose, Nikolas (1999 [1989]) *Governing the Soul: The Shaping of the Private Self*, London: Free Association Books.
Rosenau, James (2000) 'Governance in a globalizing world', in David Held and Anthony McGrew *The Global Transformations Reader*, Cambridge; Polity.
Rosenau, James and Czempiel, Ernst-Otto (1992) *Governance Without Government: Order and Change in World Politics*, Cambridge: Cambridge University Press.
Rosenberg, Justin (1994) *The Empire of Civil Society: A Critique of the Realist Theory of International Relations*, London: Verso.
—— (2001) *The Follies of Globalisation Theory*, London: Verso.
Ruggie, John Gerard (1996) *Winning the Peace*, Columbia Ohio: Columbia University Press.
—— (2001) 'global_governance.net: The global compact as learning network', *Global Governance* 7(4): 371–8.
Runciman, David (1997) *Pluralism and the Personality of the State*, Cambridge: Cambridge University Press.
Rupert, Mark (2000) *Ideologies of Globalization*, London: Routledge/RIPE.
Sassoon, Anne Showstack (2000a) *Gramsci and Contemporary Politics: Beyond Pessimism of the Intellect*, London: Routledge.
—— (2000b) 'Back to the future: the resurrection of civil society', in Anne Showstack Sassoon (ed.) *Gramsci and Contemporary Politics: Beyond Pessimism of the Intellect*, London: Routledge.
—— (2000c) 'The challenge to traditional intellectuals: specialisation, organisation, leadership', in Anne Showstack Sassoon (ed.) *Gramsci and Contemporary Politics: Beyond Pessimism of the Intellect*, London: Routledge.
—— (2000d) 'The politics of the organic intellectuals: passion, understanding, knowledge', in Anne Showstack Sassoon (ed.) *Gramsci and Contemporary Politics: Beyond Pessimism of the Intellect*, London: Routledge.
—— (2000e) 'Gramsci's subversion of the language of politics', in Anne Showstack Sassoon (ed.) *Gramsci and Contemporary Politics: Beyond Pessimism of the Intellect*, London: Routledge.
—— (2001) 'Globalisation, hegemony and passive revolution', *New Political Economy* 6(1): 5–17.
Schechter, Michael G. (1999) 'Globalization and civil society', in Michael G. Schechter (ed.) *The Revival of Civil Society*, Basingstoke: Macmillan.
Schiller, Herbert I. (1996) *Information Inequality*, London: Routledge.
Schlesinger, Philip (1991) *Media, State and Nation: Political Violence and Collective Identities*, London: Sage.
Scholte, Jan Aart (1999) 'Globalisation: prospects for a paradigm shift', in Martin Shaw (ed.) *Politics and Globalisation: Knowledge, Ethics and Agency*, London: Routledge.
—— (2000a) 'Cautionary reflections on Seattle', *Millennium: A Journal of International Studies* 29(1): 115–21.
—— (2000b) 'Global civil society', in Ngaire Woods (ed.) *The Political Economy of Globalization*, Basingstoke: Macmillan.

—— (2000c) *Globalization: A Critical Introduction*, Basingstoke: Palgrave.

—— (2001) 'Civil society and governance in the global polity', paper presented to 'Global Civil Society: Critical Engagements and Ethical Encounters' conference, 10–12 September 2001, Gregynog, Wales.

—— (2002) 'Civil society and the governance of global finance', in Jan Aart Scholte and Albrecht Schnabel (eds) *Civil Society and Global Finance*, London: Routledge.

Scholte, Jan Aart and Schnabel, Albrecht (eds) (2002) *Civil Society and Global Finance*, London: Routledge.

Scott, James C. (1990) *Domination and the Arts of Resistance: Hidden Transcripts*, Yale: Yale University Press.

Scruton, Roger (1984) *The Meaning of Conservatism*, London: Macmillan.

Seckinelgin, Hakan (2002) 'Civil society as a metaphor for western liberalism', Civil Society Working Paper 21, Centre for Civil Society, London School of Economics, January 2002 (www.lse.ac.uk/Depts/ccs/pdf/CSWP21.pdf).

Seligman, Adam B. (1992) *The Idea of Civil Society*, Princeton: Princeton University Press.

Sen, Amartya K. (1999) *Development as Freedom*, Oxford: Oxford University Press.

—— (2001) *Development as Freedom*, Oxford: Oxford University Press.

Shapiro, Ian and Hacker-Cordon, Casiano (eds) (1999) *Democracy's Edges*, Cambridge: Cambridge University Press.

Shaw, Martin (1994) 'Civil society and global politics: beyond a social movements approach', *Millennium: Journal of International Politics* 23(3): 647–67.

—— (ed.) (1999) *Politics and Globalisation: Knowledge, Ethics and Agency*, London: Routledge.

—— (2000) *Theory of the Global State: Globality as Unfinished Revolution*, Cambridge: Cambridge University Press.

—— (2001) 'Social democracy in the global revolution: an historical perspective', in Luke Martell and Christien van den Anker (eds) *Social Democracy: Global and National Perspectives*, Basingstoke: Palgrave.

Shue, H. (1996) 'Solidarity among strangers and the right to food', in William Aiken and Hugh LaFollette (eds) *World Hunger and Morality*, Englewood Cliffs: Prentice Hall.

Sinclair, Timothy (2000) 'Reinventing authority: embedded knowledge networks and the new global finance', *Environment and Planning C: Government and Policy* 18(4): 487–502.

Smith, Anthony D. (1995) *Nations and Nationalism in a Global Era*, Cambridge: Polity Press.

Soldatenko, M.A. (1999) 'Made in the USA: Latinas/os? Garment work and ethnic conflict in Los Angeles' Sweat Shops', *Cultural Studies* 13(2): 319–34.

Somavia, Juan (1999) 'Trade unions in the 21st century', Keynote Speech, WTO Ministerial Meeting, Geneva: ILO.

Soros, George (2002) *On Globalization*, New York: Public Affairs.

Sparks, C. (1998) 'Is there a global public sphere?', in Daya K. Thussu (ed.) *Electronic Empires; Global Media and Local Resistance*, London: Arnold.

Spybey, Tony (1996) *Globalization and World Society*, Cambridge: Polity Press.

Sreberny, Annabelle (1998) 'Feminist internationalism: imagining and building global civil society', in Daya K. Thussu (ed.) *Electronic Empires; Global Media and Local Resistance*, London: Arnold.

—— (2000) 'Media and diasporic consciousness: an exploration among Iranians in London', in Simon Cottle (ed.) *Ethnic Minorities and the Media*, Buckingham: Open University Press.

Stallabras, Julian (1996) *Gargantura: Manufactured Mass Culture*, London: Verso.

Stammers, Neil (1999) 'Social movements and the challenge to power', in Martin Shaw (ed.) *Politics and Globalisation: Knowledge, Ethics and Agency*, London: Routledge.

—— (2001) 'Social democracy and global governance', in Luke Martell and Christien van den Anker *Social Democracy: Global and National Perspectives*, Basingstoke: Palgrave.
Stevenson, Nick (1999) *The Transformation of the Media: Globalisation, Morality and Ethics*, Longman: London.
—— (2002) *Understanding Media Cultures; Social Theory and Mass Communication*, London: Sage.
Stiglitz, Joseph (2002) *Globalization and Its Discontents*, New York: W.W. Norton.
Strange, Susan (1988) *States and Markets*, London: Pinter.
—— (1996) *The Retreat of the State*, Cambridge: Cambridge University Press.
—— (1998) *Mad Money*, Manchester: Manchester University Press.
Taylor, Charles (1992) 'The politics of recognition', in Charles Taylor and Amy Gutmann (ed.) *Multiculturalism and 'The Politics of Recognition'*, Princeton, NJ: Princeton University Press.
Taylor, Charles and Gutmann, Amy (eds) (1992) *Multiculturalism and 'The Politics of Recognition'*, Princeton, NJ: Princeton University Press.
Tester, Keith (1995) 'Moral solidarity and the technological reproduction of images', *Media, Culture and Society* 17: 469–82.
—— (1997) *Moral Culture*, London: Sage.
—— (1999) 'The moral consequentiality of television', *European Journal of Social Theory* 2(4): 469–83.
—— (2001) *Compassion, Morality and the Media*, Buckingham: Open University Press.
Texier, Jacques (1979) 'Gramsci, theoretician of the superstructure', in Chantal Mouffe (ed.) *Gramsci and Marxist Theory*, London: Routledge.
Thatcher, Margaret (2002) *Statecraft: Strategies For a Changing World*, London: HarperCollins.
Thompson, John B. (1994) 'Social theory and the media', in David Crowley and David Mitchell (eds) *Communication Theory Today*, Cambridge: Polity Press.
—— (1995) *The Media and Modernity: A Social Theory of the Media*, Cambridge: Polity Press.
Tomlinson, John (1999) *Globalization and Culture*, Cambridge: Polity Press.
Tooze, Roger and Murphy, Craig (1996) 'The epistemology of poverty and the poverty of epistemology in IPE: mystery, blindness, and invisibility', *Millennium: Journal of International Studies* 25(3): 681–707.
Traxler, Franz and Schmitter, Philippe C. (1995) 'The emerging Euro-polity and organized interests', *European Journal of International Relations* 1: 193–8.
Tribe, Keith (1988)/(1995) *Governing Economy: The Reformation of German Economic Discourse 1750–1840*, Cambridge: Cambridge University Press.
Urry, John (2000a) *Sociology Beyond Societies: Mobilities for the Twenty-First Century*, London: Routledge.
—— (2000b) 'Global flows and global citizenship', in Engin F. Isin (ed.) *Democracy, Citizenship and the Global City*, London: Routledge.
Van den Anker, C. (2002) 'Global justice, global institutions and global citizenship', in Nigel Dower and John Williams (eds) *Global Citizenship: A Critical Reader*, Edinburgh: Edinburgh University Press.
Van Dijk, Jan (1999) *The Network Society*, London: Routledge.
Van Steenbergen, Bart (1994) 'Towards a global ecological citizen', in Bart van Steenbergen (ed.) *The Condition of Citizenship*, London: Sage.
Villa, Dana (1992) 'Postmodernism and the public sphere', *American Political Science Review* 86(3): 712–21.
Virilio, Paul (1997) *Open Sky*, London: Verso.
—— (2000a) *The Information Bomb*, London: Verso.

—— (2000b) *Polar Inertia*, London: Sage.

—— (2000c) *Strategy of Deception*, London: Verso.

Virilio, Paul and Shugaar, Antony (2002) *Republicanism*, New York: Hill and Wang.

Walker, R.B.J. (1994) 'Social movements/world politics', *Millennium: Journal of International Studies* 23(3): 669–700.

Waltz, Kenneth (1965) *Man, the State and War*, Columbia Ohio: Columbia University Press.

Walzer, Michael (1992) 'The civil society argument', in Chantal Mouffe (ed.) *Gramsci and Marxist Theory*, London: Routledge.

—— (1994) *Thick and Thin: Moral Argument at Home and Abroad*, London: University of Notre Dame Press.

—— (ed.) (1995) *Toward a Global Civil Society*, Oxford: Bergham Books.

Warkentin, C. and Mingst, K. (2000) 'International institutions, the state, and global civil society in the age of the world wide web', *Global Governance* 6: 237–57.

Warren, Mark E. (2001) *Democracy and Association*, Princeton, NJ: Princeton University Press.

Waszek, Norbert (1988) *The Scottish Enlightenment and Hegel's Account of 'Civil Society'*, Dordrecht: Kluwer.

Waterman, Peter and Wills, Jane (2001) 'Introduction: Space, place and the New Labour internationalisms: beyond the fragments', *Antipode* 33(3): 305–11.

Waters, Malcolm (1995) *Globalization*, London: Routledge.

Weber, Max (1978 [1922]) *Economy and Society: An Outline of Interpretive Sociology* (many translators), Berkeley and Los Angeles: University of California Press.

Wendt, Alexander (1994) 'Collective identity formation and the international state', *American Political Science Review* 88 (2): 384–96.

Weymouth, Tony and Lamizet, Bernard (1997) *Markets and Myths*, London: Longman.

Wheeler, Nicholas J. (2000) *Saving Strangers: Humanitarian Intervention in International Society*, Oxford: Oxford University Press.

Wilkinson, Rorden (2000) *Multilateralism and the World Trade Organisation*, London: Routledge.

—— (2002) 'Global monitor: The World Trade Organization', *New Political Economy* 7(1): 129–39.

Williams, R. (1962) *Communications*, London: Routledge.

Williams, Robert R. (1997) *Hegel's Ethics of Recognition*, Berkeley and Los Angeles: University of California Press.

Wood, Ellen Meiskins (1995) *Democracy Against Capitalism: Renewing Historical Materialism*, Cambridge: Cambridge University Press.

Woods, Ngaire (2001) 'Making the IMF and World Bank more accountable', *International Affairs* 77(1): 83–100.

World Bank (2000) *Consultations with Civil Society Organizations: General Guidelines for World Bank Staff*, Washington, DC: World Bank.

—— (2000/01) 'Attacking poverty', *World Development Report*, Oxford: Oxford University Press.

World Federalist Association (2002) http://www.wfa.org/ March (2002).

Wyplosz, Charles (1999) 'International financial stability', in Inge Kaul, Isabelle Grunberg and Marc A. Stern (eds) *Global Public Goods*, Oxford: Oxford University Press.

Yam, Joseph (1997) 'Asian monetary cooperation', *BIS Review*, accessed via www.bis.org (28.11.02).

Young, Iris Marion (1990) *Justice and the Politics of Difference*, Princeton, NJ: Princeton University Press.

—— (1996) 'Communication and the other: beyond deliberative democracy', in Seyla Benhabib (ed.) *Democracy and Difference: Contesting the Boundaries of the Political*, Princeton, NJ: Princeton University Press.

—— (2000) *Inclusion and Democracy*, Oxford: Oxford University Press.

Young, Tom (1995) '"A project to be realised": Global liberalism and contemporary Africa', *Millennium* 24 (3): 527–46.

Zacher, Mark W. (1992) 'The decaying of the Westphalian Temple: implications for international order and governance', in James N. Rosenau and Ernst-Otto Czempiel (eds) *Governance Without Government: Order and Change in World Politics*, Cambridge: Cambridge University Press.

Index